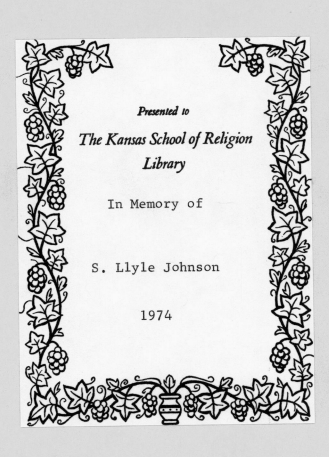

The Devil's Bride

The Devil's Bride

Exorcism: Past and Present

Martin Ebon

Harper & Row, Publishers
New York   Evanston   San Francisco
London

Library of Congress Cataloging in Publication Data

Ebon, Martin.
   The Devil's bride; exorcism, past and present.
   Bibliography: p.
   1.Exorcism. 2.Demonology. I.Title.
BF1559.E26   133.4′27   73–18699
ISBN 0–06–062114–1

Acknowledgments

In addition to the sources listed in the Selected Bibliography, I should like to acknowledge the help I received from others who shared their special knowledge with me. First, I want to mention two men who died at the time I completed research on this book, in 1973; they are Dr. Lawrence Kubie, Baltimore, Maryland, who provided me with material on his work with Dr. Milton Erickson, Phoenix, Arizona, and Father Celestine Kapsner, O.S.B., St. John's Abbey, Collegeville, Minnesota, translator of the material relating to the exorcism in Earling, Iowa. My fellow-writer, Mr. Raymond Van Over, was instrumental in compiling the data on which the chapter on exorcism in China is based. Canon John D. Pearce-Higgins, Putney, London, England, was generous with material and guidance, as were Dr. Jule Eisenbud, Denver, Colorado, Dr. Marie Coleman Nelson, Smithtown, New York, and Dr. Stanley A. Freed, The American Museum of Natural History, and Dr. Ruth Freed, Seton Hall University. Needless to say, I am solely responsible for views expressed and any possible failings in accuracy, selection or emphasis.

Contents

I. Devils, Demons, Evil Spirits

1. The Demons Among Us

In a small town in Iowa, a middle-aged woman is writhing on the floor, her distorted voice utters obscenities. A tall bearded priest counters the blasphemies with prayers and threats addressed to the devils that appear to possess the woman's body; after twenty-three days, he succeeds.

In China, a demon seems to possess several women in the same household, one after the other. Even the domestic animals respond to the invisible evil force which persists until prayerful exorcism drives it out.

Jesus Christ encounters a man who suffers physical and mental tortures because he is possessed by so many demons that their "name is legion." Christ commands the demons to leave the man and they enter a herd of pigs which, in a frenzy, drown themselves.

A Siberian shaman permits himself to be possessed by a powerful disembodied spirit, so that its force will help him heal others who are possessed by evil entities.

In Switzerland, a couple is imprisoned because they abused and beat a teen-age girl so severely that she died. Their defense is that the girl had become "the devil's bride," had confessed to immoral relations with Satan, and had merely been struck to drive the devil out. Her death, they claim, was accidental.

In Brazil, a man goes into a trancelike state during which he is "possessed" by an ancient African divinity who disports himself in an eccentrically arrogant manner, makes forceful demands and awes the spectators. When the possession ceases, the man becomes once again his usual meek and retiring self.

3

In New York, a medium goes into a trance and is controlled by the spirit of a Near Eastern physician. She faces another woman who feels possessed by one of the Salem witches. In a dialogue of ghost with ghost, the physician spirit urges the witch to leave the possessed woman's body.

A British clergyman is called to a farmhouse where he frees the spirit of a seventeenth-century soldier. When he sets him free, frightening phenomena suddenly end.

In France, a nun filled with thoughts of sexuality is told by a priest that the devil may be manipulating her, and the woman's personality becomes violent and destructive. But a Catholic psychiatrist diagnoses her condition as "demonopathy," an emotional disturbance imitating demonic possession; he cures her by psychomedical means.

These and many other cases of possession and exorcism are narrated in this book. They show the wide panorama, through history and geography, of man's concern with a seemingly inexplicable experience: he feels compulsions to thought and action that are in violent conflict with everything he consciously wants to be, think, and do. What has happened to him? Have his mind and body been taken over by an outside force? Has another personality taken control of him? Perhaps, to use traditional terms, he is possessed by a devil, a demon, or an evil spirit?

Our language, which is as much a depository of the past as an archeological site, knows such phrases as: "I don't know what possessed me" and "If the spirit moves me . . ." We speak of being "bedeviled," of being "enthusiastic" (which originally meant being filled with a divine spirit), or of being "inspired." We say that "pandemonium reigned," meaning that all the demons have been unleashed. We cover our mouth when we yawn, having learned that this gesture is well-mannered, but unaware that it was designed to keep a demon from sneaking into our bodies, from which it would have to be driven by exorcism, with the mouth and other openings prayerfully sealed off.

In terms of human history, it is only very recently that we have learned to explain most physical and some mental illnesses in terms of medical rationale. We are, for the most part, both too arrogant and too ignorant to admit that our rational thought patterns are like thin ice covering a raging river of chaotic fears that prompted us in the past to blame all illness or misfortune on demons or on the witchcraft of others. This past is still all around us, be it in the automatic response of blaming our troubles on others, or in the so-called primitive societies which are still combating or appeasing demons in one form or another.

We are almost incapable of totally abstract identification; we personify invisible powers and influences. God the Father has, in all religions, been a superpaternal figure. Below him, ancient civilizations pictured many deities who governed such otherwise unimaginable forces as the winds and waters, the sun and the planets. Death is still pictured as a skeleton with a scythe. Small wonder that a man or woman suffering from inexplicable symptoms was thought to be in the power of an invisible entity, which was given a name and identity, addressed in person—and, indeed, which began to talk back through the mouth of the suffering, "possessed" person.

This book should be read as an effort to raise questions about interpersonal relations, cultural influence, group conditioning, emotional fads and epidemics, and, above all, the crucial relations between physician and patient, clergyman and uneasy parishioner, parent and child. We are touching the shifting, complex contact between people who are dependent on one another, demand attention, respect, fear, or love of each other, and who play various parts in the drama of daily life.

The demons among us have many psychological, sociological, political, and even economic names. We are each other's demons. We are, above all, our own demons. The person who feels possessed by a demon is simply a few steps beyond the many irrational acts of compulsion and taboo that most of us practice almost automatically and unknowingly. Special circumstances, so varied as to be almost unique with each man or woman, may push these relatively harmless idiosyncracies beyond the point of self-control.

The traditional view of possession by a demon is that the possessed person has, in some way, become open to invasion by an outside entity, or several such entities. Each culture has its own definitions, just as there are innumerable variations of group reaction to the mentally ill, ranging from abuse to awe. The "inspired" prophet of one period may be the harmless eccentric of another, the demon-ridden heretic of still another, and the raving madman of a fourth.

In biblical times, having a demon appears to have been tantamount to being emotionally disturbed. In the Gospel according to John, those listening to Jesus accused him of what today would be called paranoid thinking when he suspected them of wanting to kill him: "The people answered, 'You have a demon! Who is seeking to kill you?'" (7:20) When he persisted in upbraiding them and speaking in what appeared to them highly extravagant terms, they added, "Are we not right in saying that you are a Samaritan and have a demon?" (8:48) But "Jesus answered, 'I have not a demon; but I honor my Father, and you dishonor me.'" (8:49) And when he said that "If anyone keeps my word, he will never see death," they were puzzled and shouted, "Now we know that you have a demon." (8:51, 52) And still later: "Many of them said, 'He has a demon, and he is mad; why listen to him?' Others said, 'These are not the sayings of one who has a demon. Can a demon open the eyes of the blind?'" (10:20, 21)

The Jerusalem of the first century was a cultural descendant of the civilization of Sumer, Assyria, and Babylon. Even the most elusive written records do not go beyond that point, although they indicate that the ancient civilizations of China and Babylon would seem to have a great deal of possession-exorcism in common. In fact, there is hardly any oral or written tradition in the world that does not show signs of demonological thinking: When something befalls us that we cannot otherwise explain, it must be due to an evil force; at all cost, man tries to envisage an antagonist whom he can comprehend—the unknown must become known, the invisible at least visible to the mind's eye.

From there, it is only one step to the eliciting or creation of the demon, complete with facial expression, body movements, speech, and action. Again, the various components are remarkably universal. They are so dramatic, so real, so convincing that the question might as well be asked, in all unselfconscious seriousness: Are there really demons? The material in the following chapters is presented with as much objectivity as could be achieved. Certainly, the Roman Catholic church, the Anglican and Episcopal churches, the Greek Orthodox church, and various Protestant denominations accept the reality of the devil, and with it the possibility of possession and exorcism. Islam, by itself and in interaction with African religions, accepts the existence and activity of demons and devils. Religions and cults throughout the world follow practices that are similar in emotional content and actual possession-exorcism performance.

From ancient Babylon, a cry of despair has come down to us over thousands of years. In a clay tablet found in the Temple of Asurbanipal, the Babylonian ruler, at Nineveh, the prayerful appeal of a man to his gods has been preserved. He asks, "How can I rid myself of a tyrannical ghost who seems to possess my body and soul?" Written centuries before the Christian era, this appeal is addressed to three deities: Ea, Shamash, and Marduk. The prayer shows that the man who composed it was tormented by physical and mental suffering. He pleaded with his gods to free him from the possessing ghost, asked that it be clothed in the nether world, appeased, and so securely bound that it could never return.

The tablet, now in a London museum, says that the man was persecuted by "a horrible spectre for many days," which "fastened itself on my back and will not let go of me." During the night, the prayer reads, "he strikes terror into me, sends forth poison and he makes the hair on my head stand up. He taketh

the power from my body, he maketh mine eyes stand out, he
plagueth my back, he poisoneth my flesh, he plagueth my whole
body." After this description of symptoms of apparent spirit
possession—severe anxiety, skin disease, bulging eyes, exhaustion—the supplicant pledges that whoever the ghost may have
been in life, he is willing to do whatever is necessary to appease
him. But why, he wonders, did the ghost choose him? Is he perhaps the ghost "of one of my own family and kindred," or "of
one who was murdered"?

Finally, the desperate man urges that the ghost be consigned
to the nether world, to be locked up "with a bolt and bar" to
prevent his return to earth. Before this, he had asked the Babylonian deities whether the ghost needed clothing, food, or drink.
This is a universal theme. To this day, the "hungry ghost" is
feared in parts of Asia, and such Chinese communities as those of
Hong Kong set aside a day for the pacification and symbolic
feeding of hungry ghosts that might otherwise roam restlessly and
attach themselves to living people. The theme that a spirit may
be restless, perhaps because of improper burial or of an unsettled
grievance, is still quite common in Western spiritualism and in
so-called primitive societies.

Records of early antiquity are scarce. There is little direct
reference to possession and exorcism in the Old Testament. King
Solomon, identified with great knowledge and wisdom, was described as a skilled exorcist only by the first-century Jewish historian Flavius Josephus. Writing in his monumental *Antiquities
of the Jews,* Josephus stated that Solomon's gifts were so varied
that "God also enabled him to learn that skill which expels
demons, which is a science useful and healing to men." King
Solomon, according to this historian, "left behind him the manner of using exorcisms, by which they drive away demons, so that
they never return and this method of cure is of great force to this
day."

Josephus cited several people who "were demoniacal in the
presence of Vespasian," the Roman emperor who governed from

A.D. 70 to 79, as well as before "his sons and his captains, and the whole multitude of soldiers." The exorcist, a man named Eleazar, used this method: he took a ring to which was attached "a root of the type mentioned by Solomon," held it to the nostrils of the possessed person, "after which he drew out the demon through his nostrils." Eleazar, seeing the man fall to the ground, warned the demon not to return to his body again, while "making still mention of Solomon and reciting the incantation which he composed." Josephus added: "And when Eleazar would persuade and demonstrate to the spectators that he had such a power, he set a little way off a cup or basin full of water, and commanded the demon, as he went out of the man to overturn it, and thereby to let the spectators know that he had left the man: and when this was done, the skill and wisdom of Solomon was shown very manifestly."

The Arabic word *djinn* ("spirit," "demon") goes back to the Assyrian-Babylonian vocabularies, and possibly even to Sumerian. We know it from the *genii* Aladdin lets out of his bottle in Near Eastern folklore, and from *genius*, by way of Latin. Similarly, Babylon's other category of demon, not a ghost but more a personification of evil in nature, was *shedu*, from which Arabic derives *sheitan*. Thus we have *Satan*, and presumably also an earlier meaning of *shadow*, as in "shade of the dead," an archaic way of speaking of ghosts.

The labyrinth of language also leads us back to Babylon's concept of semihuman demons: the *lilu, lilitu*, and *ardat lilit*. The first is male, the others female. These night demons symbolized sexual fear and desire. They were said to force themselves upon sleeping members of the opposite sex in order to have sexual intercourse with them. One Babylonian tablet speaks of a man "with whom an ardat lilit has had union." The seductive and fear-inspiring legendary figure of Lilith, as it was later spelled, moved from antiquity into Jewish folklore and was to be found in literature as late as the seventh century. Lilith was also said to have been Adam's wife while he was separated from Eve, but who then flew away and became a demon. She was credited with special power to entice children and emerged as an image of the woman who has died in childbirth—a restless spirit in many civilizations—and who seeks to abduct a child.

In Arabic tradition, the hoot of a night owl may be that of a woman's ghost looking for her lost child. Fascination, tragedy, and evil mix in the symbolism surrounding demonic entities. The "demon lover" concept had a revival in the Middle Ages where monks, in particular, felt tempted by a female entity, a *succubus.* Many such experiences were recorded in the eleventh and twelfth centuries. Conversely, a male incubus was said to seduce women, and witches and demons were supposed to be born from such a union.

Greek antiquity, which interacted with Babylonian and Judeo-Christian traditions, left literary-philosophical records that added a gloss of sophisticated interpretation to early, crude beliefs in demonic entities. Professor E. R. Dodds, writing on "Supernormal Phenomena in Classical Antiquity," puts the classical Greek experience into a wider framework: "States of 'possession' are everywhere viewed with a mixture of fear, curiosity, repulsion and religious veneration, compounded in proportions which vary with the nature of the symptoms displayed and also with the belief-pattern current in each society." He notes that "where the condition is persistent and accompanied by gross pathological behaviour, the possessing agent is assumed to be an evil spirit and ritual techniques of exorcism are developed—often with the effect of inducing by suggestion the symptoms they are designed to cure."

This concluding observation is a crucial point in evaluating the patterns of possession and exorcism. People who feel they are possessed tend to act within the framework of the words and actions dictated by their specific upbringing and culture. They are likely to respond, quite unconsciously, to expectation and precedent. If they are expected to vomit or to blaspheme a deity, the possessing demons are likely to oblige, perhaps reacting to the overt or covert suggestions of the exorcist. This interaction may be therapeutic in that it offers a ritualistic and tolerated outlet for hostility and internal conflict.

Professor Dodds reminds us that "in antiquity exorcism was practised by Jews, Egyptians and Greeks before it was taken over and institutionalized by the Christians." Where possession symptoms were mild, the possessed were sought out as channels to the supernatural. The Oracle of Delphi gained its fame from the individual woman, the Pythia, who spoke prophecies and advice in a state of trance. Dodds feels that the belief, "almost universally held by pagans and Christians alike over a period of more than a millennium, that through the lips of the Pythia an alien voice spoke in the first person, cannot be dismissed as a simple product of conscious fraud or even as a *fable convenue.*" Plutarch recorded that one oracular woman spoke with a hoarse voice and threw herself about as if possessed by an evil spirit. Dodd notes that this Pythia "rushed screaming from the sanctuary, and actually died within a few days."

Neither possession nor exorcism is without grave risks. The exorcist himself is in danger of psychic contagion; he may "catch" the demon as one catches a communicable disease; the element of contagion is often rather strong, and there are several cases of nuns experiencing possession as if a demonic epidemic had struck the nunnery. Official exorcism rites, of the Roman Catholic church as outlined in the *Rituale Romanum,* and by the Anglican church as recently as 1972, emphasize the need for mature responsibility on the part of the priest, as well as diligence in ruling out psychophysical illnesses that might mimic possession. But while there are numerous cases on record that show exorcists as virtually guiding the demon or devil into statements that comply with ecclesiastical concepts, it would be wrong to assume that all similarities are due to such patterns of suggestion.

The uniform character of possession, through various cultures and at various times, is striking. The Tungus of eastern Siberia, whose traditions resemble those of Alaskan Eskimos and of Indians in North and South America, have shown a form of spirit possession that rather cruelly illustrates the influence group attitudes can have on the individual. Weston LaBarre, in *The Ghost Dance,* says that "whatever the religious rationale the Tungus may have in terms of the supernatural," the phenomena of alleged spirit possession seem plainly to originate "in the human influence of persons on persons."

LaBarre notes that "the premise of Tungus religion is simple animism," which assumes that "spirits separable from the body exist," alien spirits "may invade the body of a person" and "while there, these alien spirits may act through the body in a strange manner." During a state of such possession, or "arctic hysteria," the person shows "intensified suggestibility or quasi-hypnosis." LaBarre adds: "That is, he may be compelled 'against his will' to copy the words and acts, often obscene, which bystanders force upon him for their amusement. Tungus society is brutal and pitiless. Preoccupied as the Tungus are with invidious power, the forcing of words and acts on the suggestible and helpless 'arctic hysteric' is almost a paradigm of human relations among them."

Depending on one's outlook, the underlying sameness of possession and exorcism may either be interpreted as proof of the universal presence of devils, demons, or possessing spirits, or as clear indication of the basic identity of the human psyche. As it happens, LaBarre's observations on the Tungus can be applied, with appropriate qualifications, to the possession-exorcism pattern that has existed or does exist just about everywhere. The *shaman* ("priest-witchdoctor") plays nearly identical roles in northern and southern Asia, and he has equivalents elsewhere in the Far East, in Africa, and the Americas. LaBarre observes "a psychic resonance between the shaman and his clientele," as if "mass assent were spread by psychic contagion." The shaman, in his trance, speaks as the voice of a possessing spirit.

LaBarre uses "arctic hysteria" to describe a passive state of possession, "during which the person is helplessly exploited by the spirits or the people about him." He speaks of *olonism* as "an active and self-induced state," during which the person "exploits the spirits and the people around about him." An "active" state of possession can be found in parts of Africa, in Brazil and the Caribbean, notably Haiti.

The distinction between the two types of possession is not always clear-cut. In the passive state, LaBarre writes, "the person may relax, weep, or loudly express himself," either directly or as the mouthpiece of the spirits: "Spirits often say things that ordinarily could not be said either before the elders or before children. They represent a naive 'return of the repressed'; the cult is the therapy of the culture." Further:

"Thus, typically, a young person might express a secret sexual wish openly and without fear of consequences. When holding a spirit, the olonist may require personal attention, sacrifice, prayer to himself or herself, express sexual desire for a named individual, either directly or in conventionally understood symbols, or otherwise break the usual taboos of behavior, without personal blame."

LaBarre notes that both states are "rationalized as being due to 'spirits,'" but sees their origin "in the enculturational and other psychic pressures by other people on the individual." LaBarre cautions against the all-too-easy view of such possessions and exorcisms as mere chicanery or as "a naive disclaimer of psychic responsibility for one's own wishes and acts." He writes that, "given the premises of animism, the belief in such spirit behavior is entirely sincere, however it is exploited."

Dr. Henri F. Ellenberger, interviewed in *Psychology Today* (March 1973), linked exorcism with psychotherapeutic technique. He stated: "Man always has made therapeutic use of the unconscious; shamans and medicine men of primitive societies used it. The unconscious has two traditional therapeutic uses. In the first, the healer brings out aspects of the patient's unconscious and uses them to cure him. Exorcists did this when they caused a supposedly latent possession to appear and cast out the induced spirit along with the disease. In the other form, the healer cures his patient by using a state of ecstasy that he brings about within himself (this is the method of some shamans who travel in the spirit world to recapture a soul supposedly escaped from its body). These healers often go through long periods of 'initiatory illness' to learn their art."

Let us not assume for one moment that possession is, in most cases, anything but a seriously and sincerely experienced—deeply frightening and debilitating—encounter with what vividly appears to be the supernatural world. At the same time, the exorcist who is himself convinced of the reality of possession is clearly the most potentially successful. The woman or man who is possessed by a demonic entity is quite literally "at odds with himself." Pierre Janet, the French pioneer of psychiatry, is quoted by Walter M. Horton (Union Theological Seminary) in a paper on "The Origin and Psychological Foundation of Religion According to Pierre Janet" in *The American Journal of Psychology* (January 1924) on the reality of this dilemma. Janet noted the bewilderment of someone troubled when actions "performed obviously by himself, are so contrary to his own habits and character that they seem to be those of a foreign person, hostile to himself, who has somehow got possession of him."

Possession is, in this aspect, closely related to yet another unusual psychological phenomenon: multiple personality; here, several distinctive personalities emerge alternately within one person, often hostile to each other and to the "host" person whose body they occupy. Another related phenomenon is that of spirit mediumship. The medium, in a trance, becomes the vehicle for many seemingly discarnate personalities who speak and at times act through the medium. Often, the medium's mannerisms and even facial expressions are strikingly altered and correspond to those of the spirit personality. The same thing can happen in possession. Other psychic phenomena that show kinship with possession are poltergeist phenomena; telepathy and clairvoyance, as we shall see, have also been related to the possession phenomenon.

The significance of successful exorcism lies not only in the field of religion or abnormal psychology, but, in my view, most importantly in the areas of psychosomatic medicine and psychotherapy. Shaman and exorcist are ancestors of modern psychotherapy, just as alchemy is the forerunner of chemistry and physics. In terms of scientific evolution, we are only a hair's breadth away from the thought habits of so-called superstition; we still have many more questions than answers on mental illness and on the physical illnesses that seem to have an emotional base.

Gregory Zilboorg, M.D., writing on "The Restless Surrender to Demonology" in *A History of Medical Psychology,* pointed to the vast gap between ancient Greek medical thought and "the revival of scientific curiosity during the Renaissance." Medical thinking in Arabic civilization, Zilboorg writes, "was free from the demonological theories which swept over the Christian world and was therefore able to make clear-cut clinical observations on the mentally ill." At the same time, western European medicine "became an art for the healing of bodily ills only," having "divorced itself completely from the consideration of mental phenomena." During this interim, "the medical man dared not look independently into normal or abnormal psychology. Those suffering from psychological difficulties were treated as heretics, but the few who were fortunate enough to be considered 'naturally' ill were for centuries treated with exorcisms."

By the thirteenth and early fourteenth centuries, a physician facing a psychopathological problem "put together as best he could the traditional and somewhat garbled physiologies of old Greece and Alexandria and the astrology, alchemy, demonology, and simple prayers of his own day." But the idea that "physical illnesses were natural and that mental illnesses were mostly supernatural became more crystallized." The term "devil sickness" came into use. Zilboorg felt that "the ecstatic religious tradition, the faith in the miraculous and the cultural monotony of medieval life must have contributed a great deal toward the spreading of mental illness."

By the fifteenth century, "the magician, the sorcerer, the heretic, and the psychotic began to be perceived as one and the same, the servants of Lucifer." Soon after, "fear of the invading cohorts of Lucifer which threatened to overrun the Christian world" had become consolidated, and Zilboorg notes that "medical psychology became a part of codified demonology." Western Europe was setting up a legal-theological system of exorcism techniques, unaware that similar methods had been practiced in yet-to-be-discovered continents consistently for millennia. Whether facing demon or pathology, or even "demonopathology," the practice of exorcism has always incorporated elements of such modern concepts as psychodrama, encounter therapy, or the engaged therapist's alliance with his patient in a struggle with an unseen antagonist.

There are two main areas on which history and individual cases of exorcism throw light. The first is the relationship between patient and exorcist, which is parallel to that of the psychiatrically oriented clergyman and his disturbed parishioner, as well as the relationship between psychotherapist and patient. To begin with, the exorcism ceremony is never perfunctory; the exorcist is deeply involved, as may be others who stand by to drive out the demon. The possessed person has uncensored opportunity to act out his "demon," to be accepted at face value. The encounter exposes vanity, violence, and playacting in the most seriously therapeutic meaning of these words. It is a no-nonsense battle for a human soul. Satan is real; the antagonist can be pictured; the Demon Within emerges, resists, is cornered, banished.

The second point which emerges is that of our interdependence and our inner multiplicity. There are many personalities inside of us, and these are exposed in varying mixtures to those around us. We are at each other's mercy. Arthur Koestler, in his novel *Darkness at Noon,* writes of the ambivalent intimacy between the interrogator and the accused; it is as if the exorcist is urging a demon to reveal himself or appealing to the possessed's unconscious to clarify itself and to yield. The exorcist is never engaged in "nondirective" therapy: he has an aim and, while his own vanities and quirks are ever-present, he is a man in active combat, not in passive observation.

In specific religiocultural settings, exorcism may well be more effective than any other procedure. The roads to the human soul are without number. We are, everyone of us, unique. Our demons are personal. They may be the creation of examples, pressures, expectations from those around us. Or they may be our private escape from a bewildered self. We may be, to use a common phrase, "possessed by an idea," or compelled into actions totally alien to our standards. Quite likely, these foreign impulses will be the very opposite of our carefully structured civilized identity. Small wonder that the exorcist may hold up a metaphoric looking glass and say, "Behold, here is the demon: he is your mirror image!"

2. Jesus as Exorcist

Christian concepts and practices derive directly from the words and works of Jesus Christ. His ministry of healing is central to the narratives we find in the Gospels. Yet, theologians of various denominations disagree when they face the question, "Was Jesus an exorcist? Did he, in fact, cause demons to leave the bodies of the afflicted?"

The original biblical accounts are usually brief and fragmentary. Voluminous interpretations and commentaries have created a superstructure that nearly prevents us from seeing the underlying events with full clarity. In addition, successive selection and sifting of translators add to obscurity, and to the task of searching for exactness.

One striking example is that of the Gadarene demoniac. We have narratives of this event in Mark, Matthew, and Luke. They vary in some details and phraseology, but there can be no doubt that the basic facts are identical. Let me tell it as I read it.

Jesus and the disciples crossed a lake from Galilee by ship and arrived in a place where the Gerasenes, or Gadarenes, lived. Christ fell asleep during the crossing, resting on a pillow near the ship's stern, while high winds tossed the boat around. The disciples woke him. "Master, we are sinking," they cried. "Do you not care?"

Christ awoke. He addressed the water and the wind, and the storm abated. According to Mark, in the New English Bible translation, he said to the sea, "Hush! Be still!" The wind dropped and there was a dead calm. Jesus asked the disciples,

18

"Why are you such cowards? Have you no faith even now?" The disciples were awestruck, and said to each other, "Who can this be? Even the wind and the sea obey him?"

They put the boat ashore, presumably where the village of Khersa is now located. It was getting dark. Mark tells us that as Jesus stepped ashore "a man possessed by an unclean spirit came up to him from among the tombs where he had been dwelling." Luke, in the same translation, calls him "a man from the town who was possessed by devils." The bedeviled man had lived in the town before, but now he stayed in the graveyard. Matthew describes him "as exceedingly fierce," apparently trying to block their way.

The man had been bound and chained before, but he had broken these fetters, escaped from the town and hidden in the tombs. "And so, unceasingly," writes Mark, "night and day he would cry aloud among the tombs and on the hillsides and cut himself with stones." He ran around naked. Luke wrote, "He was driven off by the devil into the wilderness," according to the King James Version; or, as in the New English Bible, "with the devil in charge, made off to the solitary place."

The three accounts indicate that the "unclean spirit" or "devils" were many. Luke says that when Jesus asked the man to tell him his name, he replied, "Legion," because "many devils were entered into him." The man also cried out, "What do you want with me, Jesus, son of the Most High God? In God's name, do not torment me." This plea was made, according to Mark, because Jesus was already saying to him, "Out, unclean spirit, come out of this man!" Luke says he "commanded the unclean spirit to come out of the man." Matthew states the plea was addressed to the "devils," which urged Jesus not to "torment us."

The three versions agree that not the man, but the possessing entity or entities suggested a way of ridding the man of their presence. A herd of pigs was feeding on the hillside, and the entities asked Jesus to cast them out of the man and let them go into the swine. He commanded the "unclean spirits" (Mark) or "devils" (Matthew and Luke) to leave the man and go into the pigs. Mark says there were 2,000 of them; Luke says there was "a herd of many." When the entities entered the pigs, they rushed into the lake and drowned.

The swineherds ran away and told all and sundry of what had happened. When the news had spread, others came to the lakeshore to see for themselves. Mark says, "They came to Jesus and saw the madman who had been possessed by the legion of devils, sitting there clothed and in his right mind; and they were afraid. The spectators told them how the madman had been cured and what had happened to the pigs. They begged Jesus to leave the district. As he stepped into the boat, the man who had been possessed begged to go with him. Jesus would not allow it. He said, 'Go home to your own folk and tell them what the Lord in his mercy has done for you.' "

Regardless of small discrepancies among the three accounts, or differences in translation, the basic outline of this dramatic incident is clear. Jesus and the disciples encountered a madman who had suffered much, believed himself to be inhabited and tormented by unclean spirits or devils; Jesus succeeded in ousting the entities, and the man was cured.

Was Jesus, then, an exorcist?

J. H. Crehan, S.J., writing on "Exorcism in the New Testament" in the pamphlet *Exorcism,* published by a Commission Convened by the Bishop of Exeter, England (London, 1972), reminds us that "it was to be expected that the Messiah when he came would show that he possessed the power of an exorcist" and that "the primitive preaching," such as that of Peter in Acts (10:38) which said Jesus "went about doing good, and healing all that were oppressed by the devil," gave "as one of the chief characteristics of the mission of Christ the fact that he freed men from the power of the devil."

Interpreters emphasize that Christ's healing techniques differed from the traditional exorcising rites of his time. Some

current commentators see in his approach a sophisticated understanding of the afflicted, particularly the mentally ill, that fore-
casts modern methods of psychotherapy. Certainly, an air of
patient understanding, unlike the dramatics of the shamans of
all ages, pervades the accounts of Christ's exorcisms. It illustrates
that treatments of mental illness, be it "possession" by real or
imagined demons, by complexes, compulsions, uncontrolled
drives or personality segments, have a great deal in common.

Prof. Merrill F. Unger, Dallas Theological Seminary, notes in
Biblical Demonology (Wheaton, Illinois, 1952) that "the simplicity and effectiveness of the method of Jesus and his disciples
in casting out demons, and the loftiness of their demonological
conceptions in general, stand in the more arresting antithesis to
current thought and usages, when it is realized that the lower
range of ideas and practices actually prevailed among the people
with whom the Lord and His followers came into constant
contact."

Unger finds that "Jesus' method of setting the demonized free"
contrasted with other approaches because it "consisted neither in
magical means nor in ritualistic rigmaroles, but in His own
living word of infinite power. He spoke and the demons obeyed
Him as Lord of the spirit world. In one respect all those who
were demonized exhibited the same phenomenon. They all
recognized Jesus and owned his power . . ."

The Reverend Leslie D. Weatherhead, minister of the City
Temple, London, uses the case of the Gadarene demoniac to
illustrate his concept of Christ's essential psychotherapeutic mo-
dernity. He may have spoken to the madman by the lake as if he
were addressing devils, but he was really drawing him out,
putting him at ease, bringing his own knowledge and powers to
bear in a way the man could comprehend.

Weatherhead, in *Psychology, Religion and Healing* (Nash-
ville, 1954), analyzes the Gadarene case against the background
of his own visit to the historic spot of Christ's successful exorcism,
which struck him as "strangely uncanny, weirdly desolate." He

recreates the mood of the "superstitious disciples, who thought pigs were unclean and graveyards full of devils." Gadara is actually twenty-five miles from the lake, and so, Weatherhead reminds us, we are probably inaccurate when we speak of the "Gadarene demoniac." He doubts that the pigs would have traveled twenty-five miles from Gadara to the lake, crossing the deep Yarmuk river on their way, to throw themselves into the sea. As Weatherhead reconstructs the event, Jesus had chosen to come to the shore for a bit of rest, but instead devoted "Himself to this poor, wild patient driven into exile, and spends the night with him." He believes that Jesus first tried suggestion when he told the "unclean spirits" to leave the man. Next, by asking him his name, he used "another method which to the modern psychologist is full of significance."

By asking the man's name, Weatherhead says, Jesus was seeking "power" over him, since, within a given tradition names were often kept secret because having knowledge of a name meant gaining a strength and advantage which Jesus used to advance the healing process. Weatherhead goes still further, interpreting use of the word "legion" as pointing to the madman's possible abuse by, or "some shock at the hands of the Roman legion." Perhaps the unfortunate man had witnessed a massacre of the innocent, as a child, which had been "quite sufficient to drive him into psychosis."

Dr. Weatherhead adds: "And now the community had exiled the patient right out of the security of their own fellowship into a wild graveyard in a foreign land, where he is left to live amongst the pigs, terrified by spasms of fear which leap up from his repressed memories into consciousness, and express themselves in maniacal frenzies and in loud cries. The destruction of the herd of swine is simple to understand. It is well-known that pigs easily panic." He assumes the pigs may simply have panicked as the madman shrieked, and "everybody in Jesus' day believed that Devils hated water." If they were driven into the pigs, and the pigs drowned, the devils would be finished. Also, "the demoniac interpretation" was probably "useful to the swineherds when they had to account for the loss of apparently the whole herd." Lastly, Weatherhead notes, the cured psychotic tried to become one of Jesus' followers, and he attributes this to the man's "transference" experience in psychoanalytic terms.

Weatherhead does not "wish to explain away a miracle by using familiar psychological mechanisms," but feels that while "the energies released belonged to a supernormal plane, Christ took pains to suit His method to His patient." This method, he says, far more complicated than a mere laying on of hands, was one "with which analytical investigation has made us familiar."

The Reverend Gebhard Frei notes in his article "Probleme der Parapsychologie" that biblical accounts "leave the conviction that Jesus of Nazareth was the greatest exorcist known to the history of religion." He feels, just as Weatherhead, that Jesus had a manner all his own when dealing with possession cases. "His technique always amounted to a categorical command, and the result was sudden. He dealt with the spirit world in a royal manner."

Whether by miracle or a form of psychotherapy suitable to the mores of his society, Jesus did fit many of his healings into an exorcistic pattern. The instances themselves are numerous. Mark (1:33–39) refers to a series of exorcistic healings: "And even when the sun set, they brought unto him all that were diseased, and them that were possessed by devils. And all the city was gathered together at the door. And he healed many of them that were sick of diverse diseases, and cast out many devils; and suffered not the devils to speak, because they knew him. . . . And he preached in their synagogues throughout all Galilee, and cast out devils." Luke (7:21) writes that Jesus "cured many of their infirmities and plagues and of evil spirits; and unto many that were blind he gave sight." Obviously, not all illnesses were attributed to demonic possession, nor treated by exorcism, or Mark would not speak of "diverse diseases" and then refer to devils separately. Luke also lists infirmities, plagues and "evil spirits" separately.

What is striking, translation differences not withstanding, is the casual way in which "evil spirits" or "unclean spirits" are equated with "devils" or "demons." The various hierarchies of possessing entities that we encounter in so many civilizations and in so much interpretive literature are not reflected in the Gospel accounts of Christ's healing miracles.

One is probably justified in assuming that cases of demonic possession mentioned in the Gospels were either emotional or emotion-linked. The devil is held responsible not only for symptoms of illness, but also for states of mind and attitudes. Thus, Luke (8:12) notes that "those by the wayside are they that hear; then cometh the devil, and taketh away the words out of their hearts, lest they should believe and be saved." In other words, the devil is held responsible for those who vacillate and change their minds.

Mark links two accounts, one which specifically mentions possession and another that implies exorcism (7:24–37). Jesus, to get away from public attention, went "into the territory of Tyre." As in the boating trip that led him to the Gadarene demoniac, he was unable to keep his anonymity. He went into a house near Tyre, hoping to remain unrecognized, but "almost at once a woman whose young daughter was possessed by an unclean spirit heard of him, came in, and fell at his feet." The woman, a Phoenician from Syria, "begged him to drive the spirit out of her daughter." Jesus said to her, "Let the children be satisfied first; it is not fair to take the children's bread and throw it to the dogs." The woman answered, "Sir, even the dogs under the table eat the children's scraps." To which Jesus replied, "For saying that, you may go home content; the unclean spirit has gone out of your daughter." This exchange is taken from the New English Bible. (It is not clear why the woman's reply should have been instrumental in getting rid of the possessing spirit, but I will cite one interpretation later on.) When the woman went home, "she found the child lying in bed; the spirit had left her."

Immediately following this incident, Mark narrates an event

which Weatherhead says "implies a demon." Returning from the Tyre area to Galilee, Jesus passed through the Ten Towns. There he was brought another patient, a deaf man with a speech impediment, "with the request that he would lay his hand on him." Instead, Jesus took the man away from the crowd, "put his fingers into his ears, spat and touched his tongue." He then looked up to heaven, sighed and said "Ephphatha," which meant "Be opened." The man's ears "opened" and he was able to speak clearly. Jesus told his followers to keep quiet about the case, but the more he cautioned them, the more they spread the news of his healings.

The use of spit, like blowing or breathing on a person or a possessing demon, is an exorcism method of long standing. I have seen it, to this day, often enough in modern Greece, where a woman will admire a pretty child, for example, and immediately make spitting sounds in order to keep away demons, the evil eye, or other influences that might be jealous of the child and seek to do it harm.

While with the man in the Ten Towns exorcism is implied, Luke makes it specific (11:14) when he speaks of a case in which Jesus "was driving out a devil which was dumb." He says that, once the devil had come out, "the man could talk." This is an instance much cited in theological literature, because Luke quotes some people who witnessed this healing of accusing Jesus of using Beelzebub, the prince of devils, to drive the devils out. (From this remark the saying "driving out the devil with Beelzebub" has entered common language; it is now used as a casual metaphor, much like, "jumping from the frying pan into the fire.")

Accusing Jesus, in effect, of being in cahoots with the prince of the devil aroused his ire. In his reply he said, "If it is by Beelzebub that I cast out devils, by whom do your own people drive them out?" This was clearly designed to put his skeptical audience on the defensive. Beyond this, it indicates that exorcism was being practiced by others ("your own people") at the time of

Jesus, although the Gospels strongly suggest that he was far more successful than others in casting out devils, as in other healing practices. Unger notes that Christ "does not defend or attack these exorcists in this passage," but merely refers to them in his argument. He adds, "As regards Jewish exorcists specifically, it does seem clearly implied by Jesus' allusion to them that they did, in some cases, at least, expel demons, and that not by evil power."

In Acts (19:13) there is a reference to a group of traveling exorcists, who appear to have moved from town to town as itinerant healers. The men, whom the New English Bible calls "strolling Jewish exorcists," decided to see whether they might not get better results by using the name of Jesus to drive out evil spirits. They said, "I adjure you by Jesus whom Paul proclaims." Among those who were, so to speak (and to use a pagan Greek phrase), trying to "steal his thunder," were seven sons of the Jewish chief priest Sceva. They had no luck with at least one evil spirit, who answered back, "Jesus I acknowledge, and I know about Paul, but who are you?" The evil spirit flew at the would-be exorcists and gave them a beating.

The account continues: "This became known to everybody in Ephesus, whether Jew or Gentile; they were all awestruck, and the name of the Lord Jesus gained in honor. Moreover, many of those who had become believers came and openly confessed that they had been using magic spells. And a good many of those who formerly practiced magic collected their books and burned them publicly."

On the whole, the Gospels indicate that Jesus used only his words, his commands, to oust the demons; that he did not utilize the traditional magical devices which the Jewish people, to whom he belonged, had inherited from earlier civilizations. But when the disciples awoke him, on the way to the Gadarene demoniac, he did address the wild waters and winds as if they were demonic entities. This is reminiscent of the exorcistic pleas to the demons or gods of the elements to be found on the clay tablets of Sumeria and Babylon; and, as we have noted, Jesus' spitting at the devil that possessed the deaf-and-dumb man is a timeless ritual.

When he addressed the distraught Phoenician woman in Tyre, who asked him to drive the devil from her daughter, Jesus objected to the mother throwing bread to the dogs. This may have been a reference to the belief that demons hid in food remnants. Dr. William Menzies Alexander notes in *Demonic Possession in the New Testament* (London, 1902) that Jesus had, at one point, asked his disciples to gather up food fragments, "discouraging the idea that demons lurk in crumbs." Alexander noted that Jesus had "no faith in the ceremonial washing of hands, so repelling the notion that spirits may rest on unwashed hands." Considering the age-old and universal nature of some neurotic compulsions, of which frequent hand washing is probably the most common, some compulsive washing may have been unrelated to exorcistic ideas.

Dr. Alexander points to other differences between Christ's exorcism methods and the magical traditions of his contemporary society. He was not afraid of "drinking borrowed water," and made a point of asking for water from a woman in Samaria; he went off and fasted in the wilderness, rejecting the idea that deserts were "the special haunts of evil spirits;" and he acted to dispel "the association of demons with animals."

Weatherhead writes that "if Jesus had been the child of His age in the matter of what we are pleased to call superstition, He would have shown the fact in other matters. In opposition to this, He went out of his way to show His own disbelief in the popular demonology of His day, save in so far as disease caused by alleged demon possession was concerned." The Reverend Weatherhead says that "apart from the contest of disease and the possible exception of the storm on the lake [he ignores the symbolic spitting] Jesus makes no reference to devils, though the conversations around Him were full of references to them. He makes an exception when He talks about certain types of illness. Then He does seem to accept the view of demon possession."

Weatherhead deals with Christ's manner of address to the

storm on the lake, noting that he said, "Be muzzled!" or, depending on the translation, "Hush! Be still!" much as he would have
spoken to the demon possessing a person. The writer gives us five
alternative explanations:

"The use of the word may be accounted for by (a) the possibility that Jesus believed in the storm demon, (b) that Jesus
made a concession to the disciples who thus believed, (c) that
Peter thought Jesus was exorcizing the storm demon, and used
this word when telling Mark the story, (d) that Mark introduced
it himself or (e) —the interpretation I favor—that Jesus addressed
the words 'Peace, be still,' to the men in the boat who spread
panic and uselessness in a storm by giving expression to the
'demon' of fear."

The question of whether Jesus believed in demons and exorcised them, or whether he didn't, is so basic to all of witchcraft,
demonology, possession, and exorcism that it calls for further
exploration. C. H. Dodd wrote in *The Authority of the Bible*
(New York, 1929) that "He could not have spoken so effectively
to His time if He had not spoken in its terms." And Weatherhead, who views Christ as a skillful and empathic therapist,
suggests that "He was unwilling to act or speak in a way which
might make His patient suppose that He thought the patient's
malady 'mere imagination.' The patient, then as now, would lose
that confidence and rapport which are so essential, unless the
healer, for the time being at any rate, accepted the patient's own
story of his troubles. If the healer of a mind, then or now, gave
the patient the idea that in his—the healer's—opinion that
demons were the result merely of a disordered imagination, the
patient would be driven farther into the dark recessess of his
illness and be more difficult to heal. In the early stages of mental
treatment, at least, the physician must not contradict unneces-
sarily the patient's interpretation of his symptoms."

These erudite and facile interpretations are worthy of consideration. While it is no longer quite fashionable to speak of
"demythologizing" Scripture, such post facto commentaries con-

tinue to be popular and can, in their own way, be enlightening. Still, there is no substitute for that primary of primary sources, the Bible itself. And, when all is said and done, it is well to go back to the original source. Here is a case of spirit possession—or epilepsy—that is characteristic of Jesus' methods.

Mark, in one of his most moving passages (10:10), speaks of Christ's transfiguration on a mountain, witnessed by Peter, James, and John. Returning to the disciples, they encountered a large crowd that engulfed them. A man told Jesus, "Master, I brought my son to you. He is possessed by a spirit which makes him speechless. Whenever it attacks him, it dashes him to the ground, and he foams at the mouth, grinds his teeth, and goes rigid. I asked your disciples to cast it out, but they failed."

The account states that the boy was brought before Jesus and "as soon as the spirit saw him," it "threw the boy into convulsions and he fell on the ground and rolled about foaming at the mouth." Jesus asked the father, "How long has he been like this?" The man answered that his son had suffered this way from childhood, and that the spirit had "often tried to make an end of him by throwing him into the fire or water." The man added, "But if it is at all possible for you, take pity upon us and help us."

Jesus replied, "If it is possible! Everything is possible to one who has faith."

The boy's father cried out, "I have faith; help me where faith falls short."

The people were crowding around them, and Jesus "rebuked the unclean spirit," saying, "Deaf and dumb spirit, I command you, come out of him and never go back!" Mark says, "After crying aloud and racking him fiercely, it came out; and the boy looked like a corpse; in fact, many said, 'He is dead.' But Jesus took his hand and raised him to his feet, and he stood up."

3. Chinese Complexities

The family of Mr. Chang, in the village of Chang-Chwang Tients, was invaded by a demon. It seemed to possess female family members in turn, or even two at a time. What did it want? The demon asked to be worshiped, to have its own shrine in the house, wanted public rites performed in its honor, and generally to be obeyed.

Chang, a man of fifty-seven, a fairly well-to-do landowner with a good literary education, was incensed by it all. He told the women who had at first followed the demon's instructions, spending a good deal of money to abide by its wishes and commands, to ignore the demon and to go about their business.

In the contest of wills that developed, the demon took complete control of one of the women and confronted Mr. Chang. Again, he refused the demon's demands. Speaking through the woman, the entity threatened revenge. As reported by John L. Nevius, a Christian missionary, in *Demon Possession and Allied Themes* (1894), the possessed woman tried to burn down the house, went on a rampage of destruction and stealing, and kept the household in an uproar. Nevius reported:

"Food, clothing and valuables were stolen from the house in the most mysterious way, even when they were secured by lock and key; furniture and dishes shook and rattled without any perceptible cause; and three women in the family were, at different times, possessed. Fires broke out without apparent cause, and, on one occasion, destroyed a number of buildings."

Chang had heard that the Christian converts had received "immunity to the inflictions of evil spirits," and he asked for help. A Chinese Christian, Mrs. Fung, visited the family, and for a while things were fairly quiet. But a few days later, the Chang family advised another Christian, Mrs. Liu, that the demon was getting out of hand: two women had been possessed and were unconscious.

Mrs. Fung and Mrs. Liu found the Chang place in an uproar. Buckets of water stood in strategic spots, so that fires could be extinguished quickly. Mrs. Chang's eldest daughter-in-law, about forty years old, was "under the influence of the demon and demanded wine, which she drank in large quantities, though ordinarily she would not touch it." She was lying on her bed, tossing her arms and "staring wildly and unnaturally." The two women spoke to the possessed, addressed the demon and at first found it defiant. But when they left, the daughter-in-law went to sleep peacefully.

The second possessed woman, a widow, was being guarded by her daughter, as she had tried to kill herself by drowning or hanging. The visitors held an informal exorcism service with her. On the way out, they ran into the daughter-in-law, who seemed fully recovered but did not remember what had happened during her possession state. The report continues:

"About this time, just before dark, an extraordinary commotion occurred among the fowls, which rushed and flew about in great consternation without any apparent cause, the family and servants having great difficulty in quieting them and restraining them from running away. After a while, they cowered in the corner of the yard in a state of fright. The swine belonging to the family, more than a dozen in number, occupying a large pen or walled inclosure near by, were put into a singular state of agitation, rushing about the inclosure, running over each other and trying to scramble up the walls." The people in the family assumed that the demon "had taken possession of the fowl and swine." Dr. Nevius refers to the biblical account of Jesus' ousting the Gardarene demons (see pp. 18–22), which entered a herd of swine.

I have presented this story in some detail, because it has a number of universal elements, as well as intriguing psychological undertones. To begin with, as in some other possession cases, there is a good deal of similarity to what are called poltergeist phenomena: shaking furniture and dishes, mysterious fires, valuables disappearing. Then too, the family constellation must have made for certain strains, with some of the women perhaps unconsciously lined up against or demanding the attention of Mr. Chang. The wine-drinking daughter-in-law reminds one of possessing entities in the Macumba cults of Brazil, who frequently ask for liquor and cigars for the persons they possess. Interpersonal strains in the Chang family do not rule out, of course, that the impact of an outside force or faith could be strong enough to change the psychological climate and thus oust the demon, real or imagined, and end its multiple-possession performance.

Missionary reports are, of course, subjective and selective. Although the Nevius book is a particularly valuable document in the literature of exorcism, the cases in it—as, indeed, can be said for the majority in the field—do not answer the crucial question: How long did the effect of the exorcism last? There is, in exorcism, an element of faith healing or spiritual healing, with strong psychosomatic undertones. However, as in other borderline healing techniques, such as hypnosis, symptoms may well recur, so that the exorcism or its equivalent may have to be repeated.

So far, with this illustration, we have been able to observe that a case reported in the summer of 1883 bears a remarkable resemblance to elements of possession and exorcism that are age-old as well as contemporary, and that know no geographic limitations. China, however, has its very own complexities. While most other contemporary societies show either remnants of traditional exorcism patterns, or even a revival of interest as in England, emergence of the Communist regime in 1949 created a break with all past activities categorized as "religious superstition." Among these, prominently, is ancestor worship, with its strong spiritualistic aspects, a tradition which was to be abolished to facilitate effective application of Marxism-Leninism.

Because of internal warfare and the events of World War II and after, the pattern of Chinese society has been in flux since the overthrow of the Manchu dynasty in 1912. We have noted that Sumerian traditions of exorcism, reflected in Babylonian tablets, may go back as far as 3000 B.C. No one knows how far back Chinese practices extend. That Babylonian and Chinese possession fears are identical in their concern about "hungry ghosts" is fascinating. There is, however, no evidence to link these two civilizations. China is unique in its spiritualistic traditions as in so much else. Ancient patterns are intricate, complex, and permit a multiplicity of approaches. Let's try to sort them out.

Whenever anyone delves into China, its mysteries are frequently not clarified as one might expect, but multiplied. Not only is the Chinese pantheon of gods and demigods the fullest of all ancient people, but folklore, myth, legend, superstitions, and magical tradition are incredibly complex. A Chinese ghost, for example, has physical as well as ethereal characteristics; it can die. If it does die, this ghost of a ghost, a *chien,* initiates a whole new set of variables in myth, legend, and popular religious belief.

There are two basic spirit influences in Chinese popular religion: good and evil, the *shen* and the *kwei.* The shen are beneficent influences; they are good and intelligent, an integral part of the universe using spiritual energies for the betterment of the world. The kwei are evil, malignant, disturbers of the law who play a leading role in distributing evil throughout the world. The shen are traditionally the Chinese peasants' allies in their constant battle with the kwei, for they have always believed that demons surround them day and night. The spirit world is intimately interrelated with the physical world. Every bush, stone, leaf, insect, wind, road, mountain, and animal is the possessor of a spiritual being. All of nature partakes of the dangers and benefits of such a clear dualism between good and evil. This spirit world is modeled largely after man's own. Spirits may appear in human or animal shape, have human passions, may be tantalized, caught, and even killed. When an evil spirit is exorcised, it most often simply flies off to do evil another day. But when a kwei is killed, it becomes a *Tsih,* something so horrible that it terrifies even other evil spirits.

Information about Chinese religious beliefs and practices predate the last several decades. Most information, even before this, came from missionaries who had little use for Chinese pantheistic and animistic inclinations. Still, reports from missionaries, especially English, French, and American, agree that spiritism was almost universal in China. Chinese belief in, affection, and concern for their gods are complex and pervasive. There are even special ordinances in Chinese ethical behavior (as described in the *Yu Li Ch'ao Chuan,* or *Divine Panorama,* something like a Chinese version of Dante's *Inferno*) in which the walls or stove of a home are not to be altered during winter or spring, as the "Spirits of the Hearth and Threshold are liable to catch cold." One missionary wrote in exasperation at his lack of success in converting the Chinese to Christianity: "There is no driving out of these Chinese the cursed belief that the spirits of their ancestors are ever about them, availing themselves of every opportunity to give advice and counsel."

While this plentiful pantheon of spirits and demons is founded to a large extent in the Chinese religious belief of "ancestor worship," it has further been expanded by two thousand years of coexistence among the "three religions" of China: Taoism, Confucianism, and Buddhism. The corruption of Taoist religious beliefs, however, must be considered the primary foundation upon which most of the Chinese occult tradition is based. But even Confucianism, as ancient as Taoism, often fell prone to demonological persuasion over the years.

In their purer forms, Confucianism (basically an ethical and social system) and Taoism (a mystical religion more prone to corruption because of its proximity to pantheistic and animistic beliefs) dominated ancient Chinese religious life. Buddhism, introduced into China from India near the end of the Han dynasty (206 B.C.–A.D. 220), brought its own contribution to the Chinese magical pantheon, such as metempsychosis, or transmigration of the soul. Chinese attraction to animism and pantheism initally favored Taoism over Confucianism and Buddhism.

While Confucianism appealed to the educated more than to the peasant, even emperors, philosophers, and the literati succumbed to animistic demonology. The peasant found personal solace in the world of spirits and demons, for they were both good and evil and gave him some influence over a harsh and baffling world. He placed crackers by his door to ward off demons, he glanced in mirrors fitfully to get glimpses of the future from friendly spirits, he listened to the first words spoken anywhere within earshot after walking seven steps to help divine the answer to his troubles when he couldn't afford a soothsayer. He possessed numerous gods upon whom he could call in times of difficulty or disaster. He had a god of the village gate, a god of the moat, and he even had a grasshopper god pictured generally in a diminutive skirt.

The sheer number of deities—in the thousands—that dominated the countryside was overwhelming. As Taoism became corrupted by its very popularity, its magical properties expanded. (This is not to imply that Taoism was itself a form of magical religion. Evidence that magic was a corrupt form of Taoism can be seen in Lao Tzu's own writings: The *Tao Teh Ching* is almost completely free of magic-ritual. The *tao-shih,* or Taoist magician-priest, was a later development as Taoism became influential. As the practical use of magic by the people and its systematization developed, corrupted forms of Taoism were eventually used by government and religious authorities for their own ends. Taoism as a mystical philosophy and religion should be kept separate from the occult-oriented popular religious forms. See Max Weber's *The Religion of China,* chap. 7, "Orthodoxy and Heterodoxy," The Free Press of Glencoe, 1951.) It was commonly believed that the Taoists held the secret of the philosopher's stone and the elixir of immortality. Taoist priests were actually called "the Immortals." This not only attracted the great mass of people who suffered brutally difficult and short lives; emperors themselves often found such ideas irresistible—despite the fact some were supposed to be already immortal.

The theme of magical beliefs and influences runs through popular literature, including the supernatural tales (*ch'uan-ch'i*) of the Tang dynasty (618–906), and especially popular forms of Taoism. The state even paid for magical services. The *Feng Shui* (geomancers), officially recognized, were frequently called upon to counteract evil influences or locate the propitious spot for a new building or road. Other magical undertakings include astrology where the magician obtains the person's nativity sign (everyone has eight characters associated with his birth) and places the appropriate characters on a piece of paper and burns them in a candle, muttering an incantation of whatever disaster one wishes to befall an enemy.

While there are substantial differences, traditional Chinese belief frequently has a familiar ring. For example, if one wishes to bewitch one's enemy, the prescription is universal: it is done by making a figure of the person to be bewitched or injured, and burning it slowly in a fire. A popular method for contacting dead ancestors is the planchette or ouija board. Before the planchette became the craze of nineteenth-century European society, China had used it for hundreds of years. The planchette was used not only for contacting departed spirits, but for directly contacting demons and gaining from them a prophecy of what the future held.

Worship of prophetic demons was so common in some provinces that Christian missionaries labeled these areas "Demon Land." One returning educational missionary, Mrs. Montague Beaucham, reported to a fascinated London society that she personally knew of one instance where demons had foretold a flood through the planchette. Other claims for the efficacy of the planchette included the prophesying of the famous Boxer Rebellion at the turn of the century. Often, planchette use was not as innocent as believed in the West. There were many reports of planchette users becoming "possessed," of being thrown into a fit and "frothing at the mouth" as one report described it. Missionaries also reported cases where some users suffered a complete breakdown and insanity; this, too, is a universal experience.

This brings us back to the most common traditional beliefs in China: "possession" and "exorcism." Possession occurs in a wide variety of ways. A rock, insect, or any animate or inanimate object can be possessed of a man's spirit, and vice versa. Either a shen or kwei can possess a human being. Animals are frequently animated by a spirit or demon who can change its shapes at will. The fox, tiger, and wolf represent the most malignant beings and are considered equivalent to evil demons. It was especially the fox, however, that constantly kept the countryside in fear. People believed that fox demons might enter into men and children, and fell them with disease, insanity, and even death.

When the fox changed his form, he often became a pretty girl, and it was in this form that he did most mischief. In many places, the fox demon was suspected of arson and other disasters. Rural shrines and temples were erected for fox spirits, and in private homes his name was written on a tablet charm. While the fox was believed to be a powerful and dangerous demon, he was regarded more as a pixie or brownie than a wild animal. It was also generally believed that fox witches in human form had sexual intercourse with animal demons. Such superstitions and fears have traditionally pervaded all classes and ranks of Chinese society, and have been known on occasion to cause whole villages to be thrown into a panic.

Like belief in possession, exorcising magic is very old in China, and some trace its use back 2,700 years before the Christian era. But exorcising rituals were performed not only for fox demons, but to control most problems encountered by the peasant: pestilence, bad weather, dangerous animals, unsuccessful crops, difficulties in love, illness. Exorcism was also used to combat evil spirits, ghosts, specters, and generally to influence the mysteries of heaven and earth.

When illness struck, doctors might come and go, priests could plaster charms on the door and chant incantations. Still, the Chinese believed the evil spirit causing the illness feared and hated the exorcist most. A case reported (August 20, 1878) in *The Peking Gazette,* a quasi-official publication reporting on legal and cultural matters of the Chinese community, related just such a belief. The Military Governor of Heh-lung-kiang had investigated the case of a young girl who suddenly began having fits. She took on the appearance of "a dangerous lunatic," the report said, danced wildly about, singing crazy songs and cursing. Her father asked a doctor friend to treat the child. The doctor, Chao Shih-sheng, who found normal medicine did not work for the child, decided that she was possessed.

When this sort of thing happened, normal procedure required the intercession of a Taoist priest or exorcist. However, Chao, though not an experienced exorcist, took it upon himself to frighten the evil spirit from the girl's body. The father agreed. Chao found two large farmer's knives, set out a table with incense and candles, and had the father and mother lay the girl down flat, face up. Chao then put knives horizontally across the girl's stomach, the edges touching the skin. The handles of the knives were held by two of Chao's friends, while the father prayed that his daughter's madness would be cured.

Chao took one of the knives and left the room to pray to the spirits for aid. Returning, he approached the nearly unconscious girl, chanting and muttering incantations to the spirits to use their powers to drive out the demons. In order to frighten the evil spirits within the girl, he lifted the knife threateningly, then brought it down on the child's stomach with the back edge first. The knife, unfortunately, was two-edged, and Chao cut so deeply into the girl's stomach that her bowels protruded and she died, after writhing for a short time.

Court record shows that the doctor, or would-be exorcist, was convicted of manslaughter and sentenced to strangulation, a sentence which ultimately was carried out. The story became famous, and most people believed that the demon had revenged itself for its exorcism. If it was to be driven out, the reasoning went, the demon wanted to take the child and the exorcist with it. If Chao had not performed the exorcism himself, had an exorcist-priest been called, the ritual would have been somewhat different—if not successful, at least less bloody.

A more typical case of possession occurred in China in 1907 as an epidemic fever swept the country. Several thousand people had already died of this fever, and the following incident became widely known. A young man of twenty-two crossed a field near a small market town, accompanied by several people from his village, and carrying two baskets of beans on a pole suspended over his shoulders. While passing through a large cemetery, surrounded by tombs, the young man stopped suddenly, frozen in his tracks. He said the baskets had become so heavy he could no longer hold them. His concerned companions, thinking him ill, took over the baskets, when the young man began to tremble and twist in spastic, wild gestures.

As the villagers took him home, he began to speak in "tongues," claiming through the gibberish that he was being possessed by the fairy-fox sister, *Eul-ku*. The fox in China is regarded as a potent force of the "other world," but as there are good and bad devils, there are also good and bad fox spirits. This was apparently a "good" fox spirit. At home, the voice speaking through the young man claimed to have the power to cure all afflicted with the disease then decimating the countryside. Word of the possession spread quickly and soon people flocked to the village. Crowds clamored for attention, begging the fairy-fox sister to cure them or their relatives. Presents and money were lavished on the youth. The prefect of Hwo Chow, a nearby village, sent his sedan chair and had the "fairy sister" brought to his official residence where he begged her to cure his son, then suffering an acute attack of fever. The prefect offered the fairy-fox sister almost a hundred dollars; whereupon rituals were carried out and the prefect's son recovered.

With this "cure," Eul-ku was hailed as a deliverer. So many

begged for her attentions that the young man refused to visit anyone in his private home, and advised all those offering money to take some ashes from the censer burning before her image (the tablet of the "Fairy of the Golden Blossom," a charm established for the Eul-ku), mix these in some water and take the potion, and "you will be infallibly cured." It was everyday practice in China to burn charm papers, steep the ashes in tea or hot water, and drink the potion as a potent force against bad influences or demons, and with this advice the youth succeeded in having numerous temples and altars set up in private homes for the worship of the fairy-fox sister. So great was his success that he received much money and was able to construct a handsome brick building as a shrine to the fox demon that had so luckily possessed him that day in the cemetery.

While the success of the fairy-fox demon and the rags-to-riches story of the possessed youth are exceptional, his methods of possession and exorcism were not. As elsewhere, the Chinese concept of possession is based on the idea that sickness and diseases result from an evil spirit or demon having entered the person. The exorcist's battle with the offending spirit possessing an ill or insane person revolves around whether it is the shen or the kwei. Whichever it is, the opposing power is called upon to neutralize the disturbing influence.

There are two types of exorcising witches (mediums—those possessed by shen, or good forces) with slightly differing techniques in diagnosing illness or possession: Taoist witches, the *Tao Nai-nai,* who generally find the pulse and utilize charms, prayer chanting with musical accompaniment (drums, cymbals, etc.) ; and those known as "Magic Grannies," the *sien-nü,* who shampoo the whole body of the possessed person in order to expel the demon. In certain areas of southern China and Indochina the possessing demon was believed to reside just between the skin and the flesh of the possessed. The thumbs were regarded as the door by which the demon makes its exits and entrances. In line with these beliefs, the possessed person's thumbs were held tightly by the exorcist in order to prevent the demon's too-early escape. In Japan, where foxes are also regarded as possessing demons, these are believed to enter the body under the finger nails.

Objects universally used to dispel demons in Chinese exorcism range widely from coins taken off the lips of a corpse, a knife that has been used in killing a person, iron nails used in closing a coffin, to the cloth bearing the mark of a mandarin's seal, peach-wood, willow branches, mugwort, and blowing on one's hands upon leaving the privy.

Once possessed by her favorite exorcising demon, or in a mediumistic trance, a witch will mutter inarticulately. Those present ask the entranced witch whether the sick person will recover. "If you will kindly restore him," the dialogue usually goes, "we shall make you a present of money; we shall celebrate a feast in your honor." The medium's spirit generally waits until something of value is offered or given, then replies to questions and begins to give advice on cures and family problems.

Another form of possession, not part of the shen-kwei spirit forces, is that by wandering ghosts. The Chinese peasant fears these "hungry ghosts" greatly. They are regarded as the malevolent, wandering spirits of those who have come to violent or unfortunate ends. Contrary to popular Western belief, the Chinese are not prone to violence or barbarism. This unfortunate view developed perhaps from the fact that many crimes which we in the West consider minor, such as theft or types of assault, are capital crimes in China. Strangulation (popular in the West in the exotic form of *garroting*) was generally the punishment inflicted upon the Chinese felon.

The average Chinese abhorred violent death and believed that the virtuous man will always die either of illness or old age. So when the nonvirtuous met a violent end, their avenging spirits wandering over the countryside were doubly feared. Another reason wandering ghosts were feared was the common belief that if the spirit of a murdered man can bring about the violent death of some living person, he may then return to earth alive and well, as if nothing had ever happened. The spirit of the person whom he just helped to a violent death passes into the lower world and suffers all the misery and anguish of a disembodied soul—while the first spirit resides snugly in its new, healthy body.

A case believed by the populace to have been caused by such a wandering ghost occurred in Canton to the wife of a government official. The official's wife, jealous of two female domestic slaves, had brought about their death. In order to cover up her guilt, she tried to make the girls' deaths look like suicide and hung their bodies from the neck in their rooms. But apparently the woman's conscience tormented her to the point of a nervous breakdown. She became hopelessly insane, frequently impersonating the victims of her jealousy. The Chinese supposed that the avenging ghosts of the girls possessed her and used her own mouth to confess her guilt. The report comments: "In her ravings, she tore her clothes and beat her own person with all the fury of madness; after which she would recover her senses for a time, when it was supposed the demons quitted her, but only to return with greater frenzy, which took place a short time previous to her death."

Many of the facets of traditional Chinese demonology have equivalents in other parts of the world, although involvement with possession and exorcism shows varying degrees of intensity in different places and at different times.

II. Where Psychology Ends

1. The Devil as Father Symbol

"Somebody who becomes severely depressed by the death of his father must surely have loved this father very deeply. It is very strange that a man like that should have turned the devil into a substitute for the beloved father." That is how Sigmund Freud, our century's most influential psychologist, analyzed the contradictions represented by a case of devil possession which ended in successful exorcism. Dr. Freud's classic paper dealing with this case, entitled "Eine Teufelsneurose im Siebzehnten Jahrhundert" ("A Devil Neurosis of the Seventeenth Century"), originally appeared in *Imago* in 1923 (vol. IX, no. 1) and is regarded by many as a key document in psychoanalysis; Freud's concepts, as expressed on this case, have been cited by supporters as well as antagonists of his ideas.

Freud's attention was first drawn to the case by a noted Viennese librarian and researcher, court councilor Dr. Rudolf Payer-Thurn, who had come across a document dealing with "miraculous rescue from a diabolical pact through the mercy of the Holy Mary." The document had been prepared at Mariazell, a village about three hours from Vienna, for centuries a center of pilgrimage, where a visitor today can find many gifts and notes of thanks deposited at the church. Dr. Payer-Thurn, noting that the possessed man, Christoph Haizmann, had experienced convulsions and hallucinations, asked Freud for a medical opinion. The two men published separate analyses of the Haizmann case, and Freud wrote: "This story of demonological illness represents a truly valuable find. It shows clearly, and without much interpre-

45

tation, what its essence is; just as some mines furnish pure metal which elsewhere has to be refined from ore with much difficulty."

Who was the victim, and what had happened to him?

Johann Christoph Haizmann had been born at Traunstein, Bavaria, in 1652. At the age of sixteen, he lost one or both of his parents—Freud assumes that it was his father—and found himself destitute, cut off from all moral and financial support. Haizmann, a painter, represented his encounters with the devil on eight occasions in a three-part painting: the left panel shows the devil accepting a pact in black ink; the right panel, a pact in blood; the center is the scene of exorcism at Mariazell.

The bedeviled young artist went to the parish priest of the village of Pottenbrunn in Lower Austria in 1677 and told him of his dilemma: he had made a pact with the devil, and the time was drawing near for the devil to come and claim his body and soul; now he wanted to be freed of this debt and to retrieve the written document. The village priest, Father Leopold Braun, responding to the plea of the twenty-five-year-old man, addressed a letter of recommendation to the father superior of Mariazell, dated September 1, 1677. In it he mentioned that Haizmann had been working as a painter at Pottenbrunn Castle for several months. On the previous Sunday, he suffered convulsions during church services; then made his confession and took Communion. The convulsions returned, becoming more severe and continuing into the following day. Haizmann, questioned by the local prefect about his condition, was asked whether he was practicing "the forbidden arts or was somehow involved in a pact with the Devil." Following the somewhat suggestive questioning, Haizmann asked to be alone with the prefect and confessed that nine years earlier, when he was worrying about finding work and was hard-pressed financially, "the Devil came to him in the forest" and urged him to surrender.

According to Father Leopold's letter, Haizmann refused the devil nine times but then consented. A pact written in blood specified that Haizmann would give himself to the devil after nine years, "body and soul." The period was to end on September 24, and now, wrote Father Leopold, "this despondent man eagerly desires to free himself through recovery of this pact"—a favor he hoped to gain through the Virgin Mary at Mariazell. The parish priest urged the Mariazell monastery to help the unhappy man in his efforts.

Haizmann was cordially received at Mariazell, where he presented Father Leopold's letter and was given asylum by the monks. After some initial delays and difficulties, exorcism undertaken by them was successful: in a dramatic scene in the church, close to midnight on September 8, the feast of Nativity of the Virgin Mary, Haizmann was released from his pact with the devil. Contemporary accounts allege that the very document written by Haizmann was recovered from its diabolical possessor; it appeared inside a window of the chapel. The exorcism ritual, about which the records give no details, was conducted by Father Sebastian Meitinger, aided by three other monks, Father Heinrich Pitz, Father Leopold Donagello, and Father Basil Finckeneis.

Christoph Haizmann, returning to Vienna, stayed at the home of his married sister. However, instead of the serenity he had hoped to achieve, he suffered a series of horrifying visitations, visions, or hallucinations which drove him anew to despair, and greatly upset other members of the household. There had, it appeared, been two written pacts: one he had recovered; another one, perhaps an earlier draft, he regarded as still in the devil's possession and therefore as a threat and a commitment.

Haizmann returned to Mariazell, and new exorcisms took place. On May 9, 1678, following extended rituals of exorcism, the second version of his pact with the devil was returned to Haizmann: contemporary accounts state that the pact appeared, torn into four pieces and rolled into a ball, on the steps of the church altar. These events and, no doubt, Haizmann's own emotional needs, prompted him to give up his secular life as a painter and turn to the monastic life. On February 9, 1681, he joined the Order of the Brothers Hospitaller in Vienna. On

March 14, 1700, he died in a monastery of this order in Neustatt, Bohemia, at the age of about forty-eight.

Some details of Haizmann's possession and exorcism have been recorded carefully by several sources; others have proven elusive and have given rise to lively controversy among scholars.

Dr. Gaston Vandendriessche of the Belgian Foundation for the Advancement of Scientific Research has presented much documentary material in *The Parapraxis of the Haizmann Case of Sigmund Freud* (Louvain, 1965) "to test a psychoanalytic hypothesis developed by Sigmund Freud." Two British psychologists, Drs. Ida Macalpine and Richard A. Hunter, differ with Freud's conclusion that Haizmann's devil visions were a father substitute in their work *Schizophrenia* (London, 1956) ; they see Haizmann's emotional difficulties in his unconscious preoccupation with human procreation (conception, pregnancy, and birth) as well as in "confusion about his sex identity."

There is room for such varying interpretations in accounts of Haizmann's experiences that go beyond the brief outline of experiences at Mariazell. The material Payer-Thurn found and showed to Freud included various texts, supplemented by Haizmann's paintings made during the period of his possession and visions. A folk song dealing with the first, seemingly successful exorcism, popular throughout the area, was presumably carried from village to village by itinerant ballad singers. Vandendriessche cites it. The song speaks of a "painter boy" who was "freed of a pact signed in his own blood, miraculously, at Mariazell." The song relates Haizmann's suffering (the name appears as Christoph Holzmayr) and various attempts to kill himself "with gun and knife," trying to "hang himself with a rope" and "drown himself off a small pier."

The metamorphosis of the devil in Haizmann's visions show how his own emotions changed from easy agreement to fear and terror. Eight images show the devil at the time of the initial pact in the figure of a respectable citizen. The scene is pastoral—not really a forest but a clearing—a picture postcard scene in blue and green tints. Satan looks eminently respectable, his hat and coat reflecting quiet affluence, his beard well trimmed. He is accompanied by a small black dog. Haizmann pictures himself in a rather admiring pose, smaller than the devil and looking up as the devil hands over the pact written in black ink. Unquestionably, this self-portrait makes the painter look blandly feminine, giving some support to Freud's view that homosexual elements, no doubt fiercely suppressed, played a part in Haizmann's delusional pattern.

Soon, the image of the devil changes. Successive pictures show him as a terror-inspiring figure: in blood-covered brownish red, partly naked, horned, with birdlike claws instead of feet, and with two rows of breasts, one above the other. He also has a long tail, which in one picture ends in a sort of arrow. In another, Freud writes, is "a penis that ends in a snake." The prevalence of breasts, "this emphasis on female sexual characteristics," Freud notes, "must appear as a notable contradiction to the assumption that our painter regarded the devil as a father substitute." Freud felt that the devil was usually pictured as "masculine, even supermasculine." Macalpine and Hunter disagree and reproduce medieval drawings showing diabolic figures with both masculine and feminine characteristics.

In picture after picture, Haizmann's devil becomes less and less human. Finally, painted as he appeared during the final exorcism, he is a satanic dragon figure and truly terrifying.

Freud lists multiple breasts in the paintings as one clue to Haizmann's sexual associations with the devil figure. A second clue, the number nine, is repeated in the nine-year gap between the pact and its implementation and the nine days Haizmann resisted diabolic temptations. Freud writes: "The number nine is well known to us from neurotic phantasies. It is the number of pregnancy months, and wherever it appears, it draws our attention to pregnancy phantasies. With our painter we are dealing with nine years, not nine months, and one can say that it is a significant number in other respects as well." But, Freud says, we know that, in dreams for example, unconscious-mind activity takes certain liberties with numbers: "Five dollars in a dream might represent fifty, five hundred or fifty thousand dollars." The pregnancy association, together with the image of a penis painted on the devil in almost every picture, prompted Freud to make the following observations:

"These two small indications do, after all, permit us to guess which specific element dictates the negative aspect of his relation to the father. He recoils from a feminine attitude toward his father which has its climax in the phantasy of giving birth to his child (nine years). We are quite familiar with this resistance from our analyses, where, during transference, it takes on peculiar forms and creates much difficulty. Mourning for the lost father, heightened by yearning for him, our painter's repressed pregnancy phantasy is reactivated, against which he must defend himself through neurosis and by degrading his father."

Freud knew full well that this sort of interpretation would not endear him to a lot of people: "Hardly any other element of psychoanalytic inquiry into the psychic life of the child strikes the average adult quite as repelling and unbelievable as a feminine attitude toward the father and the resulting pregnancy phantasy of a boy." The two pacts Haizmann wrote with the devil were differently worded. The one in black ink read: "I, Chr. H. write myself over to this Lord as his indentured son for nine years." The second version, written in blood, stated: "Chr. H, I, write myself over to this Satan to be his indentured son and to belong to him in the ninth year with my body and soul." The phrase "indentured son" is awkward, but the best possible translation of the German words *sein leibeigener Sohn,* which Haizmann used. Others have translated it as "bodily son," which fails to convey the utter self-abandonment inherent in the word *leibeigener,* used to refer to serfs (or slaves) owned outright by their masters.

Haizmann sold himself to the devil—but in return for what? Freud notes that, traditionally, such bargains promise power, riches, and sexual conquest. Haizmann was buying something else: peace of mind. He had become depressed and destitute, as a contemporary Latin document put it, *ex morte parentis*. Freud says: "This means his father had died, he had become melancholy, and the devil, who came along and asked him why he was upset and mournful, promised to help him in every way and lend him his support. Here we have someone who gives himself to the devil in order to be free of an emotional depression. Certainly, this must be regarded as an excellent motivation by anyone who can empathize with the suffering in such a condition, and who also knows how little the art of medicine can do to lessen this suffering."

Macalpine and Hunter think that Freud made it too easy for himself, that he selected from the Haizmann records what bolstered his own psychoanalytic structure, including the father-devil correlation and the bubbling-up of infantile homosexual fantasies; they see it as an example of "the easy transition in psychoanalytic writings from speculation, to hypothesis, to theory, to established fact, without supporting clinical evidence." The two British psychologists do not see a penis in Haizmann's devil painting, but rather an "obvious umbilicus." The dog accompanying the sedate-looking devil in the first painting reminds them that the dog is "widely accepted as a symbol of rebirth."

The two psychologists write that "Freud's emphasis on and preoccupation with the phallic significance of the devil led him into a corresponding error regarding the evidence in the manuscript on the painter's father." *Ex morte parentis,* they say, "simply means that a member of the painter's family had died, who may well have been a parent; but the manuscript does not allow a more precise definition of the relationship." Vandendriessche, also quite critical of Freud's "accuracy, selectivity and objectivity," suggests that the key Latin word "should most probably be translated as 'father.' "

Freud's critics feel that he had built a glittering edifice of conjecture on a minimum of selected facts. Macalpine and Hunter charge that Freud's treatment of the Haizmann case not only illustrates his own tendency to fit information onto the Procrustean bed of his own theories but, beyond that, his Haizmann paper "has exerted an important and direct influence on present day psychiatry, because it provided some of the fundamental evidence for the psychoanalytic theory of psychosis." According to them, Freud based his theory of a persecutory symptom formation on unconscious homosexual wishes, which then became "the psychoanalytic model of delusional symptom formation in general, as if no other types of delusions existed." Macalpine and Hunter counter with the observation that the most common delusions "do not concern the patient's relation to the outside world" but "his relation to himself, his mind and his body." The two psychologists had been disappointed by Freud, whose theories had given them "much less help in understanding and treating patients than we had been led to expect." Childhood homosexual yearnings, even if reawakened, they conclude, could not have driven Haizmann into his severe emotional state and prompted him to make a pact with the devil; it was due to confusion about his own body and his fear-fascination with procreation.

As a matter of fact, Freud's Haizmann paper does not read dogmatically, but rather as exploratory, tentative, rather apologetic and good-natured. He acknowledged that psychoanalysis is always being accused of "complicating plain facts by fanciful interpretations" and added: "It is not my intention to use this case to prove the validity of psychoanalysis: I go on the assumption that psychoanalysis is valid and use it to clarify the demoniacal illness of this painter." Freud assumed that Haizmann's pact with the devil was "a neurotic phantasy" and wrote: "But if someone does not believe in either psychoanalysis or the devil, he will have to be left to his own devices in dealing with the painter's case, whether he has his own means of doing so, or whether he thinks that no explanation whatever is necessary."

Freud noted direct and personal analysis of Haizmann, who

had been dead for well over two centuries, was not possible. But the bedeviled painter's diary of the period between the two exorcisms provides many clues to his state of mind. Let us remember that he left Mariazell following the first exorcism on September 8, 1677, and went to Vienna to stay with his sister and her son. He also joined the Holy Rosicrucian brotherhood. All went well until October 11, when he had the vision of "a well-dressed gentleman" who asked him to give up this membership, throw away the brotherhood's "nonsensical" literature and acknowledge that he had been "abandoned by everyone." Haizmann wrote that he refused to listen to this, and the apparition faded away.

The Mariazell exorcism had not changed the conditions of Christoph Haizmann's life. He was as destitute as before, felt as abandoned as before and was torn between desire for a good life and religious pressure for self-denial. These contradictory elements could easily be dramatized by Satan and Christ. And that is what happened. On the twelfth of the month, between two and three in the morning, Haizmann saw himself in a gorgeous banquet hall, lit by candles in silver chandeliers, and surrounded by well-dressed men dancing with beautiful women. The "gentleman" who had tempted Christoph Haizmann in his previous vision now asked him to destroy paintings of the diabolical apparitions he had made and offered him "a substantial sum of money." He also asked him not to make an altar painting, presumably of the Mariazell altar, where the exorcism had taken place.

Haizmann's response to this was: "I refused to listen to him; I went on my knees and said the Rosary. Then I put myself down on the floor, said the Lord's Prayer five times, five Hail Marys, one Creed, and then all the images disappeared."

The dreamlike hallucination recurred between three and four o'clock on the morning of October 14. Again, Christoph Haizmann found himself in the banquet hall. Tables were set with exquisite cutlery and golden goblets. Among the elegantly dressed gentlemen was the one who had previously tempted

Haizmann. He now invited the painter to sit between him and the woman next to him. When Haizmann refused, the woman approached him to lead him to the table. The painter fought off this temptation, shouting over and over, "Jesus, Mary and Joseph!" The family heard the painter's cries, came into the room, found him awake and terrified. His sister, brother-in-law and others tried to exorcise the vision by sprinkling holy water throughout the room. Finally, as the diary reports, they "came up against these hellish monsters in disguise," who retreated slowly, were pushed against the wall, and disappeared.

Haizmann's hallucinations of diabolical temptation grew more grandiose. Two nights later he found himself in the hall once again. This time, a throne was part of the setting, made of gold and flanked by lions that held a royal crown and a scepter. Gentlemen were standing around, talking agitatedly and apparently awaiting the arrival of the king. When the expected royalty did not arrive, the tempter approached Haizmann, urged him to occupy the throne, and offered to honor him eternally. When the painter shouted the names of Jesus and the Virgin Mary, the vision disappeared.

From then on, the visions varied a great deal, seesawing between divine urgings and diabolical temptations. At various times, Haizmann felt himself in the actual presence of the Virgin Mary and Jesus Christ, and on visits to hell and a community of violent sinners. On October 20 and 21, the painter had an angelic vision, experiencing such "eternal bliss and eternal pain" that he could not find words to describe his experiences. An angelic or divine voice urged to "go into the wilderness" for six years. He saw hell, a large cauldron from which he could hear the moaning of human souls, and he saw the devil torturing them. On November 1, the radiant angelic-divine figure became visible to Haizmann after he returned from church service of All Saints' Day. It led him to a rose-covered meadow where he saw a flowering lily with three blooms on which were written the words Father, Son, and Ghost; on the stem was the word God.

On November 6 he fell into a visionary trance, even before being able to say his nightly prayers. Again, the angelic-divine entity took Haizmann away, this time into a city filled with crying, fighting, killing people. He observed immoral women and lewd acts, as well as dancing, singing, and other carryings-on. His guide said that these were "Children of Damnation." By contrast, he was then taken to a hermit's cave, inhabited by an old man who had lived in seclusion for sixty years, being "fed every day by the Angels of the Lord." While he was there, an angel brought the hermit three kinds of food, a loaf of bread, and a dumpling.

During this detailed vision, Haizmann felt himself being addressed by the Virgin Mary and saw Christ on the Cross. The Virgin said that Jesus, despite his innocence, had suffered for the painter and warned that Haizmann would suffer even more, as he was filled with sin. The angelic guide returned and asked Haizmann to become a hermit for six years. The painter decided the next morning to follow what he regarded as a divine command.

Yet temptation and torture returned. While worshiping in Vienna's Cathedral of St. Stephen, Haizmann admired and envied a well-dressed man accompanied by an attractive woman. At home again, following his evening prayers, he saw a bright form come down and strike him, and he fell into a coma. His sister came into the room, and the painter temporarily recovered. But then he felt enveloped by fire and stench, and rolled on the floor of his room so violently that blood gushed from nostrils and mouth. Smell and heat disappeared when a priest came. After the others had left, a voice warned Haizmann that he had been punished for wicked thoughts, and that he must become a hermit, as divinely instructed. On December 26 and 30, he experienced the presence of two evil spirits who tortured him with ropes and threatened that this would continue as long as he failed to join the hermit order.

Agonies of this kind took place repeatedly early in 1678.

Haizmann reported suffering at the hands of four and six evil spirits during the first half of January. On the thirteenth of the month, while painting a picture of the devil, he found Satan sitting at the table next to him; he vanished when the painter's sister came and sprinkled holy water. During Haizmann's visit to Mariazell for his second exorcism in May, he complained that he had been under constant attack by the devil.

The three-part painting in which the painter illustrated the two signings of pacts with the devil shows the satanic figure in his respectable role on the left panel. On the right panel is depicted the pact signed in blood; here, the devil is portrayed as fierce and terror-inspiring, claw-footed, horned, half naked. The painter's picture of himself is more masculine than on the left panel.

The center panel, larger than the other two, pictures the Mariazell exorcism, and is dominated by the upper part of the statue of the Blessed Virgin, much as it appears to visitors at the church to this day. A cloudlike formation covers the lower part of the figure. Before the figure, facing it, and showing only their backs in dark silhouette, are outlines of the four exorcists who succeeded in freeing Christoph Haizmann from his pact and persecutions.

There were, as is frequent in such cases, lapses in Haizmann's serenity even after he joined the Order of the Brothers Hospitaller. From this event in 1681 until his death in 1700 of slow fever, Haizmann experienced occasional temptations, as one account put it, "by the Arch Fiend," designed to foster yet another pact. However, one candid source notes that these tended to occur mainly when the painter-turned-monk had "imbibed in too much wine."

The second exorcism and Haizmann's admission to the monastic order did on the whole banish the visions and experiences that had plagued whom Freud called "this poor devil." Events following the exorcism at Mariazell implemented the visions that Haizmann had between the two exorcistic rituals. His financial difficulties were solved by joining the order, much as he had seen the hermit being fed by the angels of God. In the company of other monks, freed from the temptations of the world—with its elegant men and women, thrones, goblets, and chandeliered salons—Haizmann needed no longer feel alone and abandoned. He also no longer needed the devil for company and support, whether or not his own unconscious had conjured up a father substitute: the Church, through his Order, had taken over the parental role.

Freud put it this way: "Christoph Haizmann was sufficiently an artist and a child of his time to find it difficult to give up the sinful world. But finally, when he realized the hopelessness of his situation, he gave in. When he entered the spiritual Order, his inner struggles ended together with his material destitution." As Freud saw it, the painter had been concerned right along with bolstering his security, "first with the devil's help and at the price of his Salvation, and, when this failed and had to be abandoned, with the aid of ecclesiastical authority at the price of his freedom and of most of the pleasures of life . . . thus his road took him from his father, by way of the devil as Substitute Father, back to the devout Fathers."

2. Exorcism as Encounter Therapy

The possessed man or woman is writhing uncontrollably, uttering warnings or cries of prophecy, performing a wild dance, falling to the ground, blaspheming or praying, demanding or begging. It is the same everywhere, and it has been this way for thousands of years. The ghost-possessed Babylonian, the Gadarene demoniac who faced Jesus, the demon-possessed peasant women in nineteenth-century China, and sex-plagued nuns—what do they have in common, what psychodynamics merges with the images of devils, demons, and evil spirits that seem to use and abuse the people they control?

Let us try and find a common denominator to answer this question. To do so most effectively, one should look at possession cases from a variety of cultures, and not just sensational or awesome anecdotal fragments, but detailed and contemporary studies. I have brought together three reports that take us from India to the Caribbean and then to Germany. We will touch on Hindu traditions representative of Asia back to prehistoric times, on transplanted African religiosocial patterns, and on European Roman Catholic lifestyles. These are not cases that have reached us through parchments or much-told legends. Yet they are well within the millennia-old personality patterns we have come to recognize. A number of psychodynamic elements seem to unite these diverse settings and personalities.

An admirably thorough study of spirit possession in the north Indian village of Shanti Nagar was done by Stanley A. and Ruth Freed, now on the staff of the Museum of Natural History in

New York City. The Drs. Freed visited the village (its name and that of the people are pseudonyms) from November 1957 to July 1959. Their report was originally published in *Ethnology* (vol. III, no. 2, 1964). An object of the couple's close study was a young bride, Daya, and they were present during one of her frequent possession incidents. The ghost who spoke through Daya while she was unconscious identified herself most often as Chand Kor.

Why Chand Kor? This was the ghost of a girl who had become pregnant before marriage. The husband's family promptly rejected her and sent Kor back to her parents. But her father would not have her, saying "I won't keep you. Go jump in a well." After several days of urgings to commit suicide, the outcast bride suddenly left a group of youngsters with whom she had been playing, ran off toward a well, jumped into it, and killed herself.

The report states that Chand Kor's fate was typical of the way premarital pregnancies were handled in Shanti Nagar and nearby villages. A girl was goaded into killing herself because she had disgraced her parents. The Freeds state: "The father and other relatives may either force the girl to commit suicide, or the father may simply kill her. Village opinion will solidly support the family which takes this drastic step. Death will be reported to the police as an accident, suicide or result of illness."

Daya told Mrs. Freed of Chand Kor's fate, saying first that her death had been an accident, but quickly switching her story to suicide. The anthropologists report that when they "witnessed Daya's possession, the ghost of Chand Kor seemed to be the principle one involved, although there was some switching of names toward the end." During exorcism undertaken by a shaman, the ghost gave its name as Prem. But ghosts of people who die such deaths as Chand Kor "do not keep their promises" and are otherwise unreliable.

Daya was quietly sewing when the Freeds visited her in-laws' home. As her sewing machine hummed, a brother-in-law teased her. She remained quiet: "Although Daya's activities were perfectly proper, the aggressive teasing of her husband's older brother, against which she could not defend herself, and the fact that this was a breach of the traditional relationship could have disturbed her."

The girl's mother-in-law was telling the Freeds of Daya's physical complaints when possession began. Daya started to moan, breathed with difficulty, felt cold, and shivered. The women covered her with quilts. The girl became unconscious and the spirit took over. Immediately, family members began a crude kind of exorcism, blowing cow-dung smoke at her to drive the ghost away.

It did not work. Instead, the spirit started to speak in normal Hindi. The mother-in-law asked, "Who are you?" At first, the answer was, "No one." But when the question was repeated, the spirit said, "I am Chand Kor."

The ghost said it would remain with Daya until she could take her away into death.

The family tried another exorcism trick, putting rock salt between the girl's fingers and squeezing them together. Like other exorcism techniques, dung smoke and salt makes the possessed person uncomfortable, so that the spirit might be forced to leave her. But the salt merely caused Daya to let out a high-pitched scream, and the ghost began to talk with the women of the girl's family. The Freeds write:

"The ghost complained that it had been promised noodles (a delicacy eaten in summer) that morning but that the mother-in-law had given it none. A woman then said that she would give the ghost cow dung to eat. The ghost said, 'In the morning the girl was fed noodles, but I wasn't given any.' The woman repeated that she would give the ghost cow dung. The ghost said to the woman, 'You stop talking rot.' The woman said, 'You mother-in-law [an insult], you eat cow dung.' The ghost said, 'You eat cow dung.' The woman retorted, 'You mother-in-law, you bastard, you eat cow dung.' "

This low-level chitchat continued for a while. Once more, they put salt between the girl's fingers. This time, the ghost said it would leave before they could squeeze the fingers together. When Daya came out of her unconscious state, which seems to have resembled a mediumistic trance very closely, she saw the ghost standing in the next room. The women told her they saw only a trunk. They seemed quite convinced that it was indeed a spirit that kept seizing Daya, but they doubted that it was really the ghost of Chand Kor. Perhaps, they thought, it was an impostor spirit. The Freeds report that, in addition to the use of cow-dung smoke and rock salt, exorcistic gimmicks commonly used in the area were burning pigs' excreta, beating the girl, pulling her braids, using a copper coin, or summoning a shaman. Once, one of Daya's sisters-in-law had hit her, but a neighboring farmer told her to stop, saying Daya was not really possessed by a spirit but ill.

Finally, a shaman was called in. He had no immediate success, and other shamans tried to rid the girl of the possessing entity. At one point, two shamans worked together. The Freeds say "several treatments took place before the ghost was banished, and no one could be really sure that the ghost would not return." The anthropologists asked one shaman how he worked. He said he received his power from several Moslem and Hindu holymen or deities, notably the Hindu deity Hanuman. The shaman threatened the possessing ghost with the powers of these spiritual allies, but exorcism did not end until a virtual bargaining session between exorcist and entity had taken place.

Now the ghost identified itself as Prem, rather than Chand Kor; Prem, a girl from Daya's village, had died as the result of illness. Like Kor, Prem said she wanted to see the possessed girl dead. When the shaman asked why the spirit wanted to take Daya with her, it answered, "I just do." Then bargaining began. "Is there anything else you want in place of her," the shaman asked. When the spirit refused substitute gifts, the shaman became threatening: "You still have a chance. I haven't called my powers yet, and you can choose something else. If I call my powers, you won't be able to go even one step." There was a good deal of wrangling, with the shaman saying "some words in his heart." These, he told the visiting anthropologists, provided the exorcism with its real strength. With his inner prayers, the shaman called on Hanuman to catch the ghost.

Eventually, the spirit of Prem asked to accompany the shaman. He refused. After rejecting various gift ideas which the ghost suggested as substitutes, the shaman agreed to a payment of 1.25 rupees (about twenty-six cents), a length of red cloth, and a coconut to be taken to the Kalka temple in Chirag Delhi. Once again, the shaman threatened the spirit with the wrath of Hanuman. The Freeds write: "The shaman claimed that the ghost departed and Daya was cured. However, six days later she was again possessed and her family called two shamans." Among exorcism devices used by the different shamans were: citing mantras; a blue band around Daya's neck; cutting some of her hair and burning it; cutting some of her hair, tying it in a cloth, and taking it away; offering candy. While the other visitors might try physical abuse, the shamans seemed to avoid it. The report notes that "both styles of curing involve considerable conversation, during which the ghost can complain and insult to its heart's content," and "this might have a therapeutic effect upon the one suffering the possession."

The Drs. Freed observe that a possession victim is often in family difficulties and in a situation where "expectations of aid and support are low." I think one can safely say that in such cases the spirit, for all its abuse of the possessed person, becomes an ally in its emotional and social struggles. Daya was fearful of her husband's sexuality, separated from her family, and in an alien environment. Chand Kor, the pregnant girl who killed herself, made a dramatic ghost. The Freeds say that her spirit "was uppermost in Daya's mind and that Prem served principally to confuse the identification." They note that "deception and confusion about the ghost" held the interest of spectators and prolonged exorcism through several sessions. They feel that the possessed person "gains additional attention and has greater opportunity for expressing himself through the ghost."

The two researchers investigated four other possession cases in Shanti Nagar. They conclude that possession attacks men as well as women of varying ages, tends to relate to family problems, and occurs frequently among those who have little other support; and, "while the victim usually recovers, the condition can develop into a different and apparently permanent psychological affliction." They feel that "spirit possession may be thought of as a means of controlling relatives," at least in Shanti Nagar. In the Indian province of Uttar Pradesh the Freeds found that it may extend to nonrelatives, taking "a more general form of social control," and that the spirits are more aggressive.

The analysis notes that Uttar Pradesh women tend to ascribe "a considerable variety of illnesses and misfortune to spirit possession," such as menstrual pain, death of children, barrenness, and miscarriage. It is not clear whether women attribute these problems to spirits because of local traditions, or only when a shaman suggests it. A shaman may ask the ghost to identify itself; the woman may then accept possession, go into a trancelike state, and the spirit personality will emerge. The Freeds conclude: "Spirit possession of various kinds so permeates Indian culture that many people can become possessed, especially when aided by a skillful shaman or priest. Cases in which spontaneous attacks are lacking are probably best analyzed entirely from the points of view of precipitating events and secondary gains. Barren women, for example, can possibly convert the condemnation of relatives into sympathy by attributing their barrenness to ghosts."

Wherever we encounter possession, there is awe and fear. The Indian example of Daya has universal parallels. West African traditions that have remained alive, although with regional and language adaptations, can be found in Latin America, notably in Brazil and on the Caribbean islands. The so-called voodoo or *vodun* practices of Haiti, jazzed up to enthrall visitors, have taken on aspects of tourist attractions. But the tradition is strong, continues to hold its own among the population of Haiti, and can also be found in the Dominican Republic, the Spanish-speaking half of the island it shares with Haiti; in Jamaica; Puerto Rico; Trinidad, and elsewhere.

While Haitian vodun practices are the best known, they can be observed with perhaps less distortion and flamboyance in Trinidad, with virtually identical rites and vocabulary. While on French-speaking Haiti the possessed person who is "ridden" by the African god is called a *cheval*, Trinidad uses the word *horse*. The names of various entities, their personalities, and special roles are similar. One Haitian god, Ogun, also appears in Trinidad. Drs. Walter and Frances Mischel of the University of Colorado cite a case of possession involving this entity. Differences between Afro-Caribbean and Afro-Brazilian possession and cases elsewhere are expressed in the personalities of the entities. The gods of Haiti and Trinidad, for example, are ostensibly benign as behooves gods, in contrast to devils, demons, or evil spirits. But there is great similarity, and even identity, in the manifestations and underlying psychosocial patterns.

As the Freeds found in India, the Mischels note in their paper on "Psychological Aspects of Spirit Possession" (*American Anthropologist* 60, 1958), the possessed person "controls the activities of those around him." He or she may be humble or nondescript in a normal state, but when possessed, forceful, commanding, arrogant, and certainly the center of attention. At times, the Mischels note, "the possessed is in virtually absolute control of those around him. His slightest wish is immediately carried out, the onlookers are utterly at his disposal and ready to advance, retreat, sing, or keep silent at his command. Oil, rum, implements such as axes, swords, food, and candles, are quickly brought in response to his signals."

An unemployed laborer, not otherwise prominent in his Trinidad community, may be "master of an audience of several hundred people." Similarly, a woman who was a submissive maid only a half hour earlier, may, under possession, be transformed into and accepted as a "god." The Mischels observed an "almost direct role reversal—from passive impotence to central importance, dominance, power, and recognition." That doesn't always work, and at times attempts to "gain such stature" are met with "ridicule and rejection." Role reversal, as in other cultures, may include reversal of sex.

The Mischels described the possession of Tanti, a member of the Trinidad Shango cult. The short, heavyset woman was an average person of her age and class, pleasant-mannered, verbal, intelligent, highly active. But as the spirit began to "manifest on" or "catch" Tanti, the change in personality was striking. Her body seemed in seizure, shaking, stumbling, falling, arms rigid. She grunted and groaned. "At the same time," according to the report, "her jaw begins to protrude, her lips pout and turn down sharply at the corners, her eyes dilate and stare fixedly ahead. An expression of masculinity and fierceness envelops her face."

She is possessed by Ogun. She will be dressed like Ogun, with a red head tie and waistband, and holding a cutlass or sword and a bottle of olive oil. Her posture is erect and commanding, legs wide apart, hands on hips. Tanti is the "horse" for Ogun. His power is her power.

The Afro-Caribbean pantheon is varied. Basic personalities can be recognized, and names remain the same, but each entity is likely to vary with the horse it "rides." There have been other changes over the years in various communities and, of course, from country to country. The gods may call for obeisance, just as we have seen a Chinese spirit ask that it be worshiped in a special shrine; they may ask for worldly gifts to be consumed by the "horse," as in Brazil; they may be oracular, prophetic, uttering opinions of family and village affairs, ordering their decisions to be carried out.

The spirits aren't always taken seriously, nor are all their whims indulged (anymore than the shaman went along with the ghost that possessed Daya), but doubt is held in check by fear, ridicule by awe. Fashionable labels come to mind only too easily: hypnosis, autohypnosis, suggestion, autosuggestion, mass hypnosis, trance states, mental instability, and other general or psychological terms. As no one really knows where the validity of these terms begins or ends, they are merely convenient means of categorizing.

While Afro-Caribbean gods are regarded as relatively benign, and possession by them is invited, attitudes toward them are by no means uniform. In Brazil and Haiti, conflict and overlapping with Catholicism add to the complexity of an already intricate pattern. African gods are both feared and loved, cajoled, pacified, invited to take over a horse, or sought as supporters and allies. I think that the need for outside, supernatural backing is the strongest psychosocial impetus for conscious or unconscious invitation to god, devil, demon, or spirit.

Caribbean possession, in the African tradition, is mainly induced by drumming. The degree to which drumbeat contributes to group rhythm, group excitement, and group dancing might be compared to the interaction between rock music and a mass audience. Excitement can get out of hand. The Mischels report that some Caribbean gods may hurl their horses to the ground, "making them" roll or writhe in the dust or dance with great agitation and force. They write: "Drumming is an integral part of formal ceremonials. In combination with crowd excitement, singing, darkness, candles, circular rhythmic dancing, and other ceremonial aspects, drumming engenders an atmosphere in which possession becomes desired and usual behavior."

While drumming is a stimulus, the Mischels observed, as did the Freeds for India, that social "crisis" is vitally important. They noted that "the individual is apt to experience possession when confronted by serious marital or other interpersonal problems, by difficult decisions, by involvement in court cases, or by other severely frustrating or conflict-producing events. At such times, particular emphasis is placed on the messages and advice delivered by the power through the horse, as reported by the audience to the manifestations."

The possessed rarely hurt themselves, but often engage in aggressive and threatening behavior toward the audience, at times with sexual undertones. Some try to avoid possession, the Mischels observe, fearing "loss of self-control" or "potentially undesirable behavior publicly." Some Shango participants show "embarrassment, fear and avoidance," reflecting "ambivalent and conflicting attitudes in relation to possession."

The crosscultural role of possession is illustrated in a contemporary German case, where the priest-exorcist based much of his attitude on experiences in China and addressed the entities controlling a middle-aged woman in Chinese. This case has been reported by Klemens Dieckhöfer, M.D., and his associates at the University Mental Clinic in Bonn. In their paper "Zum Problem der Besessenheit" ("On the Problem of Possession") the authors note that Catholic and Protestant church authorities sought during the past two hundred years to "develop a detached, sober, and clear" attitude toward possession.

Writing from a psychiatric viewpoint, Dieckhöfer states that in Germany people experiencing possession, often categorized as "hysterical personalities," are likely to be "undifferentiated personalities of extreme piety." Few such cases contain enough biographical data to examine possession and exorcism from a psychiatric viewpoint, but the one cited by the Bonn psychiatrists does contain such information.

Although the German doctors give no name for the possessed woman, who was thirty-five years old when they learned of her condition, I will call her Paula, for the sake of the reader's convenience. What kind of life preconditions a person toward devil or demon possession? In Paula's case, neither parent had a recorded psychiatric-neurological illness. The girl was an ambitious high-school student, and twice came out on top of her class. She studied modern languages and education, and took an examination qualifying her to teach high school.

At the time Paula's case came to the clinic's attention, she was teaching at a Catholic high school in a major city, lived with her mother, had not married, and nothing was known about "any intimate relations with the opposite sex." She had originally shown a strong interest in religious matters when she received her first Communion. After puberty, Paula withdrew from her circle of friends. She became difficult and introspective; neighbors complained that she did not acknowledge their greetings and appeared to give herself "superior airs."

After her fifteenth birthday, Paula began to visit a local priest, whom she begged not to tell her mother of the talks. This continued for three years. When the priest, who also was her confessor, moved away, she tried to involve his successor in religious discussions, but he suggested she see a psychotherapist. One of Paula's teachers made the same suggestion, but nothing came of it.

Paula's mother heard through third persons that her daughter had told their parish priests she might kill herself during Sunday church services. When the mother confronted the priest, he said the young woman might be possessed by the devil. He recommended that she see a Jesuit who was a well-known exorcist. However, the Jesuit told Paula, after a long talk, that she was not suffering from possession and should go and see a psychotherapist.

Paula's reply to this was, "Now I am very disappointed."

She stopped visiting the parish priest and generally began to see more people of her own age group, mainly those she had met in school. After finishing high school, the girl became even more interested in other things, attended concerts and opera performances, and mixed more freely with others. During a vacation with her brother and mother, however, she became introspective once again.

In 1962, an appendix operation forced Paula to go to a Catholic hospital where a head nurse suggested that she talk to a priest. The nurse had found Paula's behavior, while praying and receiving holy water, rather odd and "suspected something evil." The priest, Father Joseph, had spent many years in China and was an expert in possession and devil exorcism. He later reported: "I asked the patient to visit me in the hospital chapel. I discovered this: She could not move anywhere near the tabernacle. She crept along the chapel wall, going backwards, and could not be persuaded to move to the front. I finally succeeded in coaxing her along the wall, away from the tabernacle, toward the sacristy. When I handed her a crucifix, she broke it into pieces."

Father Joseph concluded that possession was, on the basis of this behavior, "strongly indicated." He decided to begin exorcism rites. The psychiatric article does not state whether he obtained his bishop's permission to do so, as Roman Catholic practice currently requires. The account in the psychiatric journal continues:

"Going on the assumption that the patient's education was good enough to follow any exorcistic texts in Latin, which would enable her to mislead him, the priest said his prayers in Chinese. He felt that he encountered a significant phenomenon when he discovered that the patient understood Chinese, because she answered questions asked in Chinese by giving appropriate replies in German, although she had never learned a Chinese language. He told her in Chinese, for example, that she should not leave the room, something she tried to do quite often. She did it nevertheless. The priest uttered a special prayer in Chinese, which appeared to compel her to return."

For several years, these Chinese-language exorcism rites continued. Father Joseph told the psychiatrists, "The young lady certainly does not always reply to everything I ask or demand. At times, the devil within her had to reply, and he did reply. That was particularly the case when I demanded names. She often answered—and I didn't even know what that was supposed to mean—with the name, Tarantos." Paula wrote the name down, as well as the name Lucifer, but she could not write the name Jesus. Father Joseph's account continues as follows:

"After the various exorcisms, it was difficult to bring the young lady back to normal speech. Before I got her to react, I often had to use still another form of exorcism, so she could talk normally. Once she wrote the name of the Devil, and I then asked her to read out loud. She asked, 'What's that?' She just kept staring at the name. Finally, I read it aloud and told her, 'You just wrote this name, only about twenty seconds ago, yourself, with your own hand.' This puzzled her and I said, 'Well, if you didn't write it yourself, then he wrote it through you. Do you now agree that something is definitely wrong?' "

Holy water helped bring Paula out of her possessed state. Drinking was more effective than just sprinkling it on her. At first, Father Joseph reported, she wanted no part of it. Finally, at the end of one exhausting four-hour possession state, she drank some of it. The priest said, "Immediately afterward she fell into a most profound state of serenity. These were the most peaceful moments after the excruciating period."

During a year and a half, possession stopped, but then, in 1969, Paula tried to kill herself. Father Joseph said, "As a clergyman, I see this as the work of the Devil." Paula also took overdoses of drugs. Occasionally, she had to leave school because she had spells of fainting or unconsciousness. During exorcisms, while being blessed, Paula tried to seize the crucifix. Father Joseph once tried to force her to kiss it. She refused, and when she touched it she said it was like a burning fire. Finally, after much writhing and struggling, she did kiss the crucifix and then grew quiet.

Paula had visions of "a beautiful lady" while visiting Father Joseph at his hospital chapel. She described this event in her diary. Early in 1970, Paula encountered the vision in her mother's bedroom, carrying a cross. The vision handed the cross to her and said, "Love it." A few days later, the vision asked her to take Communion. She did so, but wrote, "I hated Jesus, although I always tried to pray." Her mother finally convinced Paula to go to the mental health clinic. There, the vision repeated itself several times. The theme of the cross also reappeared. Once, looking at it, Paula was deeply moved by remembrance of Christ's suffering and said, "I, too, want to suffer." The vision advised her that Father Joseph should take care of her: "Go with Father Joseph and be obedient." Paula asked, "Where to?" and the vision answered, "To his monastery."

Psychiatrists reported that Paula was quiet, polite, well-dressed in an unobtrusive way. They assured her that she could leave the clinic any time she wanted. Paula kept her distance from others, refused to talk about her visionary experiences, but confirmed Father Joseph's report in general terms. Thematic Apperception Tests (TAT) indicated "lack of factual orientation"—Paula interpreted drawings in terms of pain and desperation; when in situations that seemed like traps, she nevertheless "envisioned religiously motivated help"; relations between the sexes were viewed in "idealized" terms; aggression "seemed repressed." Rorschach tests showed a strongly egocentric orientation and fixed emotional drives.

On March 23, 1970, shortly before Easter, Father Joseph appeared at the clinic and demanded the immediate release of Paula. This ended all clinical observation. Paula remained in personal contact with Father Joseph, who left his religious order, was assigned to the theological education of laymen, and transferred to a distant town. Paula continued to see him. The psychiatrists report: "We were recently advised that the patient married the priest toward the end of 1970, although we are unaware of further details." Presumably, Father Joseph gave up his priesthood.

The role of exorcist is a crucial one in the course of possession. In India, as we have seen, a shaman may steer a woman who faces personal difficulties toward the possession experience. Elsewhere, from China to the Caribbean, traditions and environment direct the nature of the experience. While the Jesuit specialist urged Paula to undertake psychotherapy, it would seem that Father

Joseph was so impressed by his Chinese experience, his own exor-cistic expertise—and, obviously, Paula's feminine potential—that he set her firmly on the road to possession. The French have a word for this, *folie à deux,* which implies that two can get them-selves into trouble better than one.

Cynics will look upon the exorcism of Paula, which went on for years and at times lasted for hours, as a prolonged mating dance. If, indeed, they lived happily ever after, the priest's Chinese experiences and personal feelings may have led him to a successful procedure after all: exorcism by conjugal love.

3. For Women:
A Road to Liberation

It may sound like a poor joke, at first—but possession and exorcism provide, in certain cultural settings, a road to women's
liberation. There can be prestige in being possessed by a devil or
a god, or by anything in between; and attention is certainly
drawn to the possessed who is being dramatically exorcised. The
possessed is able to be aggressive or prophetic, insulting or awe-
inspiring, base or inspired. The meek wife becomes, for a few
hours, a vehicle of the unknown; the old maid can be invitingly
sexually passive or active; the virginal nun can escape her
anonymity, become a center of attention for male priests, while
being manhandled by "the devil."

Possession can, thus, be a form of self-assertion, of compensa-
tion for a life of mediocrity. Ioan Lewis, professor of anthropol-
ogy at the London School of Economics, states in *Ecstatic
Religions* that women in some societies consciously or unconsciously use possession "as a means of insinuating their interests
and demands in the face of male constraint." This may have the
effect of "competing against other women" or "directly striving
for more consideration and respect." These "sex war" aspects
have been most thoroughly explored in African societies, but
they can also be found elsewhere, including the Far East and the
Americas. G. Lindblom, in *The Akamba of British East Africa*
(1920), showed that possessing spirits in these early women's
liberation dramas differed from the Kamba's traditional, sedate,
and conservative spirits. Just as, since prehistoric times, the gods
of the enemy may become the devils of the tribe, so did Kamba

women become possessed by demons representing neighboring people, as well as Europeans. Possessed women spoke in the languages of these outsiders. The demons usually come to the point quickly enough: they demand gifts and attention (very similar to present-day Afro-Brazilian possession cults), as well as response to other demands and grievances the women could not simply state on their own behalf.

Another early account, by H. Koritschoner, "Ngoma y Shei-tan," in the *Journal of the Royal Anthropological Institute* (1936) described the "devil's disease" observed in Tanzania. Here, too, the possessing demon or spirit would demand gifts, such as clothes for the possessed woman. Underlying these posses-sion attacks, Koritschoner found, were often domestic strains that had created an emotionally intolerable situation for a wife who, within the dominant male society, could not express her griev-ance openly. In such cases, the "devil's disease" was being treated by a form of exorcistic family therapy. The woman was during this extended treatment the center of attention, and the husband could at times be persuaded to be more considerate toward her.

Lewis writes that possessing spirits often show "a special predi-lection for the weak and downtrodden." This does not actually make their life's burden still heavier; rather, "it is through succumbing to these seemingly wanton visitations that people of lowly circumstances secure help and succor." Lewis's own re-search took place in what is now the Somali Republic in North-east Africa, where Moslem society is rigidly masculine, women are excluded from worship in mosques and generally treated "as weak, submissive creatures." Somali possession cases may take the form of a jilted girl being "possessed" by her living lover, a form of love sickness that can be treated by a Moslem cleric. Other possession cases are diagnosed as illnesses that may range "from mild hysteria to actual organic disorders."

Professor Lewis notes that "these disturbances are unequivo-cally attributed to the ingress of a hostile spirit or demon," because, as elsewhere in Islam, Somalis "believe that anthropo-morphic jinns lurk in every dark and empty corner, poised ready to strike capriciously and without warning at the unsuspecting passerby." Characteristically, these "malevolent sprites are thought to be consumed by envy and greed, and to hunger especially after dainty foods, luxurious clothing, jewelry, perfume, and other finery." These demons, and the possession attributed to them, are known as *zar* or *sar*. Lewis writes:

"The prime target for the unwelcome attentions of these malign spirits are women, and particularly married women. The stock epidemiological situation is that of the hard-pressed wife, struggling to survive and feed her children in the harsh nomadic environment, and liable to some degree of neglect, real or imagined, on the part of her husband. Subject to frequent, sudden and often prolonged absences by her husband as he follows his many pastoral pursuits, to the jealousies and tensions of polygyny which are not ventilated in accusations of sorcery and witchcraft, and always menaced by the precariousness of marriage in a society where divorce is frequent and easily obtained by men, the Somali woman's lot offers little stability or security."

Possession thus becomes a tool of manipulation, one of the few ways in which a wife can impress her needs and grievances forcefully on her husband. Thus, women's ailments are "readily interpreted by them to possession by *sar* spirits which demand luxurious clothes, perfume and exotic dainties from their menfolk." These requests, Lewis writes, "are voiced in no uncertain fashion by the spirits speaking through the lips of the afflicted women, and uttered with an authority which their passive receptacles rarely achieve themselves."

The language of the spirits is often interpreted by a female shaman for a fee. This may lead to "beating the sar," a dancing fiesta directed by the shaman and attended by other women. It is likely to be expensive for the husband, but even after such payments, Lewis states, "relief from the *sar* affliction may be only temporary." It may return quickly, for example, if the husband shows that he plans to marry an additional woman. Whether the possession performance is only a ritualized tantrum or the real thing, the men cannot be sure. As Islam accepts the djinn, of which the zar is kin, the men are committed to show belief in these happenings. Their own fears of the zar spirits, which are locally believed to hate men, may be a factor in going along with the possession-exorcism syndrome—as long as it isn't overdone, doesn't become too expensive or happen too often.

In the Western Hemisphere, voluntary as contrasted to—at least, consciously—involuntary possession exists where African traditions have had their strongest and most lasting impact. Brazil and the islands of the Caribbean are the most widely publicized. Haiti enjoys a special position, because anthropologists and tourists have sought out the vodun ceremonies and reported on them. As the vodun priestesses are female, women's role in Haitian society has, at least partly because of it, become prominent.

At the same time, the predatory motives observed by Lewis and others in Africa have taken on a new face in Haiti. It is no exaggeration to say that, at its most visible level, Haitian possession has become a business, both within Haiti's own society and towards the awed or curious visitors to the island. Allegedly "secret" vodun rites can be visited within a short ride of Port-au-Prince, and the adventure-seeking tourist encounters ample amounts of chicken blood and mud in a ready-made ceremony for the right amount of money.

But even where monetary gain is involved, it would be unfair to assume that possession is not, in a very specific sense, "real." Too little is known about autosuggestion and its psychophysiological effects to deny that Haiti's professionals do not pass into a trancelike amnesiac state. Here, too, the mental stability of the possessed person is a factor, together with a multiplicity of conscious and unconscious motives ranging from self-assertion to cupidity.

One thing is certain, Haitian women have achieved a social position that compares very favorably with women in Africa and elsewhere in the Americas. The use of possession as a social tool has been particularly well developed in Ethiopia, where, Lewis writes, it "appears to have originated, and in the Muslim Sudan,

Egypt, parts of North Africa, and Arabia where it has penetrated the sacred city of Mecca." He notes that economically depressed women in Cairo have used it, "although *zar* possession seems to have an appeal for rich women too, when they are faced with domestic problems and difficulties," and, in Khartoum, the Sudan, spirits possessing wives "may not only demand gifts, including in one case several gold teeth, but also roundly upbraid the husbands in terms which would not be tolerated were they expressed directly by the women themselves."

The existence of possession cults dominated by women in Mecca is particularly significant, as this holy city of Islam is by definition the central stronghold of Moslem male-oriented society. The most detailed description was provided by the Dutch writer Snouck Hurgronje at the turn of the century in his book *Mekka* (1889). According to T. K. Oesterreich, because of the social stability of the area, this account "may still apply," although probably with variations and fluctuations. At the time, at any rate, the occurrence of zar phenomena was epidemic, had become "a kind of pastime for the women," and "as the customary local exorcism conduces to satisfy woman's love of dress, it is quite comprehensible that the desire to be stricken by the Zar should have become very general." Oesterreich felt that Hurgronje underrated the importance of autosuggestibility when he accused them of mere playacting during the ceremonies. Oesterreich noted that there are many cases where these phenomena are called forth by the will and then follow their course passively. Hurgronje gave these details:

"Another genus of spirits which afford the women plenty of occupation are the Zar. The fight which the Zar displays illustrates both the darkest and lightest side of the Meccan women's life. They have heard talk of the Zar since childhood, so that any illness that strikes them is quickly attributed to Zar domination of the patient's will. Sometimes this is demonstrated by the woman being thrown to the ground, sometimes remaining there for hours in convulsions. At times she may be out of control, raging and in fits. Female relatives and friends fight off sugges-

tions by men, even doctors, who want the patient to be treated
with drugs or by religious exorcism. They usually succeed in
bringing in a woman accustomed to dealing with the Zar, a
shechah-ez-Zar.

"The shechah does not question the patient herself but the Zar
who inhabits her body. Sometimes the conversation is held in a
language everyone understands, but often the woman uses the
Zar language, which only she knows and can interpret. Basically,
these dialogues follow a common pattern. After repeated urgings
by the shechah, the Zar states that he is ready to leave the body of
the woman on a certain day, provided a number of demands are
met; he may ask for a new and beautiful dress, for gold and silver
jewelry, etc.

"As the Zar himself is invisible and disembodied, these gifts
have to be made to adorn the body of the possessed woman; it is
touching how such a demon makes careful allowance for the age,
tastes and needs of the possessed. On the day of the Zar's final
exorcism the patient's women friends arrive for afternoon or
evening coffee, sometimes with a performance of flutes.

"The shechah and her assistants put in their appearance. She
chants the final exorcism rite, accompanied by drums. The
patient puts on the clothing demanded by the Zar, to the accompaniment of suitably magical music. The shechah manipulates
the body of the possessed and engages in several rites, some of
them of a pagan nature. For instance, a lamb may be sacrificed
and the forehead and other parts of the possessed woman's body
are smeared with its blood. Each method of treatment results in
certain external signs that indicate that the Zar's hold is being
loosened. The possessed has to dance, sway and possibly faint, at
which time the shechah announces that the exorcism has been
successful, and the Zar has departed . . ."

That the zar is practiced in contemporary Arab urban society
is illustrated by the observations of an American writer, Vivian
Gornick, who spent some time in Egypt and describes her experiences in *In Search for Ali Mahmoud* (New York, 1973). She
notes that official efforts to eliminate the possession practice has

been unsuccessful and relates her visit to an adobe barn-type building in a Cairo alley in the densely populated district between Midan Bab-el-Louk and the Mosque of Sayeda Zeinab. There she found "about two hundred women dressed in black *milayehs* and the shapeless housedresses of the urban poor" who come there on Tuesday and Sunday evenings "to exorcise their devils."

Miss Gornick writes that "for eight hours at a time, within the sweating wall of this barn, the drums beat, insistently with a wild culminating beat that sends the women into a whirling, fainting frenzy of the dervish," with different dances devoted to different devils, so that a woman can wait for the right beat before she joins the frenzy, "skirts flying, head thrown back, eyes closed, limbs jerking to a final paroxysm of purging ecstasy." Often, the writer states, half the women fall over in a faint, while the other half "scream with urgent, frightful pleasure and grasp those fainting in their arms." Their roles may be reversed in a later dance, and Cairo people aware of the practice say knowingly, "They use the Zar for sex."

During her visit to a zar encounter, Miss Gornick found the room "alive with the gathered stench of sweat, fear and erotic exhaustion." She writes: "I felt it moving inside me, gathering speed and power; a drunken kind of abandon begins to take hold." A few men were among the crowd, and one of them, "naked to the waist, dressed in feathers and decorated ropes of leather and silk, stands suddenly before me, dancing madly to the beat of the drums; he beckons me with a cunning finger, a wily eye, a mocking mouth. Another moment, and I think I will leap to my feet, whirling toward the center." She did not, however, join the possessed. At the end of the session, a disheveled woman who had several times participated in the evening's frenzy offered Miss Gornick and her companion a ride home. A few moments later, she joined them, dressed with sophisticated care, and when names were exchanged identified herself as the wife of an Army officer. She said, "Yes, I come often to the Zar. I find it so refreshing."

A recent study on spirit-demon possession in Ethiopia, Simon D. Messing's "Group Therapy and Social Status in the Zar Cult of Ethiopia," notes that "most patients are married women who feel neglected in a man's world in which they serve as hewers of wood and haulers of water, and where even the Coptic Abyssinian Church discriminates against females by closing the church building to them." The cult obviously acts as a social leveling device. Moreover, there is an unspoken concept that women are one of several socio-economically deprived groups. Messing writes:

"Married women in the predominantly rural culture are often lonely for the warmth of kinship relations, for typical residence is in an exogamous patrilocal hamlet. Members of the lower classes, such as the Muslim (mostly Sudanese) minority, find social contact across religious barriers in the zar cult. Ex-slaves, many of them descended from alien African tribes ('Shanqualla'), are also admitted to full membership in the zar cult. Finally, occupational and economic benefits are dispensed by the zar doctor, who also functions as treasurer of the society but does not render any financial accounting. Thus he has the opportunity, rare on the simple material level of traditional Abyssinia, to accumulate capital."

What we have here, then, is a ladies' social club with its own structure, rites, and loyalties, based on mutual defense against illness by possession. In fact, possession is equivalent to an initiation rite on entering the cult. The zar is never fully expelled or exorcised, but pacified by gifts and ritual into acting as a relatively benevolent guardian spirit.

Messing notes that "active opposition to the cult comes from husbands who fear the sexual and economic emancipation of the wife" and passive resistance from priests of the Coptic Abyssinian church, who "profess to condemn the zar cult but do little to counteract it." The priests may secretly believe in the spirit society themselves, particularly when the spirits present themselves as Coptic Christian, rather that Moslem or pagan.

Although Ethiopian society is based on masculine lineage, the zar cult accepts a matrilinear pattern. Female zar doctors claim that their knowledge and ability has been handed down to them by their mothers. Even possession itself is passed on from mother to daughter. If an individual entity has become a strong "guardian spirit," or *weqabi*, it may be cheerfully passed on from one generation to the next.

Women doctors of the zar cult have greater prestige and self-assurance than men, who are often forced to make extravagant claims concerning their experience and prowess in dealing with spirits. Messing notes that female doctors rarely show arrogance and "when not in a violent trance, they usually assume the phlegmatic composure of the Abyssinian noblewoman." When Messing visited Ethiopia in 1953 and 1954, such an air of relaxed dignity was "the usual poise of Woyzära (Lady) Sälämtew, chief zar doctor at Gondar," although "she was of low-class descent." These doctors achieve their status of healers, much as do shamans in Asian and American societies, by passing through a possession illness and having mastered their own spirits. Messing writes: "Symptoms of possession by the zar spirits include proneness to accidents, sterility, convulsive seizures, and extreme apathy. The healer is himself zar-possessed, but has 'come to terms' with the spirit."

When a woman shows symptoms of illness, her female relatives may try to treat her and look after her. But when she shows severe apathy or depression, efforts are made to cheer her and the possessing spirit who otherwise might "ride his horse to death." The horse-and-rider symbol in possession is nearly universal. A woman suffering from hysterical possession may, following a traditional pattern, threaten to run into the bush and mingle with the hyenas. While arrangements are made for the zar ritual, which is more a taming than an exorcism rite, the possessed patient is never left alone. She remains the center of concerned attention at all times. Dr. Messing provides these details of a typical healing rite:

"At nightfall the patient is conducted to the house of the zar doctor. The scene inside is warm with illumination, burning incense, and the assembled membership of devotees, all chronic cases themselves. A relative hands an entry gift, called 'incense money,' to a disciple who passes it quietly to the doctor behind a screened platform. The doctor ignores the new arrival until the spirit has taken full possession. Only then does the doctor emerge, her eyes bright and curious, her gestures commanding, for the spirit is now using the doctor as a medium. She greets her flock and orders drinks for everyone. The male reader-composer of liturgy of the zar cult intones old or new hymns of praise to the zar, accompanied by the rhythmic handclapping of the worshipers. This ritual recharges the interrogation whenever it becomes difficult.

"The zar doctor pretends that she has guessed the identity of the spirit who plagues the patient, but this spirit must be made to confess publicly so that negotiations can be conducted. The patient is asked leading questions, beginning with recent activities. If answers are not satisfactory, the patient (i.e., the zar through him) is accused of lying. Gradually, the answers become more satisfactory. The doctor alternately lauds and threatens the spirit, giving the patient no rest. The latter is made to confess shortcomings, such as neglect of family, of kinfolk, sometimes even of the church, and of course of the zar himself, who may have been insulted unintentionally. Finally, the patient dances the individual whirl ('gurri') of his particular zar, thus identifying him through minor variations in the rapid movement which ends in temporary exhaustion. Still later the patient learns to intone the proper war-chant ('fukkara') of his spirit. Sometimes several nights are needed to achieve this final expression."

The argument between zar doctor and zar contains a good deal of wrangling over such demands as gifts, designed to turn the possessing spirit from vindictive to benevolent. The psychological aspects of this method vary considerably from the sheer driving-out technique of standard exorcism. The concept underlying this method differs from that which seeks possession as the result of a vacuum (by physical accident, loss of the person's own soul, or other means) that is filled by a malicious devil, demon, or spirit. The Ethiopian and related zar cults assume the presence of some sort of spirit as more or less normal—but a bad spirit may have to be wheedled or bullied or bought into becoming protective instead of destructive.

Negotiations between zar doctor and spirit, through the patient, are a form of ritualized blackmail and bargaining. Messing states that the spirit is asked what he wants "in order to reduce the frequency and severity of the patient's suffering. Some zars have simple demands, such as ornaments, new clothing, or sandals. Many zars have symbolic requests. Thus a zar whose symbol is the lion may demand that a tawny-colored goat be sacrificed at regular times."

In some cases, out-and-out exorcism is undertaken in the Ethiopian cults as well. This is the case when spirits prove recalcitrant, or when their promises, their "contracts" are regarded as unreliable. Given the feminist undercurrent of the cults, it is interesting to note that the pledges of female spirits are regarded as less reliable than those of male zars. Messing writes: "Such exorcism is accomplished by transferring the spirit to a place near a path in the bush where he can pounce on some unsuspecting stranger. The doctor then assigns his patient another zar as a protective spirit from among the zars who are currently available in the house of the zar society and without 'horses' to serve them."

Putting the specific Ethiopian zar cult phenomena in their overall socio-economic context, Dr. Messing concludes: "The motivation is now shifting toward desire for upward social mobility. Even in the past a neglected wife could punish her husband by having her zar extort economic sacrifices from him on threat of relapse. But now ex-slave and low-class patient are increasingly being 'chosen' by the zar. The epidemiology of possession starts a chain of events that enables them to escape from their social confinement."

Just because we have become alert to worldwide trends in

women's liberation efforts, there is a danger in overemphasis on female self-assertion in possession and exorcism. The panorama of the bases and types of exorcism is wide and varied. The picture of the frustrated middle-aged housewife who throws super-tantrums in order to attract attention and blackmail her husband, all in the name of spirit possession, can easily be distorted into caricature. Similarly, the image of the sex-starved nun who seeks the masculine attention, no matter how sublimated, of concerned and agitated priests, should not be overdrawn. Hypochondria of the middle-aged and aged in contemporary society does, of course, serve the similar function of provoking compassion of relatives and friends or the paid attention of the physician. Illness is a great and common social manipulator. Possession adds the awe-inspiring element of the supernatural.

The borderline between genuine illness and simulation cannot be clearly defined, if only because simulation can get out of control and explode into uncontrollable symptoms. No one familiar with the varied jungle growths of psychosomatic disorders is today rash enough to define where conscious manipulation and unconscious "game playing" are welded together. It is easy enough to invent personality types and games that can be applied to shamanistic possession-exorcism in general and to the feminine self-assertion we have examined on the preceding pages. The zar doctor, who gives herself airs as a benign aristocrat; the possessed, who goes into uncontrollable fits but responds to promises of a gold-braided gown; the annoyed but frightened husband who must respond with money, devotion, or both; and the central creation of the whole ritual, the spirit, who is part demon, part blackmailer, part torturer, and part puppet of the possessed woman.

Professor Lewis, who is rather severe in his analysis of women who use the "wide-spread strategy" of possession to "achieve ends which they cannot readily obtain more directly," states: "Women are, in effect, making a special virtue of adversity and affliction, and, of quite literally, capitalizing on their distress. This cult of feminine frailty which, in its aetiolated form, is familiar enough to us from swooning attacks experienced by Victorian women in similar circumstances, is admirably well adapted to the life situation of those who employ it. By being overcome involuntarily by an arbitrary affliction for which they cannot be held accountable, these possessed women gain attention and consideration and, within variously defined limits, successfully manipulate their husbands and menfolk."

The crucial question must be: How real is their distress? A woman who shows symptoms of depression and withdrawal or threatens in her frenzy to join the hyenas in the jungle is paying a high price to gain her husband's attention and a few trinkets. Still, the constellation of her life may well be the cause of this illness, and a change in the constellation—by means of partial exorcism—through a series of social concessions may help to alleviate it. In other words, the anguish and its reality are likely to vary from case to case, probably even during various stages of possession and exorcism.

The shamanistic zar doctor no doubt puts on a performance well calculated to enhance her prestige, awe the possessed patient, and result in financial profit. How legitimate is her role? When is it used as a theatrical device, and when does she herself see it as a truly medico-supernatural function? In any society, it isn't only the religious follower who has a "need to believe," as William James called it; perhaps even more profound is the priest-shaman-witchdoctor's own need to believe. The spirit doctor who, like the shaman, has gone through her own period of wrestling with a possessing demon, may well have concluded that she has developed a gift that can benefit others.

Certainly, elements of social climbing, financial advantage, and community respect are likely to reinforce this conviction of her hard-won skills. With success, all these may merge into unselfconscious bravura, ease in manipulation of individuals and crowds, and an air of elegant superiority—the games mistress has filled out the role she had assumed: the stage has become life itself.

4. Possession, Illness, or Fakery?

Pretense and fraud are not inventions of the twentieth century, but neither are shrewdness and suspicion. In the sixteenth century, a French country girl, Marthe Brossier, urged her local priest to exorcise her. She screamed, cursed, and contorted her body, demanding attention from her family and the church. Marthe, the eldest of four children, had failed to find a husband. She cut her hair and wore men's clothing. In an outburst of jealousy, she attacked her attractive friend, Anne Chevion, scratched her face and blamed the outburst on the devil.

Exorcism was begun. The reports state that her stomach was swollen by Beelzebub, in a way that might later have been viewed as a psychosomatic imitation of pregnancy. Marthe was able to bend her body back in an arch and said, "I am more tormented than if I were in hell." Many of her utterances were directed against the Huguenots, the Calvinist Protestants of France whom King Henry IV had just granted complete toleration; this followed the religious wars that had lasted from 1562 to 1598.

Marthe Brossier's possession and her ravings against the Huguenots were politically convenient for the opponents of Henry IV and quite disagreeable to the king. He ordered that she have a thorough medical examination, with due regard for the theological rules concerning possession. At the Chatelet Hospital in Paris, the young woman was examined by Dr. Marescot and three colleagues. Was she able to speak in languages not normally known to her? Did the devil within her recoil from holy solids and liquids; did he respond to the Latin words of the exorcism rite?

Marthe promptly went into a fit of anger, violence, and spitting when she was given a wrapped piece of metal that was supposed to be a fragment of the True Cross. But it wasn't; Marescot had given her a broken key. She also responded to a solemnly pronounced group of Latin words, which had actually been written by the Roman poet Virgil. Faced with two bowls, of which the plainer one was filled with holy water and the more decorative with plain spring water, Marthe accepted the spring water as blessed and her possession spasm faded. Marescot concluded: "Nothing demonic; much fiction; morbid motivation." Actually, the girl's motivation had been mainly financial: both she and her father had accepted a good deal of money from well-wishers who contributed to her exorcistic healing.

In his 1599 report, Marescot quoted from the Acts of the National Synod of Rheims (1583), which contained this warning to would-be exorcists: "Before the priest undertakes an exorcism, he ought diligently to inquire into the life of the possessed, into his condition, reputation, health and other circumstances; and he should consult with wise, prudent, and well-informed persons, rather than those who might be too credulous and inclined to be deceived. Melancholics, lunatics, and persons bewitched often declare themselves to be possessed and tormented by the devil; these people, however, are more in need of a doctor than of an exorcist." F. X. Maquart, writing on "Exorcism and Diabolical Manifestations" in *Satan* (1951), spoke of these cautions as "only too clearly called for," because "the ecclesiastical world is prone to a naive credulity in this matter." He added: "When it encounters those who fall a prey to obsession, to impulses or inhibitions violently opposed to their usual temper, who labor, as they often do, under the impression that they are victims of some alien and evil power, it immediately begins to think of action by the devil and sees true possession."

A leading French authority on possession, Father Joseph de

Tonquédec, gives a picture of the apparently possessed in his book *Les maladies nerveuses on mentales et les manifestations diaboliques* (1938) : "Here is a man who normally hates sin, blasphemy, impurity, cruelty and any sort of crude behavior. Suddenly he finds himself strongly impelled to practice all that he hates. Do these promptings really come from himself, or is he the passive victim of some alien force? Or, here is a woman who is intelligent and educated, a person of high moral character, who usually speaks only in a faultless manner, but who suddenly finds her head filled with a phrase of crude obscenity, which keeps running through her mind, over and over again. Surely, she cannot possibly have phrased this sentence; she merely submits to it with pain and disgust."

This kind of experience, Father de Tonquédec explained, is most disconcerting when it is encountered by people of deep religious conviction, possibly caught in sexual conflicts regarded as sinful, who feel themselves at the mercy of evil, and who may even reach the final conclusion that they give themselves over to the devil, "calling him up from the abyss." Some, he writes, "simply believe they have done so," or "wonder whether they may have done it." In addition, there are cases of persons who find themselves physically paralyzed or emotionally repelled by the paraphernalia and procedures of religious ritual, who "are assailed by obscene thoughts about God, or Christ, or the Blessed Virgin," who may deny religious dogma with violence and blasphemy.

Maquart asks, "Why is it that the priest, faced with this kind of thing, is so ready to envisage the presence of the devil? His theological conditioning and the daily exercise of his ministry pre-dispose him vaguely to the passing of moral judgments; finding it impossible to impute moral responsibility for acts so evidently discordant with the characters of their authors, he tends to assume the presence of a preternatural cause even when there is no question of the patient's 'unconscious' or of involuntary acts. The question he asks is: Virtuous or vicious? Whereas he ought to ask: Normal or abnormal?"

And it isn't even as easy as all that. The more fundamentalist Protestant denominations, but the Roman Catholic church most of all, must face this tricornered question, "Possession, illness, or fakery?"—when it is often impossible to tell these three conditions apart, and when the affected individual can't be sure of his own state of mind, or is perhaps the last person able to reflect on his condition. The effort to delineate between demonic possession, in the traditional Christian sense, and various forms of psychological and physiological illness—as well as fraud—has been going on, formally, for several hundred years. The *Rituale Romanum*, which retains its basic validity in the Roman Catholic church to this day, was originally published in 1614. A revision was made in 1952.

Preparation of the *Rituale Romanum* was essential, because the period preceding and accompanying the witchcraft persecutions had been one of doctrinal confusion. Rules were evolving, but haphazardly. A French priest, Grosbal, recorded on April 6, 1601, that he was beginning an exorcism case; the proceedings had not been completed by September 10. Other priests, including travelers from Limoges and Savoy, tried to help. One pilgrim from Spain sought to question the demon in the language of his country, but was not understood. Two visitors from Scotland addressed him in Gaelic, and others in Breton. It was useless; this demon was no linguist and, Grosbal concluded reluctantly, conceivably not a demon at all.

A detailed study of possession, specifically in the light of the *Rituale Romanum,* has recently been made by a German Jesuit, Father Adolf Rodewyk, in *Die dämonische Besessenheit.* The author seeks to conciliate his church's traditional judgments with new scientific findings, ranging from medicine and psychiatry to parapsychology (psychical research). He begins by summarizing the case of the two brothers, Theobald and Josef, whose possession in the German town of Illfurt began in 1865 and lasted four years. After listing the symptoms, Father Rodewyk notes that church authorities at that time judged the boys truly possessed, in accordance with the criteria of the *Rituale Romanum,* and acted accordingly. But, Rodewyk asks, "Could we, on the basis of today's knowledge, come to the same conclusions? Was it really possession?"

The phenomena in the Illfurt house began when Theobald was about ten years old and Josef nearly eight. Parish records show that the boys were mostly confined to bed during the first two years of their joint "possession." Two or three times an hour they intertwined their legs in such an unnatural way that they could not be separated. At times they stood simultaneously on their heads and legs, with the rest of their bodies raised high. "No external pressure could restore their bodies to a natural position," the parish record added, "until the devil was willing to leave his victims in peace."

The two boys, while lying in bed, would turn their faces to the wall and paint repulsive devils' faces on the wall, to whom they talked and with whom they played. Even while asleep, the record stated, they were sensitive to the devil's demands, so that when a rosary was placed on their beds, they would immediately hide under the cover until it was removed. Each was also supposed to levitate: "While sitting on a chair, boy and chair were at times lifted into the air, and then dropped in such a way that the boy was flung into one corner of the room, and the chair into the opposite corner. Even the mother, when sitting on the child's bed, might be lifted into the air and hurled into a corner, although without any damage."

Among the classical possession symptoms they showed were swollen bodies, vomiting, which meant expelling such things as "foam, feathers and seaweed," so that "the children were often covered with feathers that gave off a disgusting odor." The boys were also credited with being able to climb trees with the speed and agility of cats and of "sitting on the thinnest branches, which never broke under them." The room occupied by the children was unbearably hot, although never heated by a stove. The mother, who shared the room, could not stand the heat. But when she got up and sprinkled holy water on the bed "the room returned to a normal temperature, and she was able to sleep." At times the curtains were pulled down "by invisible hands" and the windows burst open "with incredible speed, entirely by themselves." Among the phenomena reported were the throwing about of chairs, tables, and other furniture, as if "pulled about by ghost-hands," while "the whole house trembled as through a powerful earthquake."

The parish record further alleges that "when a clergyman or pious Catholic visited the house, the possessed children crawled hastily under a table or bed, or jumped out the window." But when anyone who was only "a mediocre Christian" came to visit, the youngsters showed "great delight" and shouted triumphantly, "That is one of ours. They should all be like that!"

Theobald was taken for his exorcism to an institution in nearby Schiltigheim, where "the devil was silent for three days." Finally, on the evening of the fourth day, he shouted "Here I am, and I am in a fury." The nun on duty asked, "Who are you?" The answer was, "I am the Lord of Darkness." The voice reminded her of "a calf being strangled." When angry, the boy looked "absolutely horrifying," recognized no one, not even his mother, tore his clothes and broke everything he could lay his hands on, until he was tied up. When he was given a piece of clothing with a religious medal secretly sewn into the lining, he pulled it apart and tore out the medal. He was so deaf that he could not hear a pistol fired next to his ear.

These and other details concerning the Illfurt boys indicate a general psychological atmosphere that is often found in houses and families plagued by so-called poltergeist phenomena. These frequently take place where there are youngsters around who are at odds with their families: furniture is mysteriously pushed around, crockery flies through the air, pictures fall off walls, creating tensions that bring chaos and notoriety to the household. As the German word *poltergeist* ("noisy ghost") suggests, these disturbances used to be attributed to spirits. Today, parapsychologists incline toward a psychophysical explanation based on the youngster's hostility; unless, of course, there is straightforward chicanery.

It is probably fair to say in answer to Father Rodewyk's cautious question, "Was this truly possession?" that current Roman Catholic interpretations might conclude that either a dual-hysteria, pranks, or maybe both, were involved in the case of Theobald and Josef. But to arrive at such a conclusion, even tentatively, demands that a wide array of possibilities be considered and either discarded or accepted.

Crucial points in the *Rituale Romanum* are alternatives to possession that must be eliminated before the church can definitely decide that true possession exists. With scientific advancement, which brings not only new certainties but new uncertainties as well, such decisions have become increasingly complex. They require detailed knowledge of many fields. And just as the number of "miraculous" cures at Lourdes has dropped sharply during the last half century, because psychosomatic medicine has gained new ground, so has the number of exorcism cases dwindled.

The slight 1952 revision in the *Rituale Romanum* changed one alternative to possession, originally worded as "those who suffer from melancholia or any other illness" (*qui vel atra bile vel morbo aliquo laborant*), to "those who suffer from illness, particularly mental illnesses" (*qui morbo aliquo praesertim ex psychicis laborant*). With increasing knowledge of the variety of mental illnesses and their manifold forms of expression, this revision of the ritual places a still heavier burden on bishops and other church authorities, who must define possession on the basis of a series of abilities displayed by the allegedly possessed person. This task has become still more delicate because the 1952 revision changed the statement that such symptoms "*are* signs of the presence of a demon" to "*might be*" such signs.

Central among the abilities shown by a person who, within the framework of this definition, "might be" possessed by a demon are the following: knowledge of unknown languages; knowledge of secret facts; and unusual powers. These, as well as other symptoms—such as revulsion against holy things and sayings—are given additional weight as evidence of possession when they exist simultaneously. The *Rituale Romanum* states that, "the more symptoms coincide, the stronger are the indications."

As symptoms of bodily violence, excitement, aggression, obscene or blasphemous talk may reflect a variety of mental illnesses (for which even the terminology of psychology has widely differing labels, reflecting diagnostic variations), they cannot be regarded as sure signs of possession in the current state of the psychophysiological arts. But what about the remaining symptoms: knowing foreign languages, having knowledge of the unknown, or possessing unusual powers? Here, modern specialists on exorcism have come to study closely the recent findings of parapsychology.

Father Rodewyk speaks highly of the thoughts and writings of the Vatican's best-known specialist on the relationship between demonic possession and parapsychology. Father Balducci, author of the impressively detailed volume, *Gli indemonati,* is regarded as "a champion of the Western Catholic tradition of possession and exorcism" by Henry Ansgar Kelly. In his book *The Devil, Demonology and Witchcraft,* Kelly says that Balducci exhibits a "simple and undisturbed faith" in "the concepts of medieval theology and philosophy," but also "a good deal of critical acumen in evaluating the claims of various preternatural phenomena."

The new interest in parapsychological research is based on the widened interpretation of the *Rituale Romanum's* demand that the possessed should "display powers that go beyond their age and position in life" (*vies supra aetatis seu conditionis naturam*). Until quite recently, this was seen as referring to supernatural physical strength, speed, levitation, and phenomena in the poltergeist category, such as were recorded with the two Illfurt brothers. Now, however, "powers" of a mental nature, what parapsychologists call extrasensory (ESP), are also being considered.

Just as psychosomatic healing, which can be explained in terms of suggestion or other psychological aspects, has to be ruled out when a "miraculous cure" is being investigated, so does "natural" ESP function undercut a claim to demonic possession. If parapsychologists are right in attributing the movement of physical objects in terms of a poltergeist-type phenomenon for which a psychological basis may be found, the demon hypothesis is weakened.

One of the pillars of parapsychological research is psychokinesis (the impact of mind on matter), which has been tested in laboratory settings with dice, coins, and other objects on a quantitative basis. This phenomenon is also found outside the laboratory in spontaneous situations involving movement of objects under conditions that violate known physical laws. Psychokinesis, or PK, is sufficiently fluid in definition to include virtually all physical phenomena that might earlier have been cited as proof of demonic possession.

The problem created for the demon theory by the acceptance of parapsychology as a new scientific alternative for possession phenomena lies in method of investigation. Parapsychologists are passionate in their defense of carefully controlled experiments and minutely checked claims for ESP phenomena—not only in psychokinesis, but also in telepathy, clairvoyance and precognition, all of which are significant to the possession theory. The files of the Institute of Parapsychology at Durham, North Carolina, dealing with spontaneous phenomena contain some 14,000 accounts of alleged ESP cases, of which only a small fraction are regarded as potentially valid.

Dr. Louisa E. Rhine, who assembled these files over a period of three decades, often cites individual reports of clairvoyance, for example, without full documentation, but only as being suggestive for the development of new laboratory experiments. Parapsychologists are, if possible, more reluctant to accept unsupported testimony than is a court of law. Unless phenomena, for instance in the poltergeist category, have been witnessed by uninvolved observers, including experienced parapsychological investigators, they are likely to be ignored.

Parapsychologists have a long history of investigating claims by spiritualist mediums who are allegedly able to convey messages in languages they do not command in their normal state. This phenomenon, *xenoglossy,* has been investigated over and over again. Claims of verification by authorities in obscure oriental or African dialects are often made with an air of great assurance—but when the precise name, affiliation, and address of such linguistic authorities are demanded, the informant usually becomes elusive. Or, if the information is supplied, the authority cannot be persuaded to repeat the testimony (if it was ever made) formally and in writing.

Of the Illfurt boys, for instance, the parish record claimed that they spoke and answered in several languages, conversed fluently in French, Latin, and English, and understood several French and Spanish dialects, although their mother tongue was German. Rodewyk also cites the 1907 case of an African girl, Clara Germana Cele, who was supposed to have understood Polish, German, French and all other languages, "which she had never learned and of which, for the most part, she had never heard a word spoken." The exorcising priest alleged that Germana answered questions in these languages "usually quite correctly in Zulu," and when he "ordered her to answer in Latin, this was done."

A parapsychologist would not regard this kind of partisan testimony as valid evidence. Who says so? Who else was there? What precisely was the exposure of these youngsters to foreign languages? And, once the methods and hypotheses of parapsychology are accepted, another element enters: telepathy between exorcist and possessed person. Theirs is a very close relationship, and once telepathy is admitted as possible, the exorcist's questions in a language unknown to the possessed might well be accompanied by "telepathic leakage" of the question's content from one to the other. An answer in Zulu to a question put in Polish might then be based on a telepathic tapping of the exorcist's mind.

The *Rituale Romanum* leaves a loophole for telepathy, because it asks that the demoniac be able to "speak several words of an unknown language or understand someone who speaks it." Such understanding could, in theory, be telepathic and therefore a natural means of communication. Rodewyk is aware of this. He says, however, that "the peculiarities and demands of possession are such that no telepathically gifted person or medium could fulfill them all totally."

Rodewyk is at the mercy of his outdated and amateurish information on telepathy, and his effort to draw a line between xenoglossy through possession and xenoglossy through telepathy does not reflect sophisticated and professional parapsychological thinking. Basing his ideas on telepathy on Fanny Moser's *Okkultismus* (1935), he has missed more than a generation's research. Father Rodewyk assumes that telepathy conveys data through "a slow dawning of impressions," whereas in possession there is "rapid, direct understanding." He assumes telepathy is subject to "delayed stimulation," and that possession is not. Rodewyk asserts that during possession "whatever is transmitted is correctly received, at least at first," and "many things that are not openly expressed are understood from side effects of speech." Yet, one of the very difficulties with telepathy appears to be the presence of unconscious elements in thought transmission; dream telepathy experiments at Maimonides Hospital in Brooklyn, N.Y., which span nearly a decade, had to guard specifically against such "side effects."

Finally, Father Rodewyk writes: "As long as possession continues, the performance remains even and is without weakening. The ability to understand foreign languages disappears only when the crisis is over, i.e., when possession ends, and it is therefore a sign of exorcism." Parapsychologists, wary of such flat statements, might well ask whether there is a sufficiently broad quantitative basis—aside from the reliability of data—of possession cases that have been recorded to assert that linguistic ability does not fluctuate.

Father Balducci, dealing with more recent parapsychological

data and methods, is far more cautious in advocating a sort of working alliance between parapsychology and possession study. He attended an international conference on "Religion and Parapsychology" organized by the Parapsychology Foundation in 1965, and the paper he delivered on that occasion later appeared under the title "Parapsychology and Diabolic Possession." Balducci told the parapsychologists that the Roman Catholic church continues to recommend "the greatest prudence in diagnosis of the presumed demoniacs" and is well aware that "certain well-known diseases" bring about a "strange and violent behavior." The difference between mental illnesses of this sort and possession, he said, was that they are "characterized in the demoniac by a strong abhorrence for whatever is sacred." Father Balducci makes much of a particular "tonality" of behavior which concentrates on such revulsion toward the "sacred."

Balducci sees in a combination of outwardly psychological phenomena with parapsychological ones a greater likelihood that possession exists. If a person behaves like a raving madman whose excesses have a special antireligious "tonality" and at the same time displays telepathic or clairvoyant knowledge—then, Father Balducci suggests, possession may be indicated. He writes that "the presence in the same individual of phenomenologies of both" a psychological and a parapsychological nature is, "in itself, a strong indication of diabolic possession." He summarizes this viewpoint as follows:

"*Phenomenology of a parapsychological order.* In the demoniac, it is not a principle that acts, but the devil, i.e., a being who possesses a nature purely spiritual, superior to our own, and therefore endowed with a power more extensive. In the individual's behavior, this exceptional power, this demoniacal marvel, appears sometimes in a spontaneous, distinctive way, through an ensemble of manifestations, and at other times in a forced, less distinctive and more limited way.

"Thus, we have a second group of phenomena altogether different from the previous ones [psychological disturbances] and, on the whole, beyond any possible psychical [psychological] order. The demoniac will assume, for instance, the most unstable positions: he will walk, move or act perfectly, even with closed eyes; he will perform activities never learned before—playing a musical instrument, for example, or painting, or speaking unknown languages; he will manifest an occult knowledge of hidden objects, distant persons and past events, and many other marvelous things."

Balducci refers to such demoniacal phenomena as being "of a parapsychological order" and cites various authorities to show that such ESP gifts are not abnormal in themselves. He quotes Dr. J. B. Rhine, the leading U.S. pioneer of extrasensory perception, as stating that telepathy and clairvoyance have "nothing to do with mental illness" and that experiments show "there is nothing to suggest that telepathy and clairvoyance might be abnormal."

Father Balducci states that parapsychology "not only is not extraneous to diabolic possession; it has, in itself, a relevance and an altogether specific function," being "particularly useful and altogether indispensable for a diagnosis of diabolic possession." He adds: "The exorcist (i.e., the ecclesiastic who is entrusted by competent authorities to perform the prayers that are apt to free the demoniac, and who has the grave duty of acting with circumspection and prudence in the exercise of his function with persons who are really possessed) not only must not ignore the science of parapsychology but has the moral duty to recognize its decisive function in the diagnostic criterion of diabolic possession."

But do the two links, psychology and parapsychology, when placed together, really help to make a strong chain? Obviously, Balducci thinks that they strengthen each other. He assumes that phenomena in the two fields do not overlap seriously. And he hopes that priests-exorcists will have sufficient knowledge of both fields to weigh the evidence carefully. That is a nearly impossible task. Even such a narrow field as dream telepathy or Out-of-the-

Body Experiences (OOBE), earlier known as "traveling clair-voyance," are very nearly full-time research tasks these days. And neither psychology nor parapsychology, when practiced by mature professionals, are as sure of their ground as Father Balducci would have them be.

The crucial area remains proof: observation, recording, evaluation. Kelly, who was a scholastic member of a Jesuit order for thirteen years, but is now a caustic critic of "implausible hagiographic tales of possession," feels that "all past accounts of demonic wonders in cases of alleged possession are suspect to some degree." Still, he is optimistic: "Fortunately, in this modern age it is no longer necessary to rely solely upon the testimony of observers. Scientific methods of investigation and recording are available: it is to be hoped that any further claims for genuine demonic possession will be corroborated by this kind of evidence."

Thus, politely, Kelly almost succeeds in entirely eradicating the reality of demonic possession within the Roman Catholic church. Because "this kind of evidence," conscientiously weighed, must by its nature remain tentative, inconclusive, undogmatic. Father Balducci's imaginative concept of a special "tonality" of possession, which he sees as separating its phenomena from those of mental illness, is worth examining in this context. Why should actions of revulsion against religious rites and symbols or the uttering of blasphemy be anything but expressions of some madness—perhaps just the opposite side of the coin of deranged religious fanaticism? Is not devotion akin to fear, or denial the negative twin of belief? The exorcism cases on record in the Catholic church come almost exclusively from a hothouse atmo-sphere of apparently oppressive piety. We do not know enough about the religious atmosphere in the household of the two Illfurt brothers, and it may not be fair to speculate on it, but the prankish madness of their behavior has, to borrow the word, all the "tonality" of immature rebellion against an oppressively pious mother.

Father Rodewyk states that the reaction of a possessed person against holy and blessed things is "shown particularly well in the attitude of the Illfurt boys." He quotes the parish records as stating that "the demonic character of their possession was mainly revealed when the boys came close to blessed rosaries or medals." They threw tantrums, foamed at the mouth and struggled vehemently so as not to touch these items. When Holy Water was mixed with their food, they didn't touch it and would say, "Take this garbage away, it's poisoned!" When offered figs that had been blessed by a priest, they said, "Take these rat heads away. The guy in the black suit has made faces over it."

Did they really not know, not even from unconscious clues or the conspiratorial air of their mother and her friends, that Holy Water had been mixed with their food? And if they did not know directly, could this information have come to them through telepathy or clairvoyance? An intriguing case can be made that tension in the Illfurt household created just the right atmosphere for a telepathic tapping of the mother's thoughts by Theobald and Josef. Perhaps the methods used by the French physician Marescot on the publicity-conscious Marthe Brossier might have been useful in the Illfurt household.

The special dilemma faced by a modern psychiatrist, deeply concerned with the application of his Catholic faith, is well expressed by Dr. Jean Lhermitte of Paris. His findings on "pseudo-possession" have been widely quoted and translated. They appear in the *Satan* symposium originally compiled for the *Études Carmélitaines* (Paris). As an experienced professional, Lhermitte is appropriately restrained: "It must be admitted that the science of psychiatry takes a very humble place among the other biological disciplines, for psychiatry operates on a plane where soul and body meet, and we still do not know how that 'seam of soul and body' is made." He does feel, however, that progress has been made since mental disturbances ceased to be regarded as purely supernatural in origin, but as within the area of psycho-physiological adjustment.

From this premise, Dr. Lhermitte evolves what he calls "demonopathy" and examines it to answer this question: Can we discover, in certain persons supposedly possessed by the devil, anything which would permit us to relate the idea of demon-opathic possession to an illness properly so called?

Dr. Lhermitte draws attention to "epidemics of possession which raged at a time when psychiatry had barely come into being." These cases often showed a combination of psychoneu-rosis with "simulation and mythomania." In other words, under the guise of possession, illness and fakery might interact in a manner that could be indistinguishable to priest, physician, and the possessed. Lhermitte recalls from his own practice the case of a young nun plagued by sexual obsessions and perhaps sexual compulsions since she was fifteen years old. "Unwisely," the Paris psychiatrist notes, the director of the convent told the girl that the devil was "at work," and she "suddenly felt her personality divided and spellbound by evil spirits."

Exorcism was begun. The sessions soon became daily events. Lhermitte writes: "During these exorcisms the girl threw herself into a thousand contorted attitudes and gave way to the wildest and most fantastic tricks. Worse still, in between the periods of exorcism she began to smash things and utter prophecies, so that the peace and recollection of the convent were exceedingly dis-turbed." When Lhermitte examined the young woman in the presence of "a qualified exorcist," they did not continue the exorcism ritual which, they felt, "had been somewhat immoder-ately used." But even when they merely read a prayer from the Low Mass, the nun jumped to her feet, glared at them, poured "filthy insults" on priest and doctor, tore off her wimple, "began to twirl and dance and to assume innumerable fantastic pos-tures." The same thing happened during a second examination. She was treated with electro-shock, given hospital care, and after a month was "completely free from all ideas of demonic posses-sion." Of course, as we note in the next chapter, these results might be attributed to the demon's discomfort from electric

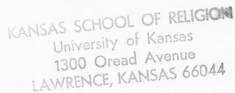

current; or, the young nun may unconsciously have regarded the shock treatment as appropriate and therefore guilt-erasing punishment.

Dr. Lhermitte is not suggesting that genuine possession does not exist; rather, he regards "demonopathy" as a form of pseudo-possession. Where the patient imitates, as Lhermitte sees it, the phenomena of true demonic possession, exorcism rites cannot be successful, because there is no devil, demon, or evil spirit to expel. He classifies as "demonopathic delirium" forms of illness that may have a specific physical basis. One such case, analyzed by Lhermitte in detail, was that of a girl named Sybil.

The Paris psychiatrist reviews this case in his paper, "Pseudo-Possession," because he regards it as "all the more remarkable in that it extends over a very long period, and that the origin and material cause of the delirium of possession are clearly traceable." Sybil had been sent to Lhermitte by a priest who had decided that "this was a pathological case and not one of genuine possession," although the girl insisted she was controlled by the devil, particularly during the night.

Whenever Sybil was about to fall asleep, she felt that the devil would come to her bed, rob her of her body and carry the "double" of her personality off into his "astral" sphere. (This, incidentally, is a variation of the Out-of-the-Body Experience, which parapsychologists seek to examine objectively.) Having kidnaped Sybil's body, "he amused himself by torturing her" with heavy blows, burns, flinging her into thorn bushes, firing revolver shots through her body, and "forcing her to endure the most terrible humiliations."

During these masochistic fantasy flights with the devil, Sybil tried to struggle against his overwhelming power and sought to regain control over her "double." Only after much begging and struggle did she get her body back—but sometimes not wholly, so that an arm or a leg might be "missing," and she would stumble out of bed and fall down because her legs "were not there." During these periods, Sybil felt that objects around her were moving and bending, and "she seemed to understand the alarm clock's mechanical language." Such feelings are common in schizophrenia and under the influence of hallucinogenic drugs.

Violent compulsions and taboos continued to torture Sybil, and she thought herself able to "understand the devil's thoughts." It did not help that she sprinkled holy water on her bed, always wore a rosary around her neck and otherwise tried to abide by religious rules. The young woman, Lhermitte writes, previously had been "reserved and pious and never fell into the sins of the flesh; it was only during her trances that she imagined that the devil defiled her by indulging with great violence in acts whose nature can easily be guessed."

Dr. Lhermitte, seeking a physiological basis of these experiences, found medical records that showed Sybil as having suffered from encephalitis lethargica (sleeping sickness), which can have disturbing aftereffects. He concluded that "the cause of the demonopathic delirium is in this case clear." Without disrespect to the insight offered by the noted French psychiatrist, one must add that—as always in these cases—another interpretation is possible: yes, some traditionalists might say, the girl was ill and the encephalitis injured her brain, and thus the devil could enter her body through the opening provided by the sickness.

Cases such as that of the young nun and of Sybil provide, according to Lhermitte, "the clearest distinguishing marks of false, as against authentic, demoniacal possession." But he does not really say just where, in his opinion, pseudo-possession ends and genuine demonic possession begins. Dr. Lhermitte notes that cases of pseudo-possession show "all the signs of an invasion by a personality alien to the individual's ego," but it is only somewhat later that the patient becomes convinced that it is, in fact, "an evil spirit who directs his actions, induces his feelings and ideas and, actually possesses him and holds him at his mercy." This foreign influence is felt as expressing the opposite of the image the patients have of themselves: "They react against this influence by all possible means, including those of the subconscious; and it is precisely by these disguised, roundabout ways that many of our patients unwittingly create a second favorable personality which fights against the evil influence, keeping the poor patients in a state of painful struggle between an influence which they consider pernicious and an influence easily attributed to the divine or to some other occult power."

Lhermitte notes that psychotherapy often reveals "some sexual disorder in patients suffering from demonopathy," because "in their eyes the greatest sin lies in carnal failings." He often finds that "this obsession with sin, which rarely leaves the person it has once gripped, also appears as a force invested with a living personality," so that the patients easily "identify the devil with the sin from which they feel the most aversion and which they most deeply dread."

In dealing with the role of illness and fraud in possession cases, we have concentrated on cases and ideas from Roman Catholic sources, but the religiopsychological aspects discussed have universal significance. Some non-Catholics as well as Catholics attribute to the Roman Catholic church a monolithic quality that it does not have, certainly not in the area of possession and exorcism. The antireligious "tonality" which Father Balducci finds so persuasive in locating genuine possession is regarded by a respected lay professional, Dr. Lhermitte, as just one aspect of mere "demonopathy" in the case of the young nun who benefited from electro-shock treatment. Clear lines of distinction simply do not exist. Balducci seeks to find added strength in bringing psychological and parapsychological phenomena together—but it is the strength of two scissor blades made of rubber, not of tempered steel. The control and evaluation methods of modern parapsychology could narrow the cases of genuine possession down to just about zero.

Sincere belief in possession may well have a specific role to play for the possessed and the exorcist, particularly if it provides the right religiocultural setting for effective psychotherapy. But psychophysiological illness, with all its fluctuation, and even conscious or unconscious fraud, cannot be effectively shut out; the walls that enclose genuine possession are as penetrable as the human mind.

III. American Varieties

1. Electronic Exorcism

The woman who came to the Burden Neurological Institute at Bristol, England, had suffered from the vision of a devil figure for decades. The devil appeared to her in the traditional manner: threatening, red, with horns and a tail. He constantly urged her to break out in rages, utter obscenities, and to strangle her twelve-year-old daughter. As her case was reported by Dr. W. Grey Walter, the institute's research director, the woman, known as Rose, had "undergone every conceivable treatment available —psychotherapy, drugs, and shock therapy and was now institutionalized."

Dr. Walter is one of the world's pioneers of a mind-changing technique that uses tiny electrodes which are implanted in the brain. Through the electrodes, the brain receives minute charges of electricity. The devices are so small that a considerable number of them can be implanted simultaneously. The procedure is painless, and a patient can wear them from one treatment to another; there are usually a number of people wearing beret-like headcovering walking the corridors of the Bristol Institute. As the electric charge is also very small, it may need to be renewed from time to time, so that its effect is heightened or maintained.

Dr. Walter was installing electrodes, each one about the thickness of a human hair, in Rose's brain, while his colleague the neuropsychiatrist, Dr. Harry Crow, talked to the patient. Walter usually has to make about 68 minute holes in the skull to place the electrodes, but in the case of Rose nearly 100 such contacts had to be made. As he reports it, Dr. Walter makes little holes, "about the size of a grain of wheat," in the "supraorbital white matter in anxiety patients and in the paracingulate region of the compulsive obsessional patient." Rose was in this second category.

The results, Walter recalls, "were magical." At a crucial point, Dr. Crow asked, "How are you Rose?"

The patient exclaimed, "Doctor, he is gone!"

"Who's gone?"

"The devil, he's gone!" Rose answered. "He's disappeared!"

Crow, as calmly and matter-of-factly as he could manage, said, "Oh, good!"

If a small amount of electricity, passed through an electrode into the human brain, can chase away a devil, modern science certainly has found a new technique: electronic exorcism. In the case of Rose, a series of treatments was necessary. At first, the devil shrank in size and was found by Rose to be less menacing. As treatment continued, he changed his obscene and violent demands to more polite urgings. His appearance also changed from the red figure with horns to a gentlemanly figure in a business suit.

Dr. Walter feels that, after some two decades of this specialized work, he can anticipate with a high degree of accuracy which brain areas are the set of specific fears and images. The human brain appears to have a special devil spot. Traditional possession and exorcism ideas aren't even totally negated by these findings and procedures. Under certain conditions, the possessed person may have opened himself, or these areas, enabling the spirit, demon, or devil to come and take over. And the electronic charges could well be interpreted—in line with age-old measures to make the possessor thoroughly uncomfortable—as being particularly effective in forcing the devil to leave.

Dr. Walter regards the supraorbital region of the brain as "part of the fear system." The Burden Neurological Institute performs the implanting of electrodes regularly on four or five inpatients at a time. He states: "If you make a little lesion here it is almost like a lobotomy in its effect on symptoms, but the lesion is minute and has no side effects." A lobotomy, an operation now very rarely performed, consists of removal of brain sections by surgery; it can have the side effect of so neutralizing the patient's emotions that he becomes unfeeling and totally lacking in initiative.

Walter says that "by causing a lesion in the paracingulate region, compulsive patients are relieved as dramatically and can function normally in their jobs." The method has also been called psychosurgery, because the electric charge does involve what Walter calls "very selective lesion." He acknowledges that "such a procedure is controversial," but summarizes the startling electronic exorcism this way: "Initially, a weak current was used for this patient. Two days later the patient reported that the devil had returned but was in modern dress without horns and a tail. Again a current was passed through the electrodes. The patient is now completely well, fifteen years after the procedure was performed."

The controversy about psychosurgery was dramatized in the United States in the spring of 1973 when a rapist-murderer, identified only as "Mr. L.," first agreed to undergo such an operation and then refused. The man, who had been imprisoned and confined to hospitals as a criminal sexual psychopath for eighteen years, had a history of uncontrolled violence. At the age of fifteen he had broken into the bedroom of a fellow high school student and beat her with a croquet mallet when she woke up. Sent to a hospital, he raped and killed a nurse five months later. In 1972, the Michigan State Department of Mental Health asked him whether he would participate in a psychosurgery experiment directed by Dr. Ernst Rodin, chief of neurology at the Lafayette Clinic in Detroit.

Mr. L. was to have been one of twelve patients, who, according to the *New York Times* (April 8, 1973) , were to have electrodes implanted in their brains for about a month "to see if an area of the brain could be isolated as a center of aggressive behavior." The Wayne County Court released Mr. L. without the brain treatment, because of a legal revision that led to the decision he was being held unconstitutionally.

While the L. case did not involve psychiatric elements of a dual personality or "possession" while engaged in a criminal act, this combination emerged quite clearly in the earlier trial of Garrett B. Trapnell, who had hijacked a TWA jetliner from Los Angeles at New York's Kennedy Airport on January 30, 1972. Trapnell, who had a long record of spectacular criminal acts, pleaded that at the time of the hijacking he was really not himself but "Gregg Ross." Two trials were held in New York City. At the first, the defense attorney's plea concerning Trapnell's dual personality prompted a mistrial on January 15, 1973. At a second trial, ending May 17, he was found guilty.

This decision interrupted Trapnell's remarkable record of convincing legal and psychiatric authorities in Florida, Texas, Maryland, New York, California, and Canada that he was subject to being taken over by "Gregg Ross" and therefore not really responsible for his actions. As a result, although arrested at least twenty times for major crimes, he spent fewer than two years in jail.

Garrett Trapnell had boasted to Cyrus Berlowitz, who was collecting material for an article in *True* magazine, that his claim of alternating personalties was "a classic Dr. Jekyll and Mr. Hyde situation." As reported in the *New York Times* (January 18, 1973) Trapnell had perfected his legal-psychiatric approach while studying works on psychology in prison libraries; he claimed that he knew "more about psychiatry than your average resident psychiatrist."

Trapnell told Berlowitz that "the temporary shot," the claim to be another personality only while a crime was being committed, "is much harder and more intricate" than a straight insanity plea, "takes a bit more finesse, but it precludes hospitalization." In claiming to be "Gregg Ross," the hijacker said, he was mimicking "paranoid schizophrenia, with a surfacing and submerging nature . . . the classic dual personality, compounded by paranoia, the sense of being persecuted. The result is an inability to differentiate between right and wrong due to this split personality."

He spoke of his alternating personalities in these terms: "Take Gary B. Trapnell and Gregg Ross. They're both the same physical person, but they are two mentally different people. If Gregg Ross commits a crime and the Gregg Ross aspect submerges, after he is put in prison, and the Gary Trapnell aspect emerges, then Gary Trapnell is not responsible legally for what Gregg Ross does." Trapnell said that it can never be proven whether such dual personality, in terms of a mental illness, actually exists, "because psychiatry as a science is the only science in the world that deals with extreme intangibles."

At Trapnell's first New York trial, one psychologist and four psychiatrists testified that he was mentally ill during the TWA hijacking designed to extort $306,800. The defense claimed that Trapnell acted as a paranoid schizophrenic who was provoked into a psychotic state shortly before the air piracy. One psychiatrist, Dr. David Abrahamsen, who testified at both trials, took the position that Trapnell was faking this possession by the Gregg Ross personality, adding, "He is not in any way psychotic or insane. He is as bright as a light."

Still, Trapnell's fantasy of being somebody else had been building up over a long time. As a child he used to dress up in his father's naval uniform. As an adult he compared his flying experience with that of Charles A. Lindbergh, and when operating a yacht he compared himself to Captain Bligh. During a string of bank robberies in Canada, he and his companion called themselves "Butch Cassidy and the Sundance Kid," and he signed a holdup note, "Butch Cassidy."

The variety of dual personalities, dramatized fantasy figures, and alter egos is conditioned by environmental and characterological factors. Yet the eviction of a demon or possessing

spirit follows remarkably similar patterns, often employing violent means. These include physical abuse of the possessed person's body, as well as treatment thought to be intolerable to the
demon but not painful to the possessed. The electronic exorcism
of Rose, mentioned at the outset of this chapter, had a forerunner in the exorcism procedure of Carl A. Wickland, M.D. His
lifelong work as a psychiatric exorcist was reported in a book,
Thirty Years Among the Dead.

Dr. Wickland's credentials included membership in the Chicago and Illinois State medical societies, as well as in the American Society for the Advancement of Science. Canon John D.
Pearce-Higgins of Great Britain has written that "a good many
patients in mental hospitals suffering from hallucinations, hearing or speaking in strange voices, or suffering from split-personal-
ities, *may* be cases of possession who would benefit from
treatment similar to that given by Dr. Wickland." Canon Pearce-
Higgins made these observations in *Spiritual Frontiers.* We shall
review his own work in a later chapter; but his views of Dr.
Wickland's work are of interest here, as the Chicago doctor
combined his medical knowledge with mediumship and exorcism
by electric current.

Pearce-Higgins feels that Wickland's work should be reexamined today by "those who have largely neglected it in the past,
namely psychiatrists, clergy, philosophers and theologians." He
reminds us that the Chicago psychiatrist played a light external
electrical current along the spine or over the head of the possessed person, which prompted the possessing spirit to flee this
body and take control of Wickland's Swedish-born wife, Anna, a
medium.

Through the medium Dr. Wickland, according to Pearce-
Higgins, was thus enabled "to interrogate and converse with the
entity, ascertain from this particulars (often exactly verified later
as correct) concerning his or her (usually frustrated) early life.
He had shed the physical body, had now entered into or got
entangled in the 'aura' of a living person, and by controlling the

victim's body and mind, was causing great injury." Canon Pearce-Higgins added:

"Eventually the 'spirit' or 'spirits'—for many were found to be possessed by more than one—were either persuaded to depart, usually in company of some near relative on the other side who was standing by to help, or removed by the spirit helpers 'on the other side' for re-education. While many 'spirits' were unwilling to go, and practically all resented at first being extruded from the patient's body and aura by the electrical treatment, which they experienced as intense heat or a flame or fire, some were glad to be set free from what they had experienced as a sort of spider's web of entanglement, from which they appeared unable to escape."

What exactly was the means of Dr. Wickland's electronic exorcism? In an article on "Static Electricity in Therapeutics" (1935), he wrote: "The static machine which I use, constructed by myself under the direction of intelligent spiritual forces, is made according to the Wimhurst pattern and contains fourteen thirty-inch diameter glass discs, all active, giving a powerful current." The electricity communicated by this instrument—about the size of a bookcase reaching two-thirds to the ceiling of a room—appears to have communicated a sparkling-tingling effect to the possessed person, with perhaps a suggestion of discomfort and potential danger. Even now, psychiatrists practicing conditioning therapy utilize low-voltage electricity in the treatment of phobias, addictions, and related emotional difficulties. Dr. Wickland had been a watchmaker and cabinetmaker in his youth, and these skills were visible in the impressive exorcism machine he constructed in 1905 and used until his retirement in 1936, the year his wife died.

A man who practices medicine, including surgery, during the day and in the evening returns to a wife who is a medium is likely to have unique experiences. During his early studies, Wickland dissected bodies. He left one morning with no intention of doing any dissecting, so that he could later say his wife's "subconscious mind could not possibly have taken any part in what transpired later."

What did happen was that he and other students had to dissect the lower part of a man's body. In the afternoon, Wickland himself began dissecting on a lower limb. When he came home in the late afternoon, he found his wife unwell, staggering and in danger of falling down. When he put his hand on her shoulder she became controlled by an entity who complained, "What do you mean by cutting me?"

Wickland replied that he wasn't cutting anyone, but was contradicted, "Of course you are. You are cutting my leg."

Things got mixed up when Wickland tried to put his wife in a chair, and the voice coming from her said he had no business touching him. When the doctor said he had a right to touch his own wife, the angry reply was, "Your wife! What are you talking about! I am no woman, I'm a man."

Wickland recalls: "I explained that he had passed out of his physical body and was controlling the body of my wife, and that his spirit was here and his body at the [medical] college." The man's spirit seemed to accept this, and Wickland told him, "Suppose I were now cutting on your body at the college; that could not kill you since you are here." The spirit found this reasonable and said: "I guess I must be what they call 'dead,' so I won't have any more use for my old body. If you can learn anything by cutting on it, go ahead and cut away." He then became chummy and demanded, "Say, Mister, give me a chew of tobacco."

Wickland refused to give the spirit, by way of his wife's mouth, any tobacco. He also refused him a pipe, although the spirit said, oddly, "I'm dying for a smoke."

After more talk about the status of a so-called "dead" person, the spirit "realized his true condition and left." Wickland found later, on examination of the body, that the man had been an inveterate tobacco user.

With this kind of matter-of-fact approach, Dr. Wickland obviously took spirit existences in his stride and regarded them as part of his common everyday routine. His wife apparently went in and out of trance with ease. Wickland found that, because of this, the majority of spirits possessing or controlling the medium failed to comprehend that they were dead and were "temporarily occupying the body of another." He explained his findings further:

"Those intelligences whose reasoning faculties are alert can generally be made to realize that their situation is unusual when attention is called to the dissimilarity between their own former bodily features, hands, feet, as well as clothes, and those of the psychic. This is especially so when the spirit is a man, for the difference will then be more readily noticed. Following the statement that the body which is being controlled belongs to my wife, spirits usually retort: 'I am not your wife,' and a great deal of explanation is required before they can be brought to recognition of the fact that they are in temporary possession of another's body."

Dr. Wickland used his electronic exorcism device on spirits who displayed "obstinate skepticism, who stubbornly refuse to understand that they have made the transition out of the physical. These will not listen to reason and fail to be convinced of their changed condition, even when a mirror is held before them." The Chicago physician said that "the transference of the mental aberration or psychosis from a patient to Mrs. Wickland is facilitated by the use of static electricity, frequently in the presence of the psychic."

It is noteworthy that Dr. Wickland, at this point, equated spirit possession with mental illness; exorcism of the spirit and transfer to the medium were, in the framework of his concepts, identical with removal of a "mental aberration" or "psychosis." He added that this electricity was "harmless to the patient," while "exceedingly effective, for the obsessing spirit cannot long resist such electrical treatment, and is dislodged."

Wickland, who used the words "obsession" and "possession"

interchangeably, explained that, once the spirit was in control of his wife, he could be addressed by the physician, educated as to his "true condition" and "higher possibilities," and then "removed and cared for by the advanced spirits," while Mrs. Wickland returned to her normal self.

It is, of course, perfectly possible that Dr. and Mrs. Wickland's electronically aided exorcism was no more than an elaborate self-delusion, a *folie à deux* that may have served a variety of their own social and psychological needs. It is also quite possible that the Wicklands cured people with their method. We either have to take the doctor's word for it, or we have to call his efforts, in the vernacular of contemporary psychology, as a special kind of "game playing."

Despite Wickland's assurance that he was offering "reliable and incontestable evidence at first hand," there is no supportive documentary data available. Canon Pearce-Higgins requested such material from people who might have known Wickland in order to validate the cases, but none was forthcoming. Wickland insisted on "the utter impossibility of fraud in these experiences," noting that "foreign languages totally unknown to Mrs. Wickland are spoken, expressions never heard by her are used, while the identity of the controlling spirits has again and again been verified and corroborations innumerable have been made."

Dr. Wickland maintained that once he spoke through his wife with twenty-one different spirits who used six different languages, although Anna Wickland spoke only Swedish and English. From one patient, brought from Chicago to Los Angeles, where the Wicklands founded their National Psychological Institute, thirteen different spirits were exorcised. Of these, seven were recognized by the patient's mother as "relatives and friends well known to her during their lives."

One dramatic incident involved a woman musician, whom we shall call Mrs. Mathews. Wickland spoke of her as a woman of culture and refinement who had "suffered a nervous breakdown" because of excessive social demands. Mrs. Mathews had become "intractable," and had been in a "raving condition" for six weeks, in need of nurses day and night. Her physician had been unable to help and the Wicklands found her sitting up in her bed, at times crying like "a forlorn child," at others screaming with fear, "Matilla! Matilla!" She also seemed to fight and struggle, as if with invisible adversaries, while talking a wild gibberish of English and Spanish. Anna Wickland's "psychic diagnosis" was possession, and she quickly went into a trance.

For two hours, Dr. Wickland spoke with the spirits that had allegedly withdrawn from Mrs. Mathews and were now inhabiting the medium. There were three of them. The first, Mary, a girl pursued by two suitors: an American whose name is not given, and a Mexican, his rival, named Matilla. As the story came to Wickland, one of the men had killed Mary in a jealous rage, and then the rivals had killed each other. All were unaware of their death, although the girl said, "I thought they were going to kill each other, but here they are, still fighting." Dr. Wickland's narrative concluded:

"This tragedy of love, hatred and jealousy had not ended with physical death; the group had unconsciously been drawn into the psychic atmosphere of the patient, and the violent fighting had continued within her aura. Since her nervous resistance was exceedingly low at this time, one after the other had usurped her physical body, with a resulting disturbance that was unexplainable by her attendants.

"With great difficulty, the three spirits were convinced that they had lost their physical bodies, but at last they recognized the truth and were taken away by our invisible co-workers. Meanwhile the patient had arisen, and speaking rationally to the astonished nurse, walked quietly about her room. Presently she said: 'I am going to sleep well tonight,' and returning to bed, fell asleep without the usual sedative and rested quietly through the night."

Dr. Wickland asked Mrs. Mathews to visit him the next day. He dismissed the nurse and discontinued medication. He then gave her his electrical treatment. She had dinner with other patients in a common dining room and in the evening attended a function in their social hall. Another spirit was removed the following day: a little girl who had been killed in the San Francisco earthquake, and who "cried constantly saying she was lost in the dark." Rest and other treatment followed. After several months Mrs. Mathews returned home to resume her normal life.

Wickland did provide data that might have been independently checked—although there is no evidence that this was ever done—in the case of a woman named Mary Rose. This happened during the Wicklands' Chicago years. The case was not one of psychiatric possession, but direct spirit possession of Anna Wickland while in trance. During one of their mediumistic home circles, the medium fell on the floor and could not be moved. Eventually, speaking as a spirit, Mrs. Wickland said as if in great pain, "Why didn't I take more carbolic acid? I want to die; I'm so tired of living."

The spirit then gave her name, as well as the address, 202 South Green Street. Her story was that life had been very bitter; she had been in great physical pain because of abdominal illness and had taken poison. The Wicklands used their standard procedure to help the spirit adjust. Beyond this, they confirmed that a Mary Rose had lived at the South Green Street address, and had died a week earlier at the Cook County Hospital. A hospital record bearing her name and the case number 341106 stated that she had died of carbolic-acid poisoning.

Skeptical psychic researchers will doubtlessly note that the information on Mary Rose was public and could have been obtained by the Wicklands before that; or, assuming that the medium had special clairvoyant powers, the data concerning the suicide might have been obtained by the medium through extrasensory perception.

Dr. Wickland's personal style of exorcism was, on the whole, rather aggressive. The force of electric currents he used to make alleged possessing spirits uncomfortable was often matched by his peremptory manner of addressing entities as they spoke through his entranced wife. The exorcist-psychiatrist emerges as a righteous, strong-minded person, who appears very sure that his method and explanations are correct. Spirits or not, it may well be that this very manner of certainty influenced his patients and resulted in either a temporary or permanent cure.

Wickland's style and approach are well illustrated in "The Case of Carrie Huntington," as he recorded the dialogue between himself and the spirit whom he regarded as possessing one of his patients, Mrs. Burton.

DR. WICKLAND: Tell us who you are.

SPIRIT: I do not wish you to hold my hands.

DOCTOR: You must sit still.

SPIRIT: Why do you treat me like this?

DOCTOR: Who are you?

SPIRIT: Why do you want to know?

DOCTOR: You have come here as a stranger, and we would like to know who you are.

SPIRIT: What are you so interested for?

DOCTOR: We should like to know with whom we are associated. If a stranger came to your home, would you not like to know his name?

SPIRIT: I do not want to be here and I do not know any of you. Somebody pushed me in here and I do not think it is right to force me in like that. When I came in and sat down on the chair you grabbed my hands as if I were a prisoner. Why was I pushed in here?

DOCTOR: You were probably in the dark.

SPIRIT: It seems somebody took me by force. [Dr. Wickland's explanation is that "guiding intelligences" in the spirit world forced such possessing spirits to communicate through his wife, so that they might gain understanding.]

DOCTOR: Was there any reason for it?

SPIRIT: I do not know of any reason, and I do not see why I should be bothered like that.

DOCTOR: Was no reason given for handling you in this manner?

SPIRIT: It has been a terrible time for me for quite a while. I have been tormented to death. I have been driven here, there, and everywhere. I am getting so provoked about it that I feel like giving everything a good shaking.

DOCTOR: What have they done to you?

SPIRIT: It seems too terrible. If I walk around, I am so very miserable. I do not know what it is. Sometimes it seems as if my senses were being knocked out of me. Something comes on me like thunder and lightning. It makes such a noise. This terrible noise—it is awful! I cannot stand it any more, and I will not either! [This comment, according to Dr. Wickland, refers to the spirit's impressions of, and reaction to, the treatment with static electricity.]

DOCTOR: We shall be glad if you will not stand it any more.

SPIRIT: Am I not welcome? And if I am not, I do not care!

DOCTOR: You are not very particular.

SPIRIT: I have had so much hardship.

DOCTOR: How long have you been dead?

SPIRIT: Why do you speak that way? I am not dead. I am as alive as I can be, and I feel as if I were young again.

DOCTOR: Have you not felt, at times, as if you were somebody else?

SPIRIT: At times I feel very strange, especially when it knocks me senseless. I feel very bad. I do not feel that I should have this suffering. I do not know why I should have such things.

DOCTOR: Probably it is necessary.

SPIRIT: I feel I should be free to go where I please, but it seems I have no will of my own any more. I try, but it seems somebody else takes possession of me and gets me into some place where they knock me nearly senseless. If I knew it, I would never go there, but there is a person who seems to have the right to take me everywhere; I feel I should have the right to take her. [This,

according to Dr. Wickland, refers to the possessing spirit's relation with his patient, Mrs. Burton.]

DOCTOR: What business have you with her? Can't you live your
own life?

SPIRIT: I live my own life, but she interferes with me. I talk to
her. She wants to chase me out. I feel like chasing her out, and
that is a real struggle. I cannot see why I should not have the
right just as well as she has.

DOCTOR: Probably you are interfering with her.

SPIRIT: She wants to get rid of me. I am not bothering her. I
only talk to her sometimes.

DOCTOR: Does she know you talk to her?

SPIRIT: Sometimes she does, and then she chases me right out.
She acts all right, but she gets so provoked. Then, when she gets
into that place, I am knocked senseless and I feel terrible. I have
no power to take her away. She makes me get out.

DOCTOR: You should not stay around her.

SPIRIT: It is my body, it is not hers. She has no right there. I do
not see why she interferes with me.

DOCTOR: She interferes with your selfishness.

SPIRIT: I feel I have some right in life—I think so.

DOCTOR: You passed out of your body without understanding
the fact, and have been bothering the lady. You should go to the
spirit world and not hover around her.

SPIRIT: You say I am hovering around. I am not hovering
around, and I am not one to interfere, but I want a little to say
about things.

DOCTOR: That is why you had the "thunder" and "the
knocks."

SPIRIT: That was all right for a while, but lately it is terrible. I
must have understanding.

DOCTOR: You will have it now.

SPIRIT: I will do anything to stop that terrible knocking.

At this point, the possessed patient, Mrs. Burton, entered the
conversation that had thus far been going on between Dr. Wick-

land and the spirit speaking through his entranced wife, Anna. Mrs. Burton indicated that she recognized the voice as that of the spirit who had been troubling her and said: "I am mighty tired of you. Who are you, anyway?"

SPIRIT: I am a stranger.

MRS. BURTON: What is your name?

SPIRIT: My name?

MRS. B: Have you one?

SPIRIT: My name is Carrie.

MRS. B: Carrie what?

SPIRIT: Carrie Huntington.

MRS. B: Where do you live?

SPIRIT: San Antonio, Texas.

Mrs. Burton had visited San Antonio several years earlier, and she now said: "You have been with me a long time, haven't you?"

SPIRIT: You have been with *me* a long time. I should like to find out why you interfere with me. I recognize you now.

MRS. B: What street did you live on?

SPIRIT: I lived in many different places there.

DR. WICKLAND: Do you realize the fact that you have lost your own mortal body? Can you remember having been sick?

SPIRIT: I last remember I was in El Paso. I do not remember anything after that. I went there and I do not seem to remember when I left. It seems that I should be there now. I got very sick one day there.

DOCTOR: Probably you lost your body then.

SPIRIT: After El Paso I do not know where I went. I went some distance. I traveled on the railroad and it was just like I was nobody. Nobody asked me anything and I had to follow that lady [Mrs. Burton] as if I were her servant, and I felt very annoyed about it.

MRS. B: You worried me to death, because you sang all the time.

SPIRIT: I had to do something to attract your attention, because you would not listen to me any other way. You traveled on the train and took me away from my home and folks, and I feel very much hurt about it. Do you understand?

MRS. B: I understand you far better than you do me.

DOCTOR: Can't you realize what has been the matter with you?

SPIRIT: I want to tell you that I do not want those knockings any more. I will stay away.

DOCTOR: Understand your condition; understand that you are an ignorant, obsessing spirit, and that you have no physical body. You died, probably at the time you were sick.

SPIRIT: Could you talk to a ghost?

DOCTOR: Such things certainly do happen.

SPIRIT: I am not a ghost, because ghosts cannot talk. When you are dead, you lie there.

DOCTOR: When the body dies, it lies there. But the spirit does not.

SPIRIT: That goes to God who gave it.

DOCTOR: Where is He? Where is God?

SPIRIT: In Heaven.

DOCTOR: Where is that?

SPIRIT: It is where you go to find Jesus.

DOCTOR: The Bible says, "God is Love; and he that dwelleth in Love dwelleth in God." Where will you find that God?

SPIRIT: I suppose in Heaven. I cannot tell you anything about it. But I know I have been in the worst hell you could give me with those knockings. I do not see that they have done me any good. I do not like them at all.

DOCTOR: Then you must stay away from that lady.

SPIRIT: I see her well now, and I can have a real conversation with her.

DOCTOR: Yes, but this is the last time.

SPIRIT: How do you know it will?

DOCTOR: When you take leave here you will understand that you have been talking through another person's body. That person is my wife.

SPIRIT: What nonsense! I thought you looked wiser than to talk such nonsense.

DOCTOR: I may seem foolish, but look at her hands. Do you recognize them?

SPIRIT: They do not look like mine, but so much has taken place lately that I do not know what I shall do. That lady over there [Mrs. Burton] has been acting like a madman, and I have taken it as it came, so I shall have to find out what she thinks of doing, and why she does those things to me.

DOCTOR: She will be very happy to be rid of you.

At this point, Mrs. Burton again spoke directly to the medium, or to the spirit addressing Dr. Wickland, asking "Carrie, how old are you?"

SPIRIT: You know that a lady never wants to tell her age.

DOCTOR: Especially if she happens to be a spinster.

SPIRIT: Please excuse me; you will have to take it as it is. I will not tell my age to anyone.

DOCTOR: Have you ever been married?

SPIRIT: Yes, I was married to a fellow, but I did not care for him.

DOCTOR: What was his name?

SPIRIT: That is a secret with me. I would not have his name mentioned for anything, and I do not want to carry his name either. My name is Carrie Huntington, because it was my name, and I do not want to carry his name.

DOCTOR: Do you want to go to the spirit world?

SPIRIT: What foolish questions you put to me.

DOCTOR: It may seem foolish to you, but, nevertheless, there is a spirit world. Spiritual things often seem foolish to the mortal mind. You have lost your body.

SPIRIT: I have not lost my body. I have been with this lady, but she does one thing I do not like very well. She eats too much and gets too strong, then I have no power over her body—not as much as I want to. [Turning to Mrs. Burton] I want you to eat less. I try very much to dictate to you not to eat this and that, but you have no sense. You do not even listen to me.

MRS. BURTON: This is the place I told you to go, but you would not go by yourself. [She was referring to the Wicklands' Institute and the electricity treatment.]

SPIRIT: I know it. But you have no business to take me where I get those knockings. I do not want to stay with you if you take those awful knockings.

DOCTOR: They are in the next room. Do you want some?

SPIRIT: No, thank you. Not for me any more.

DOCTOR: Listen to what is told you, then you will not need any more. You are an ignorant spirit. I mean, you are ignorant of your condition. You lost your body, evidently without knowing it.

SPIRIT: How do you know?

DOCTOR: You are now controlling my wife's body.

SPIRIT: I never saw you before, so how in the world can you think I should be called your wife? No, never.

DOCTOR: I do not want you to be.

SPIRIT: I do not want you either.

DOCTOR: I won't want you to control my wife's body much longer. You must realize that you have lost your physical body. Do you recognize these hands? [The medium's hands.]

SPIRIT: I have changed so much lately that all those changes make me crazy. It makes me tired.

DOCTOR: Now, Carrie, be sensible.

SPIRIT: I am sensible, and don't you tell me differently, else you will have someone to tell you something you never heard before.

DOCTOR: Now, Carrie!

SPIRIT: I am Mrs. Carrie Huntington!

MRS. B: You listen to what the doctor has to say to you.

SPIRIT: I will not listen to anyone, I tell you once and for all. I

have been from one to another and I do not care what becomes
of me.

DOCTOR: Do you know you are talking through my wife's
body?

SPIRIT: Such nonsense. I think that's the craziest thing I ever
heard in my life.

DOCTOR: Now you will have to be sensible.

SPIRIT: Are you a perfect man?

DOCTOR: No, I am not, but I tell you that you are an ignorant,
selfish spirit. You have been bothering that lady for some time,
and we have chased you out by the use of those "knocks."
Whether you understand it or not, you are an ignorant spirit.
You will have to behave yourself, or else I will take you to my
office and give you more of those "knocks."

SPIRIT: I don't want those knocks.

The seesaw dialogue between Dr. Wickland and the "Carrie
Huntington" personality continued along similar lines, with
Wickland stating that Mrs. Burton had made "a bargain to come
here and get rid of you" and telling the entity, "You have been
fired out by electricity." Again, the entity exclaimed, "I will not
have those knocks any more." The session ended, according to
Wickland's account, with "intelligent spirits" guiding the
"Carrie Huntington" personality away from Mrs. Burton.

Now, it is all too easy to read Dr. Wickland's exorcistic
dialogue with a skeptical smile and to observe his statements as a
mixture of naiveté and dogmatic self-assurance. Yet, the setting
and drama Wickland had created, the structure of treatment into
which he fitted his patients, may well have served to alleviate
their conditions. Parallels between his methods and those of
shamans in earlier and other cultures are numerous; that he
placed them into psychiatric settings, in Chicago and Los
Angeles, does not change their underlying universal appeal.

Canon Pearce-Higgins, whose contemporary work in England
closely parallels that of Dr. Wickland (see section 4, chapter 4),
feels that his own experiences convince him that Wickland's cases

"are true." Studying the American psychiatrist-exorcist's results, the Anglican clergyman observes that "case after case shows that after such treatment, and the long argument between the spirit and the doctor, patient after patient was cured and restored to sanity, or sometimes to physical health, many of them almost immediately, some after a further treatment and period of convalescence."

The position taken by Canon Pearce-Higgins even makes it possible to accommodate both the ultratechnological psychosurgery practiced by Dr. Walter—who ousted a devil image by means of electrodes implanted in the brain—and Dr. Wickland's unique exorcism by static electricity. Pearce-Higgins speaks of an "open door" in the psyche of certain individuals through which spirit entities may "enter and use the mind and body for their own ends." He notes that such "open doors" may be created by "severe illness and nervous debility, a blow on the head (very common) or some psychological trauma." Canon Pearce-Higgins urges that the Wickland method be reexamined in light of current practices. He foresees difficulties, however, "because even supposing psychiatrists were prepared to try this completely harmless experiment in 'exorcism' (for want of a better word), where shall we find the mediums who can do what Mrs. Wickland did?"

Certainly, Dr. and Mrs. Wickland were a unique team. While elements of Carl Wickland's personality are visible in his writings and in the dialogues he had with possessing spirits, little is known about his wife, Anna. Her role was similar to that of the wives of the Irish poet W. B. Yeats and of Sir Arthur Conan Doyle, creator of the Sherlock Holmes stories; all were mediums whose capacities assured a constant link with their husbands' intense interest in contact with the "other world."

It seems doubtful that the Wicklands' procedure can be duplicated at the present time, if only because electronic devices today are a good deal less awe-inspiring and pseudo-magical than during his years of practice.

2. Twenty-Three Days in Iowa

The intimate and intricate relationship between exorcist and possessed person is vividly illustrated by a twenty-three-day ordeal of exorcism that took place in Earling, Iowa. The exorcist was Father Theophilus Riesinger (1878–1962), a member of an order of Capuchin monks in the community of St. Anthony at Marathon, Wisconsin. The possessed woman, later identified as Anna Ecklund, was forty-six years old at the time of the exorcism in 1928.

Father Theophilus, strong-minded, self-assured and white-bearded, was imposing-looking in his monk's tunic. Miss Ecklund, who remained unmarried, first showed symptoms of possession at the age of sixteen. An account of her exorcism was published under the title *Begone Satan!* bearing the imprimatur of Joseph F. Busch, Roman Catholic bishop of St. Cloud, Minnesota, under the date of July 23, 1935. It was originally written in German by the Reverend Carl Vogl and translated into English by the Rev. Celestine Kapsner, O.S.B., who shortly before his death in 1973 confirmed details of the event to the author of this book.

The account stated that Anna's first possession, in 1908, took place "through her aunt, Mina, known among the people as a witch" who had "placed a spell on some herbs" in Anna's food. Father Theophilus initially "freed her from this possession" on June 18, 1912. "Curses hurled against her by her wicked father" once more put the girl into a state of possession which lasted for decades. The church pamphlet described Miss Ecklund as of "small stature" and having had only an elementary education. It added, "She preserved her virginity, though she had been exposed to severe trials."

The Earling exorcism took place at the convent of the Franciscan Sisters, in three stages: from August 18 to 26, September 13 to 20, and December 15 to 23, 1928. It was a grueling experience for all concerned; several nuns asked to be transferred to other convents. Father Theophilus outlasted them all, and the final results appear to have been positive: Anna Ecklund suffered later possessions, but these were milder and quite manageable.

Theophilus Riesinger, born in Stelza, Bavaria, clearly acted within the German exorcism traditions of the nineteenth century. Up to 1936 he claimed to have successfully exorcized twenty-two people. He maintained that he studied each case in detail "before I am willing to admit there is a case of possession." He noted that possession symptoms often "look like hysteria and insanity," but he found a number of instances where "that is not the case."

In the case of Anna Ecklund, Father Theophilus had his bishop's permission to undertake the exorcism. "Through exorcism and through the power of the church," he said, "we can force the devils to talk." As quoted in *True Mystic Science* (April 1939), he said, "I would always prefer to work in secret, but sometimes the devils make such a show that I cannot keep it quiet." That was certainly true of the Earling case, which began with a conversation between Father Theophilus and the local priest, F. Joseph Steiger. Father Steiger was not exactly overjoyed at the prospect of an exorcism in his parish. He asked his friend:

"What, another case of possession? Are these cases still on the increase? You have already dispossessed the devil in a number of such cases!"

Riesinger replied, "That is indeed true. However, the Bishop has again entrusted this case into my hands. The lady in question lives at some distance from Earling. I should like to have her brought here, since it would create too much excitement in her home and perhaps would be the cause of many disturbances to the person herself."

Exasperated, Steiger asked, "But why just here in my parish?"

"It is just here, in an outlying country district that the case may be disposed of in a quiet manner. Two places are available, either the Sisters' convent or in the sacristy here. So it is quite possible to relieve the unfortunate person of her burden without anybody out in the world becoming aware of it."

Father Steiger was not at all sure that the Franciscan Sisters would welcome the event. "My dear Father, do you really think that the Mother Superior would permit anything like that to take place under her convent roof? I don't believe it. And it would be altogether out of the question to bring the person into my own house."

Eventually, Steiger agreed, provided the mother superior was not opposed. As it happened, Riesinger had obtained her permission beforehand.

It was summertime. People were working the fields. The two churchmen could hope to keep the exorcism quiet and unsuspected. The bishop, consulted once again, cautioned Father Steiger that "the devil will certainly try his utmost to seek revenge on you, should you be willing that this unfortunate woman be relieved of this terrible oppression."

Riesinger briefed Steiger on Miss Ecklund's predicament, which began when she was fourteen years old and felt that inner forces were holding her back from church services. "Inner voices" were suggesting "disagreeable things," aroused "thoughts of the most shameful type within her" and tried to "induce her to do things unmentionable." According to the published account, "there were times when she felt impelled to shatter her holy water font, when she could have attacked her spiritual adviser and could have suffocated him." During this first exorcism, when the Ecklund girl was a teen-ager, the tall monk was thirty-four years old. The same account noted that the bishop had entrusted the Ecklund case to Father Theophilus in 1928 because of "his stainless career, as well as his successful encounter in numerous possessions." He was singled out as "the one best suited" for this case, which became his "severest experience" and would tax the monk "to the limit of his physical endurance." He was now fifty years old.

Anna Ecklund arrived in Earling by train. Her identity had not been revealed to the nuns who went to meet her at the station, nor to the train conductors who had been alerted to her unbalanced mental state. In Earling itself, precautions had been taken to hide her identity, so that later on people would not point her out as having been "possessed by the devil."

The railroad personnel had their hands full, anyway. Although Miss Ecklund had been quite willing to submit herself to the exorcism, she was hostile and unruly on the train. On her arrival, she tried to attack and choke the nuns, who nevertheless managed to take her to the convent. Riesinger and Steiger met at the rectory, next door, while Anna was taken to her convent room. But the two churchmen were soon advised that things were not peaceful with Anna. The convent cook had sprinkled holy water on a tray of food before it was sent to Miss Ecklund. It was soon reported that "the devil, however, was not to be tricked."

The woman, apparently already in a state of "possession," "was aware at once of the presence of the blessed food and became terribly enraged about it. She purred like a cat, and it was absolutely impossible to make her eat. The blessed food was taken back to the kitchen to be exchanged for unblessed food; otherwise the soup bowls and the plates might have crashed through the window."

The following morning, the exorcism ritual began, and with it a pattern that would be repeated throughout Anna's stay in Earling. Miss Ecklund passed into "unconsciousness," as soon as the exorcism rites were spoken. From early morning until late at night, a dialogue between Father Theophilus and various entities representing themselves as devils or discarnate persons spoke through the partially or fully entranced woman. At the same time, Miss Ecklund went through physical contortions, hurled herself about, uttered obscenities, made antireligious remarks, vomited, and possibly showed other physiological symptoms too objectionable to be recorded.

The very first day set the tone. Theophilus had Anna's sleeves and dress tightly bound, presumably to prevent her from stripping herself naked. The published account added: "The strongest nuns were selected to assist her in case anything might happen. There was a suspicion that the devil might attempt attacking the exorcist during the ceremony." After prayers, Anna sank into unconsciousness. The account continues:

"Father Theophilus had hardly begun the formula of exorcism in the name of the Blessed Trinity, in the name of the Father, the Son and the Holy Ghost, in the name of the Crucified Savior, when a hair-raising scene occurred. With lightning speed the possessed dislodged herself from her bed and from the hands of her guards, and her body, carried through the air, landed high above the door of the room and clung to the wall with a tenacious grip. All present were struck with a trembling fear. Father Theophilus alone kept his peace:

" 'Pull her down. She must be brought back to her place upon the bed!'

"Real force had to be applied to her feet to bring her down from her high position on the wall. The mystery was that she could cling to the wall at all! It was through the powers of the evil spirit, who had taken possession of her body."

Hopes that the exorcism might proceed quietly, without being noticed by the citizens of Earling were soon destroyed: "Satan howled as though he had been struck over the head with a club. Like a pack of wild beasts suddenly let loose, the terrifying noises sounded aloud as they came out of the mouth of the possessed woman. Those present were struck with a terrible fear that penetrated the very marrow of their bones." Father Theophilus's urgings that possessor or possessed keep quiet were ignored. The noises penetrated the convent's closed windows. People gathered in the street, wondering whether someone was being murdered. The news quickly spread through the community: "At the convent they are trying to drive the devil from one possessed."

The actual medical condition of Anna Ecklund was not recorded, so that no detailed psychophysiological account of her various states is available. Yet, body contortions, constant high excitement, vomiting, and other stresses obviously took their toll. The published account states:

"The physical condition of the possessed presented such a gruesome sight, because of the distorted members [arms, legs] of her body that it was unbearable. The Sisters, even pastor [Rev. Steiger], could not endure it long. Occasionally they had to leave the room to recuperate in the fresh air, to gain new strength for further attendance at the horrible ordeal. The most valiant and self-composed was Father Theophilus. He had been accustomed to Satan's howling displays and blusterings from experiences with him in previous exorcisms. God seems to have favored him with special gifts and qualities for facing such ordeals. On such occasions, with the permission of the Bishop, he carried a consecrated host in a pyx upon his breast in order to safeguard himself against injuries and direct attacks by the evil one."

The account added that Theophilus had several times been "twisted about, trembling like a fluttering leaf in a whirl-wind." This suggests that, by some psychophysical rapport with Miss Ecklund in her violently entranced state, the exorcist had himself been caught up in the very forces he sought to tame. Both churchmen, Riesinger and Steiger, had encounters with barely avoided dangers which they attributed to the devil's machinations against them.

The Earling exorcism was unusual in that it mixed devils with discarnate entities. Although traditionally, evil spirits, demons, and devils all have been regarded as possessing entities, it is rare to find quite as much of a mixture in a modern exorcist setting. In the Earling case, "the devils living in the possessed displayed various abilities in reactions. Those that hailed from the realm of fallen angels gave evidence of a greater reserve. They twisted about and howled mournfully in the presence of the Blessed Sacrament, acting like whipped curs who growl and snarl under the pain of the biting lash. Those who were once active souls of men upon earth and were condemned to hell because of their sinful lives, acted differently. They showed themselves bold and fearless."

While Anna Ecklund was acting as a vehicle for such discarnate entities, she was frothing at the mouth, while "vomiting forth unmentionable excrements." Outpourings would fill a pitcher, even a pail, and the stench was "most unnatural." She vomited as often as ten to twenty times a day.

The parallels between this type of exorcism ceremony and a mediumistic trance, while the trance usually proceeds with greater decorum, are striking. During the mediumistic séance, a number of entities may speak through the medium; often, a spirit acting as a "control" introduces each personality and generally serves much like a master of ceremonies. In the Earling exorcism case, as the published account puts it, "it was necessary to find out definitely whether the exorcist had to deal with one or more devils. It was also important for the exorcist to insist upon getting control over the person and of dispossessing the devil. On various occasions there were different voices coming out of the woman which indicated that un-numbered spirits were here involved." The account added:

"There were voices that sounded bestial and most unnatural, uttering an inexpressible grief and hatred that no human could reproduce. Again, voices were heard that were quite human, breathing an atmosphere of keen suffering and indicating bitter feeling of disappointment."

As to the technique and aim of Father Theophilus's questioning, these definitions were given:

"As is common in such experiences, Satan can, through the solemn exorcism of the Church, be forced to speak the truth, even though he is the father of lies from the very beginning.

Naturally, he will try to mislead and sidetrack the exorcist. It is also common experience that Satan at first does his utmost to sidestep the questions with clever, witty evasions, direct lies, shrewd simulations."

During the extended exorcism period, a variety of animal-type noises came from the possessed woman. Those present were reminded of lions and hyenas on the loose, mewing cats, bellowing cattle, barking dogs. These yelpings and howlings at times lasted for hours and were so nerve-racking that the twelve attending nuns took turns to get away from it all. Father Theophilus addressed the woman (or the devil) in English, German, and Latin. He came away from the ritual with the feeling that he had received correct replies in all three languages. The team of devils he encountered was headed by Beelzebub. At one point, the exorcist engaged in the following dialogue:

Exorcist: In the name of Jesus and His Most Blessed Mother, Mary the Immaculate, who crushed the head of the serpent, tell me the truth: Who is the leader or prince among you? What is your name?

Devil: Beelzebub.

Exorcist: You call yourself Beelzebub. Are you not Lucifer, the prince of the devils?

Devil: No, not the prince, the chieftain, but one of the leaders.

Exorcist: You were therefore not a human being, but you are one of the fallen angels, who with selfish pride wanted to be like unto God.

Devil: Yes, that is so. Ha, how we hate Him!

Exorcist: Why do you call yourself Beelzebub if you are not the prince of the devils?

Devil: Enough, my name is Beelzebub.

Exorcist: From the point of influence and dignity you must rank near Lucifer, or do you hail from the lower choir of angels?

Devil: I once belonged to the seraphic choir.

EXORCIST: What would you do if God made it possible for you to atone for your injustice to Him?

DEVIL: Are you a competent theologian?

Father Theophilus's concern with hierarchical niceties in the nether world did not, in fact, meet with significant success. His tendency toward asking leading questions, steering replies into specific channels, and at times directly suggesting answers reflects the exorcist's curiosity as well as his uninhibited self-assurance. More concrete and psychologically revealing was this dialogue between Beelzebub and Theophilus:

EXORCIST: How long have you been torturing this poor woman?

DEVIL: Since her fourteenth year.

EXORCIST: How dared you enter into that innocent girl and torture her like that?

DEVIL: Ha, did not her own father curse us into her?

EXORCIST: But why did you, Beelzebub, alone take possession of her? Who gave you that permission?

DEVIL: Don't talk so foolishly. Don't I have to render obedience to Satan?

EXORCIST: Then you are here at the direction and command of Lucifer?

DEVIL: Well, how could it be otherwise?

If Anna's father had cursed the devil into her, and thus set the whole train of mental imbalance and "possession" into motion, her personal history might provide a clue to the psychological bases of her situation. At one point, following the exorcism prayer, an entity identifying itself as Jacob spoke "with a healthy manly voice" from which "one could detect at once that he had been a human being."

Father Theophilus asked, "Which Jacob are you?"

The answer was, "The father of the possessed girl."

Later dialogue disclosed that Anna's father had led "a frightfully coarse and brutal" life and had "repeatedly tried to force his own daughter to commit incest with him." She had, however, "firmly resisted him" and he had "cursed her and wished inhumanly that the devils would enter into her and entice her to commit every possible sin against chastity, thereby ruining her, body and soul."

Whether such an incest demand was actually made, or whether the entranced girl was subject to a retroactive fantasy, is impossible to guess. Despite references to her lifelong virginity, incest may have taken place and been repressed. In addition, Anna's hostility toward Mina (the "witch" who fed her herbs on which she had placed a spell), her aunt and her father's mistress, also emerged during the exorcistic dialogue. The account states:

"As the prayers of exorcism were continued, Jacob's mistress, who was in hell with him, also had to face the ordeal and give answer. Her high-pitched voice, almost falsetto, had already been noticed among the many other voices. She now confessed that she was Mina."

She was in hell, according to the dialogue, because of her "prolonged immoral life with Jacob, while his wife was still living." But a more specific cause of her damnation was the act of child murder, mentioned in the following exchange.

EXORCIST: You committed murder while you were still alive? Whom did you kill?
MINA: Little ones.
EXORCIST: How many did you actually kill?
MINA: Three—no, actually four!

The account suggests that the murdered children were Mina's own, but the dialogue apparently did not contain that information. The picture of hell and damnation and the position of humans who had become devils were illustrated in the case of Mina and Jacob. Anna's father confessed to having ridiculed the priest who ministered the sacrament of Extreme Unction on his deathbed. However, these and other sins might have been forgiven before death, but "the crime of giving his own child to the devils was the thing that finally determined his eternal damnation." Still, "even in hell he was still scheming how to torture and molest his child" and was "not in the least disposed to give her up or leave her."

What emerged from the exorcistic dialogue, then, was Anna Ecklund's emotional and, in a very specific sense, bodily possession by her father, linked to the memory of Mina. During the exorcism, when Mina controlled Anna, "her demeanor toward the Blessed Sacrament was beyond description. She would spit and vomit in a most hideous manner so that both Father Theophilus and the pastor had to use handkerchiefs constantly to wipe off the spittle from habit and cassock."

Father Theophilus's leading questions were most obvious when he had ordered Beelzebub to bring forth the woman's father and had received the reply, "You can ask him." Theophilus had said, "Is then the father of the woman also present as one of the devils? Since when?"

To which the devil replied, "What a foolish question. He has been with us ever since he was damned."

Theophilus said, "Then I command in the name of the Crucified Saviour of Nazareth that you present the father of this woman and that he give me answer!"

A deep rough voice was heard, which had been noticed earlier beside that of the devil. Theophilus asked, "Are you the unfortunate father who has cursed his own child?"

The answer was a defiant "No."

"Who are you then?"

"I am Judas."

"What, Judas! Are you Judas Iscariot, the former Apostle?"

There followed a long drawn-out "Y—e—s. I am the one," in a deep bass voice, with much spitting and vomiting.

Theophilus asked, "What business have you here?"

"To bring her to despair, so that she will commit suicide and hang herself! She must get the rope, she must go to hell!"

"Is it then a fact that everyone that commits suicide goes to hell?"

"Rather not."

"Why not?"

"Ha, we devils are ones that urge them to commit suicide to hang themselves, just as I did myself."

"Do you not regret that you have committed such a despicable deed?"

A terrible curse followed. And then, "Let me alone. Don't bother me with your fake god. It was my own fault."

But even such limited coherence was rare during the seemingly endless days of exorcism. Much was rambling, yelling, physical self-torture on the part of the possessed, with such physiological side effects as hardness in the abdomen and extremities. Her face, emaciated and distorted, was also often suffused with blood. Anna's violence and suffering placed a strain on everyone, but particularly on F. Joseph Steiger, the parish priest who had reluctantly permitted Father Theophilus to undertake the exorcism in Earling. His long-standing friendship with the forceful monk, severely tested by the community's concern over the exorcism proceedings, turned into frustration and anger. He told Theophilus that the whole upsetting and seemingly fruitless effort was the result of his stubbornness and persistence. Naturally, the monk attributed Steiger's reaction to the devil.

Steiger was frequently taunted by the devilish voices coming through Anna Ecklund that he should never have permitted the exorcism to take place in his parish, and would suffer the consequences. Typical was this remark:

"It is the pastor! He is at fault. Had he not given you permission to use his church and convent, you wouldn't be able to do a thing. And even today you would be helpless against us, if he were to retract his assent."

At other times, Father Steiger was warned, "You will have to suffer for all this." And, "I'll incite your whole parish against you and I will calumniate against you in such a way that you will no longer be able to defend yourself. Then you will have to pack up and leave in shame and regret." Finally, "Just wait until the end of the week! When Friday comes, then . . ."

Friday came, and with it an early morning telephone call from an outlying farm. Father Steiger was asked to minister the Last Sacrament to the farmer's dying wife. The parish priest drove out, performed his clerical duties and returned the same way, on a route he had driven hundreds of times, day and night. Nevertheless, Father Steiger fervently prayed for a safe journey. But just as he was about to cross a bridge leading over a deep ravine, he was struck blind: it seemed as if a dark cloud had descended on him or he had been blindfolded. His car crashed into the railing of the bridge and stopped just short of toppling into the ravine.

Although the steering wheel had broken, Steiger was able to extricate himself from the wreck with only minor bruises. His legs were shaking; he was thoroughly frightened. A farmer drove the priest to a nearby doctor who treated him briefly, and then to the parish house. From there he went to the convent, where another exorcism session was under way. According to the published account, the priest had hardly entered the room, when the devil possessing Anna called out triumphantly, "I certainly showed him up today! How about your new auto, that dandy car which was smashed to smithereens? It served you right!"

News of the accident quickly spread. Parish members collected enough money to buy Father Steiger a new car. But the priest remained pale, shaken and tense. He was more than ever ready to get rid of Father Theophilus, Miss Ecklund, exorcism, and all its shocking, upsetting side effects.

Outwardly unperturbed, Theophilus plowed on. Minor and major devils were being exorcised, one by one. Still, the task seemed endless. Out of the welter of voices, those identified as Beelzebub, Judas Iscariot, and as Anna's father and mistress emerged as the most coherent and consistent. Father Vogl's booklet contains the comment that it was surprising "such a wicked and blasphemous father was blessed with such a virtuous child," as "even during the period of possession the devil could not disturb her inner basic disposition." Father Theophilus also encountered "dumb devils and avenging spirits" in hordes, but exorcised them as one would chase a swarm of mosquitoes. The record does not show him as being anywhere near as wrought up by the proceedings as Father Steiger, who would gladly have driven Theophilus from church and convent. Steiger's sleep was disturbed by seemingly threatening noises; he was distraught day and night.

Anna Ecklund, who awoke each morning in a normal state and apparently without knowledge of events during the exorcism periods, was greatly weakened. She had taken only liquid food. Once, pale and motionless, she appeared on the verge of death. Except for Theophilus Riesinger, everyone around her worried that she might die and her death be attributed to the exorcism.

Toward the end of the ordeal, Father Theophilus continued the exorcism through three days and nights. Even the nuns who alternated in attendance were on the edge of collapse. The exorcist himself, now frail in appearance, seemed to have aged by decades. Physical strain on the monk had been severe, despite his strong constitution. Perspiration forced him to change clothing sometimes three times a day.

Frustration had mounted. The published account noted that "questions directed to the devil and the answers given by him were by no means an entertaining dialogue between the evil spirits and the exorcist. On occasion a long time intervened before an answer could be forced out of Satan. For the greater part, only a ghastly bellowing, growling, and howling was the result, whenever he was urged to answer under the power of exorcism." Tension and irritation, mixed with fear and revulsion, characterized the atmosphere in convent and parish house, overflowed into the community.

During Anna Ecklund's brief periods of lucidity, she reported visions of fierce battles between good and evil spirits. Her visions followed biblical images, including those of the Horsemen of the Apocalypse who, led by St. Michael, drove the demons back to hell. She also reported seeing St. Thérèse the Little Flower of Jesus appear, urging Anna, "Do not lose courage. The pastor especially should not give up hope. The end is soon at hand." The nuns and the pastor's sister, Mrs. Theresa Wegerer, reported seeing a cluster of white roses on the ceiling, although the pastor himself did not see them.

In the evening of December 23, 1928, Anna Ecklund fell on her bed and gave a piercing shriek. The words "Beelzebub, Judas, Jacob, Mina," followed by "Hell—hell—hell!" emerged from her. She opened her eyes, smiled, and said in a normal voice, "My Jesus, Mercy! Praised be Jesus Christ!"

Four months later, Anna returned to Earling to make a novena of thanksgiving.

While the Roman Catholic church did not make an official decision concerning the validity of the Earling events, the exorcism did follow its traditional pattern. No doubt, it would have been more in keeping with the church's increasingly cautious attitude toward such manifestations if the Ecklund case had not caused so much publicity and even notoriety. Publication of even part of the proceedings is unusual in itself, but provided unique insights into a modern exorcism case.

The underlying psychological elements, including the alleged incest demands of Anna Ecklund's father, suggest that a similar case might today be regarded by church authorities as requiring psychiatric rather than exorcistic treatment. Still, as the woman was familiar with exorcism procedure since she was a teen-ager, some form of pastoral counseling and treatment was obviously desirable. To a devout person, a form of therapy within the religious framework and utilizing familiar concepts and images may well have been appropriate in Miss Ecklund's case. As psychotherapy has, in recent years, become more pragmatic and less dogmatic, the slogan "If it works, it's right," can be applied to Father Theophilus's treatment of Miss Ecklund. The exorcism was a frightful, and even reckless ordeal. But, as far as the public record shows, it worked.

3. Miss Damon and Miss Brown

The exorcist, facing a possessed person, is in a sculptorlike position: from the shape, texture, and grain of wood or stone, the sculptor fashions his design—imposing his own concept and vision, so that image and material join and the resulting sculpture emerges. The underlying pattern of the possessed woman or man provides the exorcist with his raw material; like the sculptor, he can literally "bring out" the latent content, give it shape and personality.

The analogy goes further. Each sculptor has his own style, approach and creative needs. No single piece of tree, slab of marble is exactly the same; at some point, the raw material may begin to dominate the sculptor's act of creation, to dictate the final result. Social and cultural pressures, traditions, and trends influence exorcist as well as sculptor. Nothing is ever quite the same. Experience may bring rigidity or maturity, narrowness or insight, tolerance or intolerance.

The mystical tradition of Judaism which created the "Dybbuk," a possessing spirit, also developed the legend of the "Golem," a clay figure that was given life by a Prague rabbi but destroyed when it fell in love with its creator's daughter. Whether he knows it or not, the exorcist plays a role—in varying degrees, of course—in bringing out the possessing entity he confronts in order to eliminate. To dramatize emotion or illness, a recognizable figure must be created. The sculptor who created "Winged Victory" gave this feeling of soaring triumph a human form. Fear, like love, must have a face.

Personalized fear played a decisive role in an experiment undertaken by Dr. Milton H. Erickson, well known for his research in hypnosis as a psychotherapeutic tool, with a twenty-year-old college girl who worked in his laboratory. Together with Dr. Lawrence S. Kubie, he reported this case under the title "The Permanent Relief of an Obsessional Phobia by Means of Communications with an Unsuspected Dual Personality." The young woman, whom Erickson named, of all things, "Miss Damon," was suffering from obsessive fears that doors of refrigerators, kitchens, laboratory rooms and lockers might have remained open. She was compelled to test the doors over and over again, waking up at night to go out and check them once more.

In addition, Miss Damon had an intense hatred of cats, whom she regarded as "horrid, repulsive things." She thought her feelings had been caused by seeing "an awful cat eating some nice pretty little baby robins." On the other hand, she liked to make pets out of such laboratory animals as white rats and guinea pigs, while being constantly afraid that she might leave the door to the animal room unlocked. The phobia was threatening to spread, with the possibility that she might begin to worry about other doors, and eventually anything similar, such as windows, boxes, filing cabinets, and thus find herself socially paralyzed in many ways.

Dr. Erickson decided to help her. His staff had experimented in hypnosis, as well as automatic writing. This practice, which spiritualists use in order to contact what they assume to be spirits of the dead—but which appears to be a direct road to the individual's unconscious—has these characteristics: it appears to be totally divorced from the writing person's conscious efforts, the hand moving as if controlled by an outside force; in fact, the individual may be able to engage in reading and talking as usual, while his hand writes in an eerie, disembodied, independent, "automatic" fashion. In mature spiritualistic circles, automatic writing is often discouraged, because it has many times led to "possession" by alleged spirit entities.

When Miss Damon volunteered for the hypnosis experiments, her first trance was, as Erickson and Kubie put it, "characterized by a marked degree of amnesia, ready hand levitation and profound catalepsy." Catalepsy is muscular rigidity—stiffness, in other words. By "ready hand levitation" the researchers must mean that the hypnotized woman lifted her hand without conscious effort. She continued to lift her hand in the office the next day and neglecting her work entirely. She was totally "absorbed in inducing hand levitation and arm catalepsy by autosuggestion." She seemed compulsively fascinated and frightened by seeing her hands go up and down, seemingly on their own, quietly talking to herself, "Do you see my hand move? How do you explain it? What does it mean? What is happening? Have you ever had such an experience? What psychological and neurological processes are involved? Isn't it funny? Isn't it queer? Isn't it interesting. I am so curious. I am just fascinated by it."

In another cultural environment, this hand movement might immediately have been attributed to an early stage of possession, a demon elicited and exorcism undertaken. As it happened, a very similar development, but with psychotherapeutic aims, took place. When Miss Damon showed the same behavior the next day, Erickson suggested that she might try automatic writing. She agreed with enthusiasm, but wasn't sure she could do it.

Miss Damon was placed at a desk, her right hand, with a pencil, poised over a blank piece of paper, while she was distracted into reading a psychology article on which she was to prepare a summary later on. She was asked to ignore anything that might be said or might happen. Once the young woman was absorbed in reading, hand levitation was suggested. Then she was asked to "write the reason for her interest in hand levitation and in catalepsy."

Soon afterwards, she started scribbling on the paper. When she was finished, her body trembled. She was tense, breathed with difficulty, the pupils of her eyes were enlarged. She also seemed to find reading difficult. Nevertheless, the two activities occurred separately and side by side. With the last words or scribbles put on the paper, Miss Damon grew pale and said she felt "terribly afraid," wanted to cry and was puzzled by her feelings as there was nothing in what she read that might upset her. Once she had said all that, the anxiety disappeared and she was able to remember what she had read.

She looked at what her hand had scribbled and was disappointed to see that it seemed to be merely senseless scrawls. Dr. Erickson decided to untangle the mystery of the handwriting on the assumption that it "represented significant material and that unconsciously she was seeking aid from the investigator." This led to twelve hours of stop-and-go activity with startling results. As the Erickson and Kubie paper reported, "the first essential step was achieved at the beginning of the investigation and was confirmed throughout: the identification of a second and unknown personality in the subject." An exorcist would have regarded this as the "naming" of the possessing entity.

While Miss Damon looked over the scribbles once again, trying to decipher some of the words, she laughed, "Did I really write that nonsense?" Her own hand, outside her vision, answered and wrote distinctly, "No."

Erickson picked up this cue and asked, "What do you mean?" Miss Damon was puzzled by his question but her hand wrote, "Can't." The next question, "Why?" was answered by the hand writing, "Damon doesn't know these things."

Erickson then asked Miss Damon a series of questions which baffled her, while her hand wrote appropriate answers, as follows:

QUESTION: Why?
ANSWER: Don't know, afraid to know.
Q: Who?
A: D [Damon].
Q: Who does?
A: Me.
Q: Me?
A: Me—Brown—B.

Q: Explain.
A: D is D; B is B.
Q: B know D?
A: Yes.
Q: D know B? [Does Damon know Brown?]
A: No. No.
Q: B part of D?
A: No. B is B; D is D.
Q: Can I talk to B?
A: Are! [You are doing it!]
Q: Talk to D?
A: Want to. [If you want to.]
Q: How long have you been B?
A: Always.
Q: What do you want?
A: Help D.
Q: Why?
A: D afraid.
Q: Do you know what D is afraid of?
A: Yes; D no. ["No" stands for "know."]
Q: Why?
A: D afraid, forgot, don't want to know.
Q: Think D should?
A: Yes, yes, yes.
Q: You know what it is?
A: Yes.
Q: Why don't you tell D?
A: Can't, can't.
Q: Why?
A: D afraid, afraid.
Q: And you?
A: Afraid a little, not so much.

While Dr. Erickson was asking these questions, which sounded quite disconnected and meaningless to Miss Damon, her hand kept writing answers; but now she wanted to know what was going on. So Erickson asked "Brown," the secondary personality, the almost conspiratorial question, "Shall I tell her?" The reply was, "Sure; she don't know."

The full set of questions and answers were given to Miss Damon, and she read them with care and increasing understanding. Finally she said, "Why, that really must mean I have a dual personality." She was quite startled when her hand wrote, "Right." The following dialogue then took place between Miss Damon and her alter ego:

"Can I talk to you?"

"Sure."

"Can you talk to me?"

"Yes."

"Is your name really Brown?"

"Yes."

"What is your full name?"

"Jane Brown."

Miss Damon then read over all the questions and answers and addressed her secondary personality, "You really want to help me, Brownie?"

And the personality she now affectionately called "Brownie" replied, "Yes, Erickson ask, ask, ask." From then on, it was up to Dr. Erickson to ask specific and relevant questions. This was not easy, as Jane Brown refused to volunteer information and insisted on writing her own type of cryptic shorthand, which needed interpretation, an understanding of peculiar spelling, and a form of emotional decoding.

In terms of possession and exorcism, Jane Brown would have been regarded with suspicion; fear and hostility might quickly have intruded into the dialogue. In spiritualistic terms, she would certainly have been regarded as Miss Damon's essentially benevolent "guide." Dr. Erickson's observations make it clear that "Brownie" was very much her own kind of person:

"Throughout the investigation, the Brown personality was found to be literally a separate, well-organized entity, completely maintaining its own identity, and differentiating to a fine degree between Brown and Damon. Brown was capable of entering into spirited arguments with the investigator, his assistant, and with Miss Damon, and of expressing ideas entirely at variance with those of Miss Damon. She would know before Damon did what Damon would say or think, and contributed thoughts to Miss Damon in a manner quite as psychotic patients bring up autochthonous thoughts."

During exorcism rituals, the spirit or demon is frequently at odds with the exorcist, criticizing him for lack of knowledge or insight, and generally showing a tendency to be stubborn, downgrading the exorcist and being haughty or arrogant. Brown had a touch of these characteristics:

"She would interrupt an attempted explanation by Miss Damon by writing 'Wrong,' and would respond to stimuli and cues which Miss Damon either overlooked completely or misunderstood. In fact she so impressed her personality upon those in the office that automatically she was regarded by the entire group as a distinct personality among them. Nor was Brown limited just to the problems at hand. She would enter readily into conversations on many other topics, often resorting to this in an effort to distract the investigator from his efforts. In addition Brown was possessed of a definite sense of personal pride; on two occasions she resented derogatory remarks Damon made about her, and thereupon refused to write anything more except 'Won't' until Damon apologized."

Brown frequently became impatient and irritable with Dr. Erickson, in traditional demon manner, because of his "inability to comprehend some of her cryptic replies; and at such times she would unhesitatingly and unsparingly denounce him as 'dumb.' " Erickson's troubles can be well understood when it is realized that Jane Brown would occasionally write "Yo"—meaning simultaneously yes and no, but being used as "I don't know." Erickson found Brown "highly protective" toward Miss Damon, "shielding her, demanding special consideration for her, offering encouragement, distracting her attention, deliberately deceiving her, and employing various other protective devices." Jane Brown's general attitude is reflected in the following detailed answer:

"Writing means a lot, B know it all. D don't, can't, afraid, forgot something a long time ago. D can't remember because she never knew some of it, she just thought she did but she didn't. B afraid to tell D, D get awful scared, afraid, cry. B don't like D scared, won't let her be scared, won't let her feel bad. B need help. Erickson ask. Ask right question, B tell Erickson right answer; wrong question, wrong answer. Right question only right question. B just answer, not tell, won't tell because D afraid, awful afraid, Erickson ask, ask, ask. Brown answer, not tell, question answer, not tell, question, answer, that help. B answer but not too fast because D get scared, cry, sick. B tell truth, all truth, Erickson not understand, don't understand because he don't know. B trying to tell, Erickson don't ask right questions. Ask, ask, ask. B can't tell, won't tell. B a little afraid; B only answer. Ask, ask."

Despite this concern, Brown at times confused and upset Damon. Once the cryptic syllable "con" was written and Brown declared that the words "subconsciously," "subsequent," "consequent" and "consequences" were both right and wrong. Miss Damon called Brown "crazy" and "a liar." Brown demanded and got an apology from Damon but was not satisfied. Instead, the hand wrote "Sleep," which was interpreted as a demand to neutralize Miss Damon by placing her into a hypnotic state.

While Damon was in the hypnotic sleep, Brown said that "subsequent" was both the right word correctly spelled and the wrong word incorrectly spelled. Miss Damon awakened with fright but relaxed quickly. She talked hurriedly about a lot of things, including that her grandfather was French-Canadian. Brown again wrote "Sleep," Erickson hypnotized Miss Damon once more and discovered from the automatic writing that the confusion about words had to do with French rather then English spellings. Miss Damon woke several times in intense terror, was hypnotized again, and Brown wrote that Damon had to pass through these fears because they were associated with the elusive French word or words.

When Miss Damon fully awoke, she was told what was going on. Referring to Brown, she exclaimed, "What does he mean?" This slip to a masculine identity for Brown did not go unnoticed, particularly as Miss Damon turned pale as she put this question and quickly ignored it. Brown, after asking that a dictionary be consulted, wrote the word *niaise,* added that Miss Damon had learned it from her French-Canadian grandfather who had called her *niaise* when, at the age of three, she had got lost. (*Niaise,* colloquially, means "idiot" or "fool.")

But Brown blocked further questions writing that she was afraid, because Miss Damon was frightened of what she might have to tell. Miss Damon, however, denied that she was afraid, and said with outward amusement that she was getting "terribly interested." As she spoke, Brown wrote in her usual cryptic fashion, "D don't know," and Miss Damon commented, "Isn't he economical?"—once again using the masculine word.

Dr. Erickson jumped on this. He asked, "Brown, what do you think about Damon's last remark? Explain it."

The answer was, "B is she. D says he because she means Da——. D don't no Da——. B no Da——."

Miss Damon said that the three dashes in the word simply stood for the *m, o,* and *n* in Damon. At this, her right hand, acting as Jane Brown, threw pencils, paper, and books on the floor, while Damon looked shocked and said, "Brownie is having a temper tantrum. And she can't help it, either."

An emotion-laden dialogue between Miss Damon and her alter ego followed:

"Please, Brownie, get the information."

"Suppose I fail?"

"Brown, will I ever know?"

In reply, the automatic writing slowly spelled out, "Yes." Miss

Damon covered her face with her hands, slumped into the chair and began to weep.

At this point, Dr. Erickson, drawing on his experience as a psychotherapist who knew that fixing a specific time for the end of a treatment can speed results, asked, "When?" The answer was, "Don't know."

Erickson said that too much time had already passed, his assistant had an 8:00 appointment and Brown should give a specific time by which she would, as it were, tell all. Brown wrote "7:30" and urged Erickson to "Ask, work." Questioned how the work was to proceed, she wrote, "Crystal."

Now, this is an exceedingly interesting element in the whole proceedings. Traditionally, mirrors, crystal balls, and calm surfaces of lakes or bowls of water have been used in divination, or simply as a point of concentration to see images, achieve mind dissociation, or otherwise pinpoint trancelike impressions. Nostradamus, the sixteenth-century physician-seer, used to gaze into a bowl of water to conjure up his prophecies; in a session with Catherine di Medici, he used mirrors to forecast the fates of her sons.

Now, here was a secondary personality asking for such a device, writing, "Brown wants you to look in that crystal and see." The device used was a horizontal mirror which reflected the room's ceiling. But as soon as Miss Damon, while in a hypnotic trance, looked into the mirror, her face contorted; she woke up, cried for help and said, "I'm so scared, just awful scared." Erickson was deeply concerned, but the Brown personality assured him that this was another phase of fear Miss Damon had to overcome to reach an understanding of her phobias. Again, Brown wrote, "Crystal."

Miss Damon, again in a hypnotic trance, reported that she saw her grandfather's face in the mirror and that he was speaking a word that she did not grasp. Brown wrote that Miss Damon was again getting "awful scared" but added a little later that by 7:30 she would tell everything she had forgotten "long ago." Out of the blue, Miss Damon asked, "Brownie, what is your first name?" When no reply came, she exclaimed, "He's crazy! *He!* Gosh!" Tension between Damon and Brown was building, and Brown explained it this way:

"First D afraid vague, then afraid to learn something, then afraid she not no; now she afraid she going no. D afraid she going to no *it*."

What was the frightful secret concerning the three-year-old child and her French-Canadian grandfather who had called her an idiot? It all sounded so harmless. How could it be linked to her phobias about open doors, cats, and even her liking for rodents? But Miss Damon was tense, and when Brown asserted Damon "would begin to remember at 7:23," the young woman said, "That's ridiculous. How can she say a thing that like that. There's nothing to remember."

But Brown insisted that she was changing Miss Damon's mind. "She is not," insisted the young woman. "She is not, there is nothing to remember."

Again, Miss Damon insisted that this was a ridiculous state-ment: "As if I didn't know if my mind was being changed." Still, she sobbed for a moment and then asked, "Have I a reason to be scared?" Firmly, Brown answered, "Yes."

At 7:30 Brown wrote slowly, and with interruptions from Miss Damon who was sobbing, the words, "Consequences of catching the muskrat to the little idiot."

Erickson and Kubie report that Miss Damon then shuddered and cowered, begging piteously for help. But at exactly 7:35 she said calmly, "I just remembered a story my grandfather told us when we were kids. A muskrat got into the pantry. Everyone chased it and knocked over all the things. I haven't got a thing to do with what my hand is doing."

While Dr. Erickson asked Brown to clarify all this, Miss Damon spoke up and said, "Every *subitement* catalepsy the con-sequences of catching the muskrat to the little idiot."

After much talk, back and forth, and checking in a dictionary, it became clear that the second word in the sentence should be "subsequent." Brown finally said that the correct phrasing was, "Trance, will my muskrat enter, also go. Every subsequent catalepsy the consequences of catching the muskrat to the little idiot."

The still-puzzled Dr. Erickson confessed, "I don't understand." But Miss Damon did. "I know what it means now but I didn't then. It's all right there. Everything, except the words mean so much. Each one means different things. You see, I thought I was interested in catalepsy; it wasn't catalepsy but the rigidity. I was just frightened by the muskrat episode." She explained further:

"You see, I was lost when I was four years old [Brown corrected and Damon agreed that she was only three years old] and I was awful scared. Grandfather scolded me when I got home; he called me *petite niaise* ('little idiot') and scolded me and said I had left the door open and I hadn't. I was mad at him and afterwards I would leave doors open to spite him and I got my brother to do it, too. Pantry door and icebox door. And grandfather laughed at me for getting lost, and then he told me, while I was still scared about how he got lost and the muskrat got in the pantry and everyone got upset, and I thought I did that.

"I was so scared I got grandfather's story about him mixed up with my getting lost. And I was so mad at grandfather and so scared and I left doors open to spite him and wondered if another muskrat would come."

Twice during this narrative, Brown wrote that Miss Damon was such a little idiot that she thinks "she is her own grandfather." Erickson regarded Brown's persistence in emphasizing the confusion of identities as "noteworthy," because it compelled Miss Damon to "keep to this important issue."

Damon was also able to clarify another point of spelling and identity: "You remember when I called Brown *he,* and Brown wrote Da—? Well, I can explain that. Brown was telling you that I didn't know who I was because my grandfather's name was David. Like my name, it begins with *Da* and has three more letters. And that's what Brown means when she says the little idiot thinks she is her grandfather."

Miss Damon explained her phobia about open doors, speaking of it in the past tense, in terms of her grandfather's accusation and her fear-defiance about leaving doors open to spite him. She said that her dislike for cats was based on an association of cats with the rats they chase. With great satisfaction, she confessed there had always been "something wrong with the way I liked the white rats in the laboratory. When I played with them I knew I didn't like them, but I always persuaded myself I did, and I did like them in an uncomfortable way." At this point, Brown wrote that Damon had "liked them, so she wouldn't no the truth." Miss Damon concluded, "I suppose rats are all right, but I'm not crazy about them anymore."

Erickson and Kubie commented on the case, which "permanently relieved this young woman of a serious and rapidly increasing compulsive phobic state," in terms of the use to which hypnosis can be put in psychoanalysis. They noted that Miss Damon felt "safe under the guardianship of her projected dual personality and of the investigator." Their summary of the case puts it neatly into focus:

"For a short time a little girl of three believes she is lost, and while lost gets into a state of intense terror. She is found again or else finds her way home and is greeted by a grandfather who scolds her, makes her feel guilty of leaving doors open, laughs at her, humiliates her by calling her a little *niaise* (idiot), and finally tries to comfort her by telling her a story of an occasion in his own childhood when he was lost and when a muskrat entered the house through an open door and got into the pantry where it did a great deal of damage.

"At this, the little girl is thrown into a state of increased terror, rage, anger, resentment and confusion. She mixes up her grandfather's story and especially the tale of the muskrat with her own experience. She feels as if it had happened to her almost as though she were her grandfather. She is angry and out of spite and revenge she deliberately begins to leave doors open as he had done and as he had unjustly accused her of doing. Then she begins to fear she will make a mistake, that she will leave doors open unwittingly and that something dreadful will come in. She begins compulsively to check up on the doors over and over again."

But what about Jane Brown, who would be regarded as a "good spirit" residing in Miss Damon in a spiritualistic culture, but whose occasional anger, impatience, and defiance might have turned into spiteful threats and psychophysical suffering for Miss Damon in less skillful exorcistic hands? Brown confessed having encouraged Damon in her defiances, saying "Damon thought of leaving doors open and Damon did that, but I helped by getting Damon to get her brother to do it." Brown called Dr. Erickson "dumb" in the manner that "Beelzebub" had called Father Theophilus Riesinger an ignorant "dumbbell" when, while exorcizing Anna Ecklund, he supposedly mispronounced Latin words.

Erickson and Kubie note that the Brown personality's protective attitude toward Miss Damon was "in striking contrast to the destructive or malicious alternative personality which has more frequently been described in the literature." They are "unable to explain the existence" of Brown, but "understand in some measure the function which this dual personality performed but not how it came into being." The two researchers have this hypothesis: "The story makes it evident that under the impulse of terror and anger, the young woman had made a very deep and painful identification of herself with her grandfather. Somehow all her later anxieties and compulsions stemmed from this momentous event. At some time she built up a protective, compassionate alter ego, Jane, who knew the things that she did not want to know, who was either unable or else forbidden to tell them to anyone but who exercised an almost continuously protective role toward the patient herself."

It is nevertheless possible that Jane Brown lay dormant in Miss Damon and emerged as a fully dramatized personality only under the influence of Dr. Erickson, no matter how carefully displayed. Just as, in hypnotic regression into alleged previous lives, fully rounded total personalities may emerge that purport to represent an individual's previous incarnation—often in direct response to the hypnotist's leading questions—so Jane Brown shows a subtle compliance with Erickson's psychoanalytic orientation.

We are not told whether the Jane Brown personality was herself exorcised, driven out together with the phobias and no longer needed as the guardian of Miss Damon's secrets. The laboratory setting, the presence of Dr. Erickson and his assistant, served as a dramatic backdrop in the shamanistic tradition. The overall pattern and result do not really differ in essentials from a successful shaman exorcism—a personality emerged from the unhappy young woman, with the aid of the shaman-therapist, and became instrumental in the dramatic curing ritual; the use of automatic writing and mirror gazing places this unique therapeutic procedure squarely into the ancient framework of occult techniques.

IV. Doubt and Danger

1. Ghost Against Ghost

A few years after I started working as administrative secretary of the Parapsychology Foundation in New York City, a lawyer acquaintance of the foundation's president, Mrs. Eileen J. Garrett, telephoned her with an intriguing request. Could she, he asked, exorcise the spirit of a witch who had invaded the mind and body of a young married woman? Mrs. Garrett heard the request in her usual gracious and matter-of-fact manner. It was a good deal less unusual to her than it would be to most people. In one way or another, she had been called upon to oust malignant forces from dozens of houses (once even from a barn, in my presence) for several decades.

But this request was no routine matter. Everything about it was modern, jet-settish and affluent. The very scene of the haunting and possession phenomena was elegant: a town house on New York's Upper East Side. I am, of course, disguising the identities of the people who asked Mrs. Garrett's help, but when I say that the husband, Walter Camden, was a successful steel executive, and that his wife was, to probably all her friends and acquaintances, a vivacious hostess and sportswoman, I am merely fitting them into the accurate social niche. Victoria Camden had, we were told, suffered a number of accidents in her home. Without forewarning, she might be thrown across the room, and pitched down on her face. At one time, she nearly drowned in her bathtub and then found herself hurled, wet and helpless and naked, against the tiles around the tub and wall. To her friends, she laughed about her obvious cuts and bruises, implying that they had been caused by her clumsiness on a tennis court or by a recalcitrant horse on the Camdens' Pennsylvania farm.

Walter Camden's lawyer friend told Mrs. Garrett that Camden had become seriously concerned about these injuries, as well as about Victoria's mental sufferings. She had lost more weight than, even in her diet-conscious set, was good for her. Would Mrs. Garrett come and talk to her; would she visit their house; would she try and explain, or explain away, the increasingly horrifying phenomena that were haunting Camden's wife?

It did not take long to agree on the arrangements. However, Mrs. Garrett had established, through long experience, that it is wise to keep detailed records of virtually all psychic experimentation, and to have witnesses, both for scientific and even possible legal reasons. The lawyer, Francis Basso, was invited to join the exorcism experiment, and I came along to help put the chronology of events in order, ask supplementary questions, and look after the recording. I looked up the Camdens' biographical notes in various reference volumes, and Mrs. Garrett and I went off into a more-than-routine Manhattan summer evening.

The evening began with dinner at a better-than-average French restaurant. The descriptions of Victoria Camden's external personality had been accurate. She had an easy way about her. Even her haggard appearance contributed to an elusive, intriguing air. Victoria did look somewhat older than Walter, and I soon realized that they were childless. Mrs. Garrett and Victoria discussed the charms of southern France, particularly Provence, while Walter Camden and I discovered mutual interest in such esoteric fields as low-grade iron ore beneficiation through the pelletizing method. Basso, the lawyer, sat back most of the time, spectator rather than participant, waiting for the next act in the unfolding play. Camden, it turned out, drove a vintage Ferrari that took us within a few minutes to his town house.

By New York standards, this was an historic house. Its actual age was a matter of conjecture, but Camden, because of the phenomena Victoria had experienced, had traced its ownership to some of the city's oldest and "best" families. The furnishings in the main living room, on the second floor, were quietly traditional; the lighting was subdued, but did not strike me as gloomy. But it obviously struck Victoria as a good deal more than gloomy. As soon as we walked through the entrance door, the woman changed into a frightened child. "She is here," she whispered. There was a tremolo in her voice. First her hands began to shake; then her whole body.

Who was "she"? We gathered that Ruth, the entity appearing to possess Mrs. Camden, had been a witch in Salem, but one of those not caught or tried. Just why she had fastened on Victoria was not clear. It had not just happened from one day to another. Victoria, it seemed, had "opened herself up" to psychic influences, beginning with writings that seemed to flow through her hand as if dictated by spirit entities. I asked whether she had done any extensive reading in the psychic, had been aware of what was happening to her. Walter denied it.

"When her writing went into its first phase," Camden explained, "she was just like a ship's operator getting messages. They seemed to come from a variety of personalities. Some came only once or twice, but there were hundreds of them. We have thousands of pages. Perhaps two-thirds came from two personalities, who identified themselves only as Richard and Mary, but the rest came from entities who purported to have existed on earth in different times and places."

I wanted to know whether the messages had any intrinsic value. "Were they interesting at all? Were they at all valuable in themselves?"

Victoria answered that some of them were: "I found one or two quite interesting or literate. For example, I don't know what I asked them, but something about were they 'always with us.' The answer, I thought, was interesting. They said, 'We walk among you unhindered and unhindering. Midnight is a fool's myth.' That was pretty coherent. A lot of them begged for my prayers and described where they were. They would say, 'Oh, it's so cold in this merciless wind.' They suffered from lack of privacy, and some said they had no lives."

Mrs. Garrett, quite firmly, said, "Oh no, we have to get rid of all this." Obviously, such an onslaught by innumerable ghosts could drive a person to total distraction. I still wondered whether Victoria had really come to these experiences entirely without outside suggestion, by persons or through reading. But she only remembered a "ridiculous story by Oscar Wilde about a haunted house that I thought was so funny. No, I've never been interested in the occult." When the term "automatic writing" was first mentioned to her, Victoria said she didn't know that she had been doing it: "I didn't know what it meant. This wasn't a hobby with me."

The automatic writing, much of it done on the Camdens' place in Pennsylvania, had been followed by seeing ghosts, fleeting things, and hearing odd noises that seemed to originate with the spirits who had dictated the writings to her. And now, in this house, right in Manhattan, it had become a nightmare of possession. Victoria said:

"Ever since we moved into this house, I have been sick. Right from the beginning. I've been ill the whole time I've been in this house, one thing after another, one thing after another. Of course, the persecution by Ruth has made me sickest of all with these violent attacks. You have no idea how violent they were—I mean, she'd throw you across the room, that kind of thing, always on the face, which is just peachy. There was always the strain of not knowing what would happen next. You'd be perfectly all right, you'd start across the room ordinarily and then—wham!—down you go."

Mrs. Garrett and I, as we had done in other instances, were acting in tandem. She expressed determination to rid the house, and most certainly the woman, of the plaguing ghost, or memory, or delusion, or whatever one might call it; I, meanwhile, was asking questions that sought to probe Victoria's own role in this drama and to compare it with similar cases. I said, "I'll tell you this. It is a very classical and established sequence. We can see the origin, the present state, and the outcome. After you have reached a saturation point, as you obviously have, then comes the time for closing it off, sealing it all off, having had it as part of your life. You'll never forget it, but you'll be done with it. That is an almost classical pattern, too, that you arrive at a peaceful conclusion: it ends; you've finished with it."

Victoria did not quite believe me: "You mean, finished entirely? Might I not become a healer, or something."

Mrs. Garrett shook her head with determination. "That is something else. You must give all this up."

Healing, I said to Victoria, calls for different qualities: "You do not receive such impulses or possessions as this. Healing makes you a battery, a channel, providing strength to others."

"I have been through all this myself," Mrs. Garrett said. "Your kind of suffering is not a preparation for healing."

"I don't want it," Victoria protested. "I truly don't want it." I think she sensed our doubts, our impression that this personal drama, no matter how painful, filled some sort of need—for attention? for self-castigation? for the concern of others, including her husband?

Mrs. Garrett then began to go slowly through the house, from room to room, from floor to floor. Walter Camden and I took the tape recorder along, so her observations could be spoken into a microphone. The Camdens had heard rumors that the house had, several generations back, been the scene of a murder. Perhaps, they thought, the possessing entity, Ruth, was not a Salem witch at all but a victim of violence, the kind of restless ghost mankind's tradition has known since the days of ancient China and Babylon. In some of the rooms, and even on stairway landings, Mrs. Garrett stopped quietly, spoke inaudibly as if in prayer or pleading with an unseen force. On two occasions she rushed ahead, giving us little chance to catch up, and then stood still, as if listening. At one point she stared at a wall; later she said there had been an opening, a window or door or connection with another building, but it had now been closed off: its memory remained, like a phantom limb. Moving about, she was taking, as it were, the building's psychic measure, searching for memories that might be felt and dramatized by a sensitive person, while seeking to put them in their proper place in time and history.

This took about one hour. It had happened many times before, and it was a method I had learned to accept as standard practice. Walter Camden, for all his tolerance and worldliness, seemed at times doubtful, at others shaken, and finally exhausted. But Mrs. Garrett was seemingly just building up energy while, as she put it, "smelling the place out." It was all in preparation for the final encounter, the meeting of ghost with ghost.

I have to explain that for most of her life Eileen Garrett had been a trance medium. She was able to place herself in a trance state, eyes closed, her own personality withdrawn and apparently unconscious of what was happening, while her "control" personality, Uvani, took over. This entity, identified as a Persian, called himself "Keeper of the Gate." When he was in control, Mrs. Garrett's voice changed markedly, as did the vocabulary used by the entity. Uvani often simply appeared at the outset and end of such a séance, while another personality, identified as Abdul Latif, an Arab physician at the Court of Saladin in the twelfth century, appeared to speak through her. Abdul Latif had a distinct personality, far less curt and occasionally peremptory than Uvani; I had come to accept him, over the years, as one accepts a kindly stranger with whom one has a number, though not a great deal, of interests in common. Tonight, obviously, Abdul Latif would be called upon for his healing skills. It was to be an exorcism of ghost by ghost, a unique situation.

We seated ourselves, as one would for an hour or so of informal conversation, in the Camdens' living room. Mrs. Garrett made herself comfortable by slipping off her jewelry, closing her eyes, and leaning her head against the couch's back. Victoria sat facing her, rigidly, in a stiff chair, while the ever-silent Basso,

Walter Camden, and I tried to be inconspicuous. Eileen Garrett entered her trance state. The voices of Uvani and Abdul Latif came through with their usual fluency. "What do you wish of me?" Abdul asked, after we had all introduced ourselves. Briefly, we described Victoria Camden's dilemma. "It is well that you have come here," Abdul Latif said.

At this point, Victoria seemed convulsed, tossed about like a ship in a storm. While her body writhed, a croaking voice uttered from her throat, "I want—I want—I want—peace!"

We did not transcribe this segment of the evening, fearing that recording paraphernalia might disrupt the psychological constellation. The scene that followed was dramatic. "Come to me, my child," Abdul Latif said through Mrs. Garrett. The writhing Victoria, speaking with the voice of her possessing entity, Ruth, stumbled over to the sofa and sank to the floor. Quietly, soothingly, a stream of reassurances came from the medium's vocal chords. "We are here to heal you, to help you find you, to bring you peace." Words of such reassurance, in a steady flow, came with Abdul Latif's characteristic voice, intonation, and vocabulary. Ruth-Victoria knelt before Abdul-Garrett, her head on the medium's knees, sobbing. Slowly, the writhing stopped. Motherly, fatherly—whatever you want to call it—the entranced medium spoke to the distraught woman as to a frightened child. The voice of Abdul Latif, addressing the witch Ruth, sought to tell her that she did not belong on this plane, and must let go of the body through which she sought contact with the world. "No," Abdul said, "you have not been abandoned, although you may be seared in your soul, but there are others here among us who can help you find your proper life, your proper existence. But you must let go of this body, of this house, for your own sake."

Basso's hands were gripping the side of his chair. Walter Camden was slumped back, just staring ahead, immobile. I did not dare lift my hand to my eyes. Was this truly ghost speaking to ghost? If so, did they need the entranced medium and the possessed woman to make contact; couldn't they meet, independently, on their own plane of existence? It is a question that, frankly, I did not formulate just then, although obvious.

Abdul Latif lifted, through the medium, a blessing hand to the possessed woman's head: "And now, you, Ruth, must go and let this child reside in her own world. She must be restored to herself, and to herself alone." Eileen Garrett leaned back once more. She shuddered, groaned, breathed heavily; she was coming out of her trance. Victoria remained kneeling. She was quiet. Camden look at me questioningly. I nodded. He went over, lifted up his wife, and guided her back to her chair.

Eileen Garrett came out of her trance, neither exhausted nor exactly rested. "What's happened?" she asked, matter-of-factly. We told her, and she listened with approval. While the rest of us were still tongue-tied, Mrs. Garrett broke the ice: "I guess we all need a stiff drink. And let's get out of here." Like the captain of a battered crew, she steered us into the large and bright kitchen. Walter Camden brought bottles from the bar; Victoria, once again the hostess, proceeded to juggle roast beef, turkey, and ham for sandwiches, while I busied myself with a beer can opener. The spell, as the ancient saying goes, had been broken. But for how long?

No one knew better than Eileen Garrett that the evening's dramatic events might be no more than just that, drama. So when we had recovered, she insisted on another round of probing talk. By now we felt like people on a cruise ship that has been on the high seas for several days. We took our plates and glasses into Walter's study—another change of scene—and sought to tie the numerous loose ends together, including the occasional presence of a male spirit entity.

"You know," Mrs. Garrett said, "there hasn't been a murder here. The knocking you have experienced, I think, comes from someone who is friendly. You talk about the feeling you get around the fireplace, but I don't. This friend is very fond of you, actually."

"Oh, is he?" said Victoria. Eileen Garrett caught this note of fascination and said, "Yes, he likes the house, he likes you, but I've asked him to go away; to please go away in the name of God and leave everybody at peace until they are strong. I see him as brash, cheerful, nonchalant, good-natured but rough."

Victoria demurred. "Not too good-natured, actually."

Tapping sounds heard in the house also were discussed. Now they had stopped, and Victoria asked, "I wonder why they won't appear anymore." She had liked the tapping and the personality behind it, and so I said, "Well, I guess you have to get rid of the good with the bad." Mrs. Garrett agreed enthusiastically, "You bet you do. You have to get them *all* out."

Eileen Garrett felt her work had not been completed. She made arrangements to come back to the house to contact whatever entities there might be about, talk to them, exorcise them out of Victoria's life. "I want to come up here again. Let's put aside some afternoon to come and give the house a treatment."

I was still puzzled by the underlying psychological factors of the phenomena we had encountered. "Could it be," I asked, "that in a house like this husband and wife might somehow interact?" Mrs. Garrett answered, "Certainly, if he is psychic, too."

By then Walter Camden had shed some of his controlled manners. "Well, that's awfully strange. Down at the place in Pennsylvania, I did see a creature, a living creature that crossed in my sight. I didn't have a feeling of seeing through him or anything odd whatever. I didn't mention it until about six or eight months later."

How did Victoria feel about these experiences, before they got really out of hand? She answered:

"I've suffered terribly with this, but I've never been afraid. Now that is the peculiar part. I don't understand it. You ride a horse that's thrown you and you may say to yourself, 'I'm not afraid of this horse,' but deep down in your soul, you are afraid but I was not afraid of this. I had some misgiving about coming back here tonight. I admit that. But still and all, when Ruth takes hold of me, as she did before, I'm still not really afraid of her, though I know she can hurt me."

Walter agreed. "It has been amazing to me, too, that with all these very real wounds, bloody and scratched, beaten and with contusions, and all that, she still kept an amazing morale. I'd be ready to shoot myself at half a dozen points; but, seriously, she took it all—well, I don't want to say nonchalantly, but with a very positive attitude."

Mrs. Garrett looked at me over the brim of her glass. She had seen too many situations like this not to have some doubts about its total reality. So I dared to say, "There is a good deal of dramatization here, because it's certainly hard to say where the realities, or, shall we say, the memories, of this place stop, and where Victoria's imagination begins."

Victoria, with candid introspection, admitted, "Yes, that's true."

Eileen Garrett, with her most cordial smile, said, "She should write fiction, this girl—very creative."

I do not know whether Victoria Camden became a fiction writer. Perhaps, under a pseudonym, she is today a successful author of Gothic novels. Anyway, Eileen Garrett returned to the Camden house and went over it by herself one afternoon.

By now, Walter Camden has retired from the rat race of the steel industry, and the couple live on a ranch in Arizona. I still get a Christmas card each year. These are cheerful, as such cards usually are. Once there was a picture of Victoria, taken in the garden she has turned from desert to flowers. Come to think of it, I don't recall getting a card last Christmas. Perhaps I am part of a past which, like many a good or bad experience, has now faded and is forgotten.

2. They Killed "The Devil's Bride"

During the second half of the twentieth century, in one of the most enlightened of European countries, a teen-age girl was beaten to death as a result of a series of "exorcism" tortures. Her name was Bernadette Hasler. The event occurred in 1966 in a village outside Zurich, Switzerland. The trial of the two major persecutors, John Stocker and Magdalena Kohler, took place three years later.

At the time of the trial, the Roman Catholic bishop of Chur testified that Stocker and Kohler had violated a number of the church's basic tenets. He emphasized that the church "assumes that human beings may be influenced by non-human evil forces," but that it does not assume such influence until all other possibilities have been "scientifically excluded." Only then, said Bishop Johannes Vonderach, "does the Church engage in the appropriate compelling prayer, whose wording is contained in the *Rituale Romanum*," in order to effect an exorcism.

Bishop Vonderach added: "The prayer may only be said by a priest who has received a specific written authorization from his Bishop. Physical force is never permitted." These safeguards had been ignored by Stocker and Kohler in their supposed exorcism of "the devil" from the soul and body of seventeen-year-old Bernadette. Following lengthy physical and mental persecution, the childlike young woman said that she had a "pact with Satan." She had been brought to an emotional state which Dr. Hans Binder, a testifying psychiatrist, described as a "sin mania." The cheerful girl, grown depressed and desperate, had come to regard her short life as a "chain of sins."

Gruesome as the fate of Bernadette Hasler was, it does provide instructive psychological insights into the role of suggestion and brainwashing in witchcraft, demonology, possession, and exorcism. Above all, it dramatizes interpersonal factors that may be involved in attitudes and actions concerning exorcism. Where many historical cases have been recorded in fragmentary terms, the exorcistic murder of Bernadette provides testimony that throws light on personalities and beliefs in useful detail.

Who were the actors in this drama? How did they arrive at their idea structures? What psychological forces prompted them to act in a sadistic, and eventually lethal, manner?

Paul Langdon, writing in *Witchcraft Today* (New York, 1970), found that Bernadette's fate was "merely the most extreme example of the religious fanaticism" which held a cult founded by Stocker and Kohler "together in a boiling cauldron of emotion." The original impetus to the bogus "Holy Family" had come from Sister Stella, a Carmelite nun known as "Sternli," or "Little Star," who met Stocker and Kohler while they were on a "pilgrimage" in Jerusalem in 1956. For several years, Sister Stella (Olga Endres) had claimed a "direct telephone to heaven."

Langdon comments that Stella's "superiors either failed to recognize her apparent mediumistic psychosis or regarded these messages, in some manner, as genuine or at least uplifting." It would not have been outside church tradition to regard such messages as the possible work of demons or unclean spirits, who pretended to offer "Messages from the Savior." As it was, Sister Stella believed she was obtaining instructions from Jesus directly, and she transcribed these in typewritten form. Such "automatic writing" has long been practiced by Spiritualists, who believe it to originate with discarnate entities.

Stocker and Kohler, following the "revelations" provided by the mediumistic nun, returned with her from the Near East. An odd symbiosis developed among the three of them. Stella became the "child" of the Stocker-Kohler duo, and Magdalena Kohler even ordered her to play with dolls. Kohler testified, "Herr

Stocker was the Father, I was the Mother, and Stella was the Child." She had once been "ordered by God," Magdalena said, to buy Stella a red teddy bear.

The relationship between Stocker and Kohler was supposedly entirely spiritual, although Magdalena gave birth to a child. Kohler had been a member of the Pallottine Order, but when his odd activities came to light, and he refused to stop them, he was ousted from it. At the headquarters of their apocalyptic cult, which after return from the Near East was set up in Singen, Germany, preparations were made for "the end of the world." One room remained empty, reserved for the Pope. Magdalena testified that "it was supposed to be his place of refuge, once the final catastrophe crashed down on mankind."

Sister Stella, ordered by her superiors to return to her nunnery, was twice abducted from the cloister by Stocker, and twice returned. Stella's mental state resembled a return to infantilism; she was something of a child-slave to Stocker and Kohler. She recalled: "Times were not as good as here in the Cloister. I no longer had a will of my own, and I was in constant inner fear. I was spoken to as if I were a child. Today I no longer play with dolls. I no longer write Messages from the Savior. I was suffering from a malignant delusion."

Professor Walter Nigg, a church historian formerly with Zurich University, said that Stella's role was, "if not in a judicial sense, at least in a religious sense, that of a key person, who bears a heavy moral guilt that cannot simply be eradicated by calculated disregard of the past." In the late 1950's, her prophecies of the world's end, complete with a rain of brimstone, guided the Stocker-Kohler cult. Nigg concluded that their cult's "Holy Work" of saving souls, which led to the death of Bernadette, was "not a straight path, which by some intrinsic force had to lead to this immensely tragic end."

As Nigg saw it, Bernadette was manipulated into a position resembling that of a witch in the Middle Ages, to the point where she "began to play the part that had been forced upon her, so that, defiantly, she accused herself of the most repulsive sexual misdeeds with the Devil." She was, he found, "abandoned by all human sentiment, without the slightest support, she died alone in the night, without any hope of divine aid, an expectation that had long before been destroyed within her very soul." Dr. Binder, the psychiatrist, added that Bernadette, feeling she had lost the support of God, followed the "logic of a defiant heart" and finally insisted that she had, indeed, turned to the devil for his satanic superpower.

The cult had been forced to leave Germany, where its head-quarters was stocked with sacks of flour and sugar, hundreds of cans of food, and even a cow that boarded on a nearby farm. The Swiss refuge was the farm of Josef Hasler, Bernadette's father, in the village of Ringwil. The Haslers, caught up in the apocalyptic delusions of Stocker and Kohler, joined their "International Family Society for the Advancement of Peace." Schoolmates of the Hasler children called the well-stocked establishment "Noah's Ark." The power which Stocker and Kohler exercised over Hasler and other of their followers was remarkable, in financial as well as human terms. Josef Hasler had turned both Bernadette and his other daughter, Madeleine, over to them. The results were a shock to him, but he acquiesced, nevertheless.

"I could not know then," Hasler told at the trial, "that this was the beginning of a road of suffering for our daughter." The girls were not permitted to speak to their parents, but were limited to "divine" education they received from their "Holy Parents." Hasler had trouble getting Madeleine to return home, even after her sister's death. He recalled that he literally had to "tear her away from there," because "she no longer regarded us as her parents, she had only eyes and ears for her 'Holy Parents,' Stocker and Kohler. After we told her of the torture death of Bernadette, her eyes opened. She told us that even the smallest children in that home were beaten to a pulp."

The "Holy Parents" gained control of the Hasler family while they moved in on their daughter. Stocker-Kohler censored the Haslers' mail, handled their money, and doled out their food. The Haslers' car, a Mercedes 300, was used by them for "missionary trips." This tyrannical atmosphere was reinforced by so-called prayer sessions which, as Hasler put it, became brainwashing sessions that lasted until early morning hours, while "satanic words were poured out and we were ordered to be silent." Josef Hasler was no longer permitted to speak to his wife. Otherwise, he was told, he would forfeit "God's forgiveness." When Mrs. Hasler was rushed to the hospital for a premature birth, her husband was forbidden to go and visit her. Josef Hasler, taken in—one is tempted to say "bewitched"—by the Stocker-Kohler approach, was in financial ruin at the time of his daughter's death. At the trial of the two people who had destroyed him, he said, "If I had to judge those two today, I would beat them to a pulp and feed them to the pigs."

Still and all: Why and how did all this happen?

Stocker, and particularly Magdalena Kohler, developed a following, a coterie, that was swept along enthusiastically in the group delusion concerning young Bernadette's pact with the devil, the need to punish her physically to exorcise the evil from her body. They questioned her, harangued her, suggested the extent and details of her alleged transgressions, and forced her to confess. Yes, she admitted, she had dealt with the devil, had impure thoughts and wicked desires. Her "religio-sexual confessions," as Langdon calls them, were statistically recorded in childlike handwriting: "I have taken communion improperly 6,000 times; I have prayed wrongly 450 times; I have given 750 tongue kisses; 1,000 times have I undertaken the sexual act in my imagination."

Langdon doubts that Bernadette could have thought up all these things by herself and writes that "the pathetic statements of the young girl reflected the sexual suggestions of her 'Mother Confessor,' rather than her own native imagination." The 330-page confession the Kohler woman extracted from Bernadette contains this tragic, bewildered statement: "I love the Devil. He is beautiful. He visits me nearly every night. He is much better than God. I would like to belong only to the Devil." By that time, the girl had obviously lost all hope in a just world, governed by a benign God. Yet, this love letter to the devil, if we may call it that, sounds hardly more diabolical than the note a teen-age girl might write to a pop singer whose picture she kisses secretly every night.

Stocker and Kohler enlisted four members of their cult to "drive the Devil out of" little Bernadette. They restricted her severely. Turned into a household slave, she was not permitted to go for walks, her violin lessons were stopped, and she could no longer talk to other children in the care of the "Holy Parents." Slowly, the noose tightened around her soul. Magdalena Kohler heaped scorn and curses on her, calling her a "perverted piece" and a "lying swine." She climaxed this by referring to the girl as "Satan's mate" and the "Devil's whore."

One of the four cult members who aided Kohler in persecuting the girl was Paul Barmettler, then in his late thirties. Just as Kohler had forbidden Hasler to speak to his wife, so she forbade Barmettler any sexual relations with his wife. He complied. The other participants in the "exorcism" orgy were his two brothers, Hans and Heinrich. The fourth cult member and torturer was Emilio Bettio, a greengrocer. Barmettler, putting his money where his induced delusions were, gave the "Holy Family" 10 percent of his income, paid the mortgage on the chalet occupied by the family, and even gave up hunting, because a "holy message" had demanded it.

Hans Barmettler, who made a modest salary as a railroad official and had five children to look after, paid a monthly sum to the "Holy Parents" and contributed to their purchase of yet another Mercedes 300. His brother Heinrich, also a railroad worker, had hoped to get married, but Magdalena told him to break his engagement, and he remained single. Altogether, Magdalena Kohler imposed sexual deprivation and control over the men in her cult, while projecting her multiplicity of sex fantasies on young Bernadette. Among these induced confessions was a "marriage to Lucifer," of which Bernadette wrote: "I wore a white dress and he had his black, shiny fur. It was a beautiful picture." She also wrote that the death of her "Holy Parents" would free her to marry ten more times, so that she could have one son and one daughter by each of the men and start her own demonic tribe.

The exorcism rites consisted of beatings, twice daily. Stocker and Kohler would take the lead, and the four men would join in. At times, they would be summoned by telephone to lend a hand. They vied with each other, took turns, and it is probably an understatement to say that these were scenes of orgasmic sadism. It all ended when, on May 14, 1966, the six participants talked themselves into a frenzy by discussing Bernadette's alleged "desire to cause the death" of the "Holy Parents" and her "pact with the Devil."

The girl was sent to her room, asked to crouch on her bed, kneeling and exposing her backside while resting on elbows and hands. The Swiss newspaper, *Blick,* reporting court testimony on January 8, 1969, said that "an orgy of brutality began, in order to drive out the devil—as the sadistic cultists put it—and to make her feel the righteous wrath of the Lord." The paper stated that "the quietly whimpering girl was beaten by all six 'devil exorcists' in turn, using whips, canes and a plastic pipe to beat her buttocks, back and extremities." Wracked with pain, the victim lost control of her bowels, was asked to "eat it," vomited, pushed into a bathtub by the Kohler woman, asked to wash her clothing outside the house, and sent to bed.

Langdon writes succinctly: "She died the next morning; according to the Judicial-Medical Institute at Basel, her death was due to an embolism of the lungs. Her body showed numerous bruises, abrasions, and broken skin. She died a virgin."

This lethal onslaught was caused by Bernadette's ultimate religio-emotional breakdown about a month before her death. When the Kohler woman denied her the privilege of Easter confession, Bernadette's desperation prompted her to turn in the one direction still open to her: the devil, at last. In defiance of a God supposedly represented by Stocker and Kohler, the girl crossed a mental borderline into the hysteria that caused her to say, and possibly even to believe, that she had indeed made a "pact with the Devil."

Magdalena Kohler, strong-willed and defiant in the courtroom, said she had "loved the girl" and had cursed her only "because she had a pact with the Devil." When Mrs. Hasler, lifting the nightgown from her daughter's dead body, saw the torture marks, she collapsed. Yet Kohler accused the Haslers of being "guilty that Bernadette was possessed by the Devil," because they "did not bring her up properly." She even tried to get Josef Hasler to accept the guilt for his daughter's death, saying "If you refuse, you become a traitor to our Holy Work. Anyway, you will only have to serve one year, at most."

Magdalena Kohler also said: "I have, in everything I did, acted under orders from God. All force, and all that has happened, was done on divine instruction. To avoid discipline, or faith, to withhold oneself from divine orders, leads the soul to punishment in hell and eternal damnation." Her defense attorney, Dr. Hans Meissner, cited this statement to show that she was "a simpleminded woman, who grew up in an environment of narrow superstition and fear of eternal damnation. She is convinced that, one day, she will have to fight a duel with the Devil." While living secretly on the Hasler farm, the attorney said, the woman had been "psychologically destroyed" and had come to believe more and more "in her delusion, in her own supernatural powers and divine mission."

The defense attorneys made the major point that the cultists, led by Stocker and Kohler, had not meant to kill Bernadette, only to beat her. They killed her, so to speak, because they were too eager in the execution of their self-appointed task of exorcism. Bernadette's father turned on the defendants at one point and cried, "You have killed my child!" Paul Barmettler pleaded, "Not killed, only beaten."

Emilio Bettio's attorney maintained his client felt he was not really beating Bernadette, but, through her person, Lucifer. Bettio was described as an "infantile, dependent" personality, who "lived in constant fear of the eternal damnation that Stocker and Kohler preached with devastating effectiveness." On February 4, 1969, the Zurich court sentenced Stocker and Kohler to ten years in prison, Bettio to four years, and each of the three Barmettler brothers to three and a half years in prison.

In his summation, State Attorney John Lohner had demanded sentences to serve as "a warning to all those still enmeshed in superstitions and in abusing religious faith." He urged Roman Catholic authorities to aid in "cleansing the soil that nurtures belief in and fear of the Devil, so that such crimes as that against Bernadette Hasler may never be repeated."

The newspaper, *Blick,* reported Bishop Vonderach's statement on the need for a careful and highly selective use of exorcism rites. In a front page story headlined, "But the Devil Exists!" Monsignor Alfred Teobaldi, vicar general of the Canton of Zurich, noting that the Stocker-Kohler cult had originated in Germany, urged the public to guard against "the influence of movements originating in foreign countries." He defended the Catholic church, saying that "no church can be protected against members who use holy works as a pretext to practice diabolic actions."

The possibility that Stocker and Kohler had themselves acted under diabolic or demonic influence was also mentioned by Dr. Nigg, the theological expert employed by the Zurich court. Nigg endorsed the following theses:

(1) "The influence of evil forces in the world cannot be denied.

(2) "If the influence of demonic power is categorically denied, world history becomes incomprehensible. Life consists of a struggle between good and evil forces. It does not matter what names we give to these powers."

Nigg suggested that the torturer-killers of Bernadette were themselves under the influence of demonic force. He said that "the perpetrators were surrounded by demons who had succeeded in confusing their minds so totally that they forgot even the most basic elements of humanity."

3. Exorcist: Victim or Victor?

At the end of William Blatty's novel *The Exorcist,* the two priests engaged in exorcising a demon from Regan, a little girl, die mysterious deaths. The old, experienced exorcist, Father Lankester Merrin, had, in the words of a colleague, undertaken an exorcism in Africa that "lasted for months" and "damn near killed him." During the hostile onslaught of the demon possessing Regan, Father Merrin dies of a heart attack. The Jesuit psychiatrist, Damian Karras, who had been treating the girl right along, then meets the demon in a final encounter. The demon taunts him, holding "his hands out like great fleshy hooks, beckoning slowly, 'Come on! Come on, loser! Try *me!* Leave the girl and take me! Take *me!* Come into . . .'" From downstairs, Father Karras is heard to shout, " 'No! I won't let you hurt them. *You're not going to hurt them!* You're coming with . . .'"

Father Karras is later found outside the building, his crumpled body lying under the window of Regan's room. Up there, the window shutters have been torn from their hinges, the window panes shattered. The child is free of the demon, at last. But what has actually happened? Novelist Blatty leaves the climactic event to his reader's imagination. Did Father Karras physically wrestle with the demon possessing the child? Did the demon leave the little girl's body, invade that of the exorcist and plunge with him to his death? He says, through one of the investigators of the death, that "exorcists frequently became possessed," particularly when they were suffering from "strong feelings of guilt and the need to be punished," with autosuggestion provided by the exorcism ritual itself.

Just as the film version of Aldous Huxley's work *The Devils of Loudun* went far beyond the historical records on the mass possession of nuns at a French convent in the seventeenth century, so do most fictional works dealing with the supernatural tend to simplify and dramatize known facts. In the Blatty novel, the demon speaks of the experienced old exorcist, shouting at the height of its fury, *"Hypocrite!* You care nothing at *all* for the pig. You care *nothing!* You have *made her a contest between us!"*

Traditionally, the devil or demon will seek to attack the exorcist at his weakest points, and will display knowledge that the possessed person could not have acquired by normal sensory means. It is therefore quite appropriate that a demonic voice might challenge the exorcist, particularly one with a record of successful expulsions or healings, and accuse him of personal pride in his exorcistic prowess.

While the death of two (or even one) exorcists in the actual process of expelling a demon is not on record, a number of exorcists have become enmeshed with the persons they sought to free from their suffering, as well as with the entities that seemed to control their bodies and voices. We have already seen that Father Theophilus Riesinger, the Capuchin monk who exorcised a forty-year-old woman in Iowa in the 1920s, spoke proudly of his many exorcisms and of his bishop's respect for this impressive record. While his twenty-three-day exorcism bout at Earling centered around the person of Anna Ecklund, the dialogue between monk and demon at times became a tug-of-war for personal dominance. The "evil spirits howled and yelped fearfully," while the exorcist continued his relentless pursuit:

"Therefore, depart at once, ye cursed! It is entirely within your power to free yourself from these sufferings. Let this poor woman in peace! I conjure you in the name of the Almighty God, in the name of the Crucified Jesus of Nazareth, in the name of His purest Mother, the Virgin Mary, in the name of the Archangel Michael!"

"Oh, yes," they groaned, "we are willing. But Lucifer does not let us."

"Tell the truth. Is Lucifer alone the cause of it?"

"No, he alone could not be. God's justice does not permit it as yet, because sufficient atonement has not yet been made for her."

Father Riesinger's own theological concern with a satanic hierarchy was frequently reflected in these exchanges, as was his picture of the devil, the demons, and hell. The devils, as stated in *Begone, Satan!*, "betrayed great fear lest they be forced to return to hell." Father Theophilus "insisted upon their departure again and again," although they pleaded pitifully, "Anything but that, anything but that." Riesinger reminded the devils, "But you are already in hell." They groaned, "True, true, we drag hell along with us. Yet it is a relief to be permitted to roam about the earth until (at the last judgment) we shall be cast off and damned to hell for eternity."

The record shows that Father Riesinger, although "almost completely exhausted," played a heroic and triumphant role, while the devils yielded in "moaning and despairing tones," as they "could not bear the tortures of exorcism" he inflicted on them. Similarly, on a secular level, Dr. Carl Wickland showed haughtiness and contempt for the "ignorant" spirits who spoke through his wife and did not understand their status of being dead.

Wickland's and Riesinger's posture as arch-antagonists of evil entities, men who banished wickedness while liberating and thus healing the possessed, reflects an attitude that can be found to varying degrees among many exorcists. No doubt, to display the strength necessary to bring about the cessation of a possession syndrome calls for more than average self-assurance. Mrs. Anita Kohsen Gregory, in an introduction to T. K. Oesterreich's *Possession: Demoniacal and Other,* outlined Dr. Wickland's exorcism pattern. She noted that the exorcist instructed the spirits on "what is what in the spirit world, and after the spirit has returned converted (whether peacefully or by threats and static electricity, or forcibly being confined to a dungeon by intelligent spirits), he usually preaches a little sermon on the truth about the world and the conditions in the hereafter, echoing precisely the doctor's own views, and quoting the same scriptural texts." Wickland's self-esteem must also have been bolstered when, through the mediumship of his wife, the spirits of Helena Blavatsky, founder of the Theosophical Society, and Mary Baker Eddy, founder of Christian Science, made their appearance. As Mrs. Gregory puts it, they were "full of contrition for the false doctrines they have taught, that is, those doctrines that clash with the opinions of Dr. Wickland"; Mrs. Eddy showed particular "repentance for her disrespectful attitude toward doctors and the medical profession generally during her lifetime."

In Wickland's case, the transfer of the confused spirit to his wife, Anna, made the entity a virtual captive of their personal symbiosis. That need not imply fewer genuine healings than in a direct exorcist-with-possessed dialogue, but it created an entirely different dramatic situation. As the setting, personalities, and paraphernalia of exorcism have a decided impact on the patient, the Wickland pattern may well have been uniquely suited to the type of patient who sought the doctor's help.

Dr. Wickland's medical degree, his standard practitioner's office and instruments, together with his no-nonsense attitude about possession, spirits, and the conditions of an afterlife, must have provided a high degree of certainty and assurance. Photographs show him, throughout his career, as a stern-faced, ramrod-straight man. Anna's relation to Dr. Wickland shows, as we have noted, parallels to those of the wives of W. B. Yeats and Sir Arthur Conan Doyle to their husbands. At crucial periods of their lives and marriages, these women developed mediumship, thus assuring themselves of their husbands' continued attention. The Wicklands appear to have been childless. Their circle of friends was probably restricted to those attending the Wickland séances, with Anna in trance and her husband in charge of the proceedings. Mrs. Wickland's spirit control, known as "Pretty Girl," had aspects of a child surrogate.

Even if Anna and Carl Wickland's involvement with the spirit world was a joint mental aberration, a *folie à deux,* it was—even allowing for Wickland's inability ever to be wrong—quite possibly effective in alleviating certain psychological disturbances. That it gave his patients a chance to rid themselves of possessing spirits (whose manifestations may have been due to Wickland's suggestive powers) who had become personifications of their illnesses, by putting them onto Anna, could have been dramatically effective. In addition, giving the patients a chance to see these entities being browbeaten by Wickland, or even themselves talking back to them through Anna's mediumship, may well have been cathartic.

Certainly, Dr. Wickland is not an unbiased reporter of his own exorcistic feats. Did his patients remain well? Or did they have to return to be re-exorcised? Did they perhaps fade from Wickland's horizon and seek out other therapists? To what degree had Carl Wickland become the unknown victim of his own rigidly structured thoughts and procedures, victim of self-delusion, or at least of varying self-deceptions? Canon Pearce-Higgins, the Anglican clergyman whose experiences somewhat parallel those of Wickland, believes that, lacking a medium of Anna Wickland's unique gifts, it is impossible to repeat Wickland's method and success; yet, Carl Wickland's forceful and unyielding personality, righteous and self-possessed (no pun intended) , was also essential to the performances he recorded. Psychic phenomena show very specific patterns in various places and at different times. The Anna Ecklund type of mediumship is nearly extinct in the TV era.

The range of interpersonal elements that enter an exorcism situation is wide. In certain shamanistic settings, a whole community may be involved, with all the varied stresses and attractions this implies. Exorcism may be entertainment; or a fierce struggle between antagonists within or outside a human personality; or a dignified rite, in a somber and awesome setting; or a cauldron of obscenity, bodily excretions, physical aberrations, sado-masochistic interactions. Many religio-cultural factors dictate the conditions under which an exorcism takes place; but the exorcist himself is the commanding figure in the dramatic confrontation.

Dr. Jan Ehrenwald, the New York psychoanalyst, has developed the concept of "doctrinal compliance." In the analytic or general psychotherapeutic setting, it suggests that the patient tends to comply with the therapist's own doctrinal orientation. On a wider canvas of patient-doctor relations, identical symptoms may suggest the need of a surgical operation to a surgeon, or the need for psychotherapy where a psychosomatic disorder is suspected. We all impose or "project" our own interests, orientations, or frames of reference on situations we encounter. One man's madness is another's nutritional deficiency (indeed, schizophrenia is being treated, in some cases, with niacin and other vitamins in large doses) ; accepted behavior in one cultural setting may be regarded as eccentric in another and as reprehensible in a third. The compulsion to comply is the reverse of this coin. People will do the oddest things in order to obtain attention, approval, affection, notoriety, to be at center stage, or to manipulate those around them.

Certainly, illness—whether real, feigned, or both—is a culturally accepted attention-getter everywhere. For mixed reasons, children cater to their ill and aged parents, and parents throw a protective mantle of affection and attention around their sick children. Illness and death are favorite topics of conversation. And a mysterious illness, particularly when it has the threatening, awesome quality of mental sickness, is certain to draw attention, commiseration, and advice of varying quality.

Illnesses imitate each other, even when there is no biological basis for an epidemic character. No one has fainting spells any longer, but nearly everyone has a nagging backache now and then. Both, together with the ever-available headache, are means to avoid certain duties, gain attention, and become agreeably dependent on the ministrations of others. The priest who tells a young nun that her sex urges may be due to the devil, the spiritist who attributes compulsive action to the intervention of low-minded spirits, the shaman who is familiar with the habits of demons—all these encourage "doctrinal compliance" that may transform psychophysiological symptoms into possession by devils, demons, or evil spirits.

Compliance is based on mutual need. The exorcism undertaken by a Protestant clergyman, the Reverend Johann Christoph Blumhardt, in the mid-nineteenth-century German village of Möttlingen, provides illuminating detail on just such a situation. Blumhardt's career was crowned, and his Lutheran parish invigorated, with the exorcism of a young woman, Gottliebin Dittus. Dr. Henri Ellenberger, in *The Discovery of the Unconscious,* calls it "a typical example of possession and exorcism, patterned exactly on the model of those performed in the early Christian Church," although it took place "in the middle of the nineteenth century—and was thus an instance of primitive healing in modern times and in a modern setting."

The would-be exorcist had been a precocious student of religion. Blumhardt had twice read the Bible by the time he was twelve years old, had studied theology, written on the subject of Christian missions, and served in several parishes. He came to Möttlingen at the age of thirty-three to succeed the Reverend Barth, who had failed to bring about a religious revival in the community. Miss Dittus had been one of his favorite parishioners, although Barth's zeal did not make him popular within his parish.

Blumhardt was ready to meet the challenge which the rundown parish offered. He arrived in Möttlingen in July, 1838, and married in the fall. Ellenberger notes that Blumhardt "had always been convinced that the devil was a dreadful reality that played a major role in human affairs." Some of his ideas, although they sound odd today, were held by quite a few of his contemporaries. Ellenberger recalls that he believed the mortar used in the construction of the pyramids had been "mixed by wizards who were helped by the devil" and that "sin was the root of most diseases."

Blumhardt, and possibly Gottliebin Dittus as well as other

members of the parish, must have been familiar with a celebrated case in the nearby Black Forest town of Prevorst, where fourteen-year-old Friederike Wanne achieved fame as a clairvoyant. Her achievements were recorded by a distinguished poet-physician, Justinus Kerner, in *The Seeress of Prevorst* (1829). The region was remote and tradition-minded, populated by farm folk who retained many earlier, even pre-Christian traditions on witchcraft, good and evil, curses and spells. So much for the would-be exorcist himself, and for the community in which he was to function.

What about Gottliebin Dittus? Her first name is the feminine form of "God-lover." Her family combined intense religiosity with folk superstition. She told Blumhardt that shortly after her birth she had twice been abducted by an invisible spirit, who dropped the baby at the door when her mother invoked the name of Jesus. One of her aunts, she claimed, was a witch and had tried to enlist her in witchcraft practices. Ellenberger suggests that the woman's experiences were provoked by a "cultural conflict between the Church and superstition."

Gottliebin Dittus was twenty-eight years old when her possession symptoms began. She was poor and lived with three unmarried brothers and sisters, including a half-blind brother. She had served in various homes and farms, but a kidney ailment and facial skin disease forced her to stop working. Curious phenomena began when the Dittus family moved into rented rooms in 1840. Gottliebin saw figures and fleeting lights, including the image of a woman who had died two years earlier; the phantom was carrying "a dead child in her arms."

Shortly afterwards, knocking sounds could be heard in the Dittus apartment, but no one paid much attention to them. By April 1842, relatives of Gottliebin told the Reverend Blumhardt the sounds had become so strong that the knockings disturbed the neighbors. On June 3, the cleric and a local physician, Dr. Späth, visited the apartment, accompanied by village officials. Blumhardt reported:

"As soon as I entered the room, we were met by two powerful

poundings. These were followed by other sounds of knocking and pounding of various types. These came mainly from the room where Gottliebin was lying on her bed, fully dressed. Those who watched from the outside and in the rooms above heard it, too, and they assembled in the lower apartment, convinced that the sounds came from there.

"The tumult seemed to grow stronger, particularly as I began a religious hymn and said a few words of prayer. During a three-hour period, we heard twenty-five poundings. Everything was carefully investigated: the sounds seemed to come from below Gottliebin's bed; but they could not have occurred by normal means, as the girl was constantly under observation. No explanation was possible."

Blumhardt was told afterwards that Gottliebin had, shortly after the knocking sounds, suffered convulsions of increasing intensity and length. The cleric visited her and made the following report:

"Her whole body trembled. Every muscle of her head and arms was either in intense motion or tight and stiff, and she often foamed at the mouth. She had been lying this way for several hours. The physician, who had never encountered anything like it, seemed at his wit's end. Suddenly she woke up, was able to sit and drink some water. It was difficult to believe that we were dealing with one and the same person."

Reporting on a later visit, Blumhardt wrote: "After what has happened, I have come to the conclusion that something demonic is involved here. With this thought, I found myself angry, jumped up and grabbed her stiff hands, forced the fingers together in a praying gesture. Though she was unconscious, I shouted her name into her ear and said: 'Put your hands together and pray, "Lord Jesus, help me!" We have seen long enough what the devil can do, now let us see what Jesus is able to do.' She awoke a little later and said the words of prayer. Much to the surprise of those present, the convulsions ceased. This was my moment of decision, forcing me with irresistible power to begin action in this matter."

Blumhardt was now being pulled into the maelstrom of Gottliebin's illness-possession. The very next day, her convulsions
returned. Meeting the woman again, the clergyman found that
"something hostile within her was directed against me. She had
fiercely bright eyes, a repelling facial expression which conveyed
rage and fury, and she threatened me with her fists." When
Blumhardt said a prayer, the girl rolled her eyes and spoke with
a voice "that could immediately be recognized as alien, not only
because of its sound but because of the attitude and expression it
conveyed."

Addressing the voice, the Reverend Blumhardt asked, "Can't
you help yourself? Don't you know how to pray?"

The voice answered, "No, I can't pray."

"Don't you know Jesus, who forgives our sins?"

"I can't bear to hear that name!"

"Are you by yourself?"

"No."

"Well, who is with you?"

The voice hesitated, then blurted out, "The most evil of all."

During this prayer struggle, a number of demons made their
presence known. At first they numbered 3, then 7, and finally 14.
Eventually, the total rose to 175 and ultimately to 425. Blumhardt tried to stem their tide with prayers and readings from the
Bible. His most difficult night, he wrote, was the eve of June 25,
1842, when "I struggled from eight in the evening until four
o'clock in the morning as never before, but without getting any
satisfaction. Whoever saw her was overwhelmed with pity. She
beat her breasts, pulled her hair, squirmed like a worm and
seemed totally lost."

At last, Gottliebin collapsed into a heap, lying on the floor as
if dead; only her upper body jerked a few times. She then "spit
out" her demons, one by one, and later in groups of 14 or 28 or
12, as if there were thousands, but without any word from the
Reverend Blumhardt or "any remarks from the demons." The
possessed woman got up off the floor, was quiet, and it seemed as
if the exorcism had been successful.

Nevertheless, the phenomena began once more a few days later. Hallucinations and bleeding took place, possibly because of the violent movement of the woman's body. The demons made themselves known, worse than ever: "The riotious shouting of the demons, accompanied by a thunderstorm of lightning and rolling thunder, pouring rain, and the deep concern of all present, as well as my own prayers, contributed to the scene during which the demons rushed out of her as they had before." It was on this occasion that Gottliebin Dittus expressed the wish to move into the Reverend Blumhardt's home, because she expected it to be more serene than the family apartment. The clergyman agreed, and there was peace for several months. However, early in February the disturbances started all over again. Blumhardt's diary reports them as follows:

"It began with her vomiting sand and small pieces of glass. Then, pieces of iron were added, particularly old, bent nails. Once, before my very eyes, she squirmed and choked for a long time, until twelve nails dropped into a bowl. She also threw up shoe buckles of various sizes and shapes, so large that it was difficult to imagine they could pass through her throat. She also vomited a large and wide piece of iron, which caused her to lose her breath and she was forced to lie down as if dead. Added to this were uncountable pins, sewing needles, and even pieces of knitting needles; these came up with difficulty, either one by one or in bunches mixed with paper and feathers."

Dr. John Mischo, reviewing the Dittus case in a paper on "Psychologische Aspekte der Besessenheit" ("Psychological Aspects of Possession") suggests that Blumhardt should have wondered "how these things that came out of Gottliebin Dittus had got into her in the first place." He cites the Lutheran clergyman's observation that the woman hung her coat on a door hook one evening, but that her sister saw a figure move to the coat during the night and remove a metal money box from its pocket; the next morning, she vomited up several coins and the metal box. Blumhardt's comment was surprisingly evasive and bland: "All this indicates that certain people know the art of moving their spirit outside their bodies and to undertake certain magical acts, although not always fully conscious at the time." Mischo suggests, instead, that "Gottliebin took these items while being in an hysterical state of semiconsciousness, in order to bring them up later on." If such conscious, semiconscious or totally unconscious sleight of hand really took place, the control exercised over the woman's movements must have been virtually nonexistent; this may well have been the case, either because Blumhardt and others in his household had preconditioned themselves into accepting the demonic theory—under the doubtlessly very strong impact of Gottliebin's genuine suffering—or were so awed by the phenomena that they did not dare to "spy" on the woman.

While Gottliebin stayed at the Blumhardts', her sister Katharina and her half-blind brother developed symptoms similar to their sister's. By then, Blumhardt felt that Gottliebin was in a fairly good state, while Katharina, "who until then had not been affected in any way, became so violent that she could only be controlled with the greatest effort." He wrote that "she threatened to tear me into a thousand pieces, and I did not dare go close to her." During the Christmas holidays, things were at their worst: "The alleged Angel of Satan yelled fiercely at two o'clock in the morning, while the girl's head and upper body twisted backwards over the back of her chair. The voice seemed totally inhuman, as it shouted: 'Jesus is the victor, Jesus is the victor.' By now the power of the demon seemed to have been broken; it grew quiet, made fewer movements, and disappeared, like the light of life in a dying person, about 8:00 A.M." After a few more flare-ups with Katharina and Gottliebin, the phenomena ceased entirely.

Six years later, the Reverend Blumhardt reported: "I simply want to note that she [Gottliebin] has been living in my house as the most loyal and understanding support of my wife, helping her in the household and in bringing up the children. My wife has been able to trust her completely with all the major and minor matters that arise in a household. She does not live with us simply as a servant, because her gratitude for what she is permitted to do prevents her from accepting payment. Rather, she views herself and feels that she was taken in as if she were our own child, something we were also able to do for her sister Katharina and her half-blind brother."

All's well that ends well, in other words. Everyone came out ahead in this two-year drama. The three Dittus family members achieved a sinecure in the pastor's house, while Blumhardt's prestige increased tremendously. Dr. Ellenberger gives this appraisal:

"As a first result of Blumhardt's victory, the religious revival that had been vainly attempted by the Reverend Barth was now becoming reality. One after the other, parishioners came to Blumhardt, confessing their sins and requesting his blessing. In an account he gave of this revival, we see him appalled at the number and gravity of sins confessed to him, to which were added superstitious practices, witchcraft, and the practice of birth control. It would seem that the Church authorities regarded Blumhardt with some anxiety and suspicion, and he was subjected to vehement attacks from some of his colleagues."

By then, Blumhardt had become a self-assured celebrity. Ellenberger notes that he had achieved the prestige of a man who, "with the sole means of prayer and fasting, had sustained a prolonged struggle against the powers of darkness and overcome them with the help of God." His motto was, "Jesus is the victor," and people made virtual pilgrimages to confess their sins to him or to be healed by his prayers. With financial help from new friends, Blumhardt bought a house and grounds in a nearby spa, Bad Boll, which he used as a center of healing and preaching. Gottliebin acted as his assistant, particularly in his work with the mentally ill.

Mischo sees Gottliebin's symptoms as an exaggerated appeal to Blumhardt, first for his attention and then as her protector. The exorcism was satisfactorily concluded when the woman was ac-

cepted into the clergyman's household. At this moment, Mischo
writes, her brother and sister "learn to play the same tune in
order to gain the pastor's attention," and their phenomena cease
when he accepts them, too: "A critical phase in the personality
development of Gottliebin Dittus has been overcome, she has
moved from the poverty level into a clerical household, moves on
with him to Bad Boll, finally marries and becomes a vocational
teacher. Brother and sister are taken care of, and it is a tribute to
the psychological empathy displayed by the Reverend Blumhardt
and his family that no one among the 'Dittus Clan' need fall
back on demonic attacks in order to provoke a readjustment of
human relations."

And so, the Dittuses and the Blumhardts lived happily ever
after. With all that, however, it is difficult to ignore that somehow, no matter how it satisfied his own needs and ambitions, the
Reverend Blumhardt had been taken advantage of by Gottliebin's presumably unconscious acts of traditional demonic possession. Later interpretations tended to be baffled, intrigued and
somewhat patronizing. Viktor von Weitzsäcker called the case
"one of the most remarkable examples of reciprocal action of
helper and help-needing individuals." In *Seelenbehandlung und
Seelenführung* (1926) he called its solution "a victory of Blumhardt over hysteria and a victory of Gottliebin over Blumhardt:
he obtained a withdrawal of the demons, and she the community
of life with him."

One psychiatrist, Gaetano Benedetti, saw strong similarities to
the cure and psychotherapy of severe schizophrenics. He wrote in
Reformation, IX (1960) that Blumhardt intuitively discovered,
more than a century ahead of others, the principle of such cures.
If that is so, then a good number of shamanistic and other exorcism rites have similar psychotherapeutic value. Benedetti wrote
that Blumhardt threw himself into Gottliebin's demoniacal
world, just as the modern therapist explores the inner world of a
schizophrenic's delusion, and that he was responsive to healthy
elements in the patient's mind-world. Ellenberger adds that

Blumhardt made "full use of what existential therapists called the *kairos;* that is, the elective point for decisive intervention or decision."

If the Reverend Blumhardt was, to a certain extent, a willing victim of the Dittuses' demoniacal displays, his fate was far less dramatic than that of one of the most outstanding exorcists in recorded history: Father Jean-Pierre Surin. He had already lived a life of determined asceticism, prolonged contemplation, and study when he joined the exorcists at the Ursuline convent at Loudun, France, in 1634, a cauldron of contagious possession which had already consumed several victims. Upon the accusations of the nuns, or their possessing devils, Surin's contemporary and fellow graduate of the College of Bordeaux, Urbain Grandier, had been publicly burned at the stake as the devil's coconspirator. His major accuser, the convent's prioress, Jeanne des Agnes, displayed a vivid mixture of suffering, self-dramatization, pleas, and writhings.

Aldous Huxley, whose book *The Devils of Loudun* provides a sophisticated account of these events, notes that Surin's life of devotion and chastity contrasted strongly with Grandier's life of worldly ambition. Surin had grown up in a cloistered atmosphere as a child; only when the plague endangered his family was the little boy sent to the country, where he could play and run wild "without having to be afraid of anyone"—a phrase Huxley called "painfully revealing." Surin was a good writer, and Huxley feels the priest would have "relished the taste of fame, would have enjoyed, while seeming of course to deprecate, the praise of critics, the plaudits of an adoring public." Instead, we have Surin's touching, self-revealing letters, which show that while engaged in exorcising the Loudun nuns, he fell victim to possession himself. He had asked for it, and he got it with a vengeance.

From fall of 1629 to spring of 1630, Surin attended the Jesuit College of Rouen to complete his second novitiate. Self-transcendence through self-denial, fasting, and going without sleep became central to his existence. Next, Surin moved to the fishing village of Marennes, where he became the spiritual guide of two locally prominent women. Both had had what they regarded as mystical experiences of deep religious impact, visions, and ecstasies that impressed Father Surin profoundly. The two women's "extraordinary graces" advanced the Jesuit father's relations with women on an ecstatic spiritual level; everyday man-woman contact was impossible, but daily exchanges on esoteric religious experiences and ideas served as fully sanctioned substitutes.

By now, Father Surin's physical strength had been undermined by years of self-imposed rigors. Emotional symptoms were added; his colleagues observed "melancholy" or neurotic behavior, including sharp muscle pains, headaches so severe that he could hardly read, and frequent attacks of confusion and depression. Still, Surin was chosen to go to Loudun to continue the exorcisms that had already caused the death of Grandier. Surin's fellow Jesuits were not at all sure that the Loudun nuns were really possessed by the devil; he had no such doubts, being convinced that the visual and invisible worlds are everywhere and continuously intertwined.

Sister Jeanne, who had asked to continue her exorcism with the Capuchin and Carmelite fathers whom she had come to know well, was obviously worried about the impact of a presumably cool and penetrating Jesuit mind. She wrote letters of inquiry in all directions and compiled quite a dossier on Surin before he ever set foot on Loudun. The much-possessed prioress need not have worried. Surin was so moved by the first exorcism he witnessed that he shed tears over the suffering of the nuns. All, however, was not pain and suffering. Sister Jeanne, who had even experienced a full-blown psychosomatic pregnancy through one possessing devil, Isacaaron, wrote later: "The devil often beguiled me by a certain pleasure, which I took in my agitations and the other extraordinary things he did to my body. I took an extreme delight in hearing these things spoken about, and I was happy that I gave the impression of being more gravely tormented than the others."

Isacaaron, devil of debauchery, quickly became Surin's tempter. The exorcism rites at Loudun were overripe with sexuality, not covert but overt. The nuns could readily confess to their attending priests just what intimate physical things the devils had done to them during the night, what whispers of indecency they had uttered, what physiological changes had taken place within the feminine parts of their bodies. This was no place for a man like Surin, who not only hoped to remove possessions from Sister Jeanne but sought to turn her into a saintlike creature whose "extraordinary graces" would testify to God's greatness. Eventually, his often-repeated suggestions sank in, and Sister Jeanne did achieve a conversion of sorts, complete with spurious miracles. But the Jesuit had no chance to enjoy this Pygmalionlike transformation, because on January 19, 1635, Father Surin became possessed.

At first, this was an inner and psychological possession. But by Easter time, the exorcist himself was rolling on the floor and uttering wild defiances, while the nun was sitting calmly by, now spectator instead of spectacle. Earlier, when witnessing a particularly vicious exercise of diabolic force, Surin had prayed that he might suffer as Sister Jeanne did, that he might become possessed, "provided that it should please the divine Goodness to cure her." He even prayed that he might suffer the humiliation of being considered a lunatic. What happened would seem to support the thesis that much of the effectiveness of prayer is a result of conscious-to-unconscious autosuggestion.

Other of the Loudun exorcists had earlier been driven into psychosomatic illness. In two cases, those of Fathers Lactance and Tranquille, this had led to their death. Huxley noted that all of the exorcists were eventually beset by the very demons they had helped to evoke and "were doing their best to keep alive." Surin's overt possession took place at a moment when, as Sister Jeanne later confessed, she was overcome by seductive, "very evil desires and sentiment of most lawless affection" for Surin. She feared the priest, Huxley says, because his perspicacity might expose her as what "in her lucid intervals she knew herself to be—half actress, half unrepentant sinner, wholly hysterical." After a three-hour prayer session, Surin referred to her "infamous temptations," which she thought she had kept to herself but may have signaled in ways the thirty-three-year-old priest perceived.

Surin's first physical phenomenon was that, as he had her tied down helplessly, he found himself unable to speak, although able to apply a consecrated wafer to her head and heart. It was at this point that the prioress yielded to Father Surin's prayers that, turning away from the diabolical, she move toward saintliness. She soon did the best she could, but Surin's image of her was of one humble and unworldly, while her self-image was oriented toward publicity and spectacular display. In one of her new-found ecstasies, she claimed to have come so close to God that she had "received, as it were, a kiss from his mouth."

Just about everyone except Surin regarded her conversion with skepticism. If they were charitable, they saw it as still another trick by the possessing devil; if not, as a new attention-getting device by Sister Jeanne. During exorcisms, presumably mouthing the words of possessing entities, fellow nuns called her "the devout devil," *le diable devot*. As she moved from the demoniacal to the divine, Isacaaron departed on January 7, 1636. Behemoth, demon of blasphemy, remained in possession. Surin continued the exorcism while himself intermittently possessed. When he had not succeeded in dislodging the demon by the following October, he was recalled to Bordeaux by his Jesuit superiors. But Behemoth assured his successor that he would yield only if Jeanne and Surin were to undertake a joint pilgrimage to the tomb of St. François de Sales in Annecy. Surin was sent back to Loudun in June, but the church authorities balked at permitting nun and priest to travel together. They had to go separately, meeting only at the tomb; Behemoth disappeared on October 15, and Surin returned to Bordeaux.

The other priests drifted away from the Ursuline nunnery. As Huxley put it, "Left to themselves such devils as remained soon took their leave. After six years of incessant struggle, the Church Militant gave up the fight. Its enemies promptly disappeared. The long orgy was at an end. If there had been no exorcists, it would never have begun." But the ordeal of Father Surin continued. He had not been well when he went to Loudun. The presence of evil there, in whatever form, deepened his psychosomatic disorders and intermittent depressions. Surin was ill during much of 1637 and 1638. Fevers, overall bodily weakness, and partial paralysis had emotional equivalents in feelings of unworthiness. Eventually, he could neither dress nor undress himself, and had great difficulty in eating. Medical treatment brought no relief. He could still write, and his letters were lucid, detailed, and specific. But by 1639 correspondence ceased, too. What Huxley calls his "pathological illiteracy"—he then could neither read nor write—persisted until 1657. He also found it difficult to speak during these years. Surin was sure that the devil had taken control of him, was preparing him for death and damnation.

Like others among the Loudun exorcists, the Jesuit father was haunted by the memory of Urbain Grandier. Now Surin thought he, too, had become a sorcerer. Once, standing beside the bed of a dying man, he felt the irresistible compulsion to call upon the devils he had known so well at Loudun to enter the body of this man. Soon the man no longer spoke prayerfully of God, Christ, and mercy, but of flapping black wings and unspeakable terror. Surin was overwhelmed by the thought that here was proof that he had, indeed, become a sorcerer who could command devils. What are we to make of this? Telepathy? Surin's private delusions?

In 1645, Surin tried to kill himself. He jumped out of a window but only broke a thigh bone. The pull toward self-extinction remained. He retained a fear of high places, of knives and ropes. He also felt an urge to set fire to buildings. But, even if there had been another chance at suicide or arson, he was now the prisoner of his brothers. Watched and tied, he spent three years in humiliation and further disintegration. That the man came out of all this, still able to write carefully and well about his ordeal, seems almost more a miracle than any phenomena Sister Jeanne—then living out her pseudosaintly self-image—was able to produce as a voyaging relic during this period.

Surin was rescued by Father Bastide, who took over the Jesuit College at Saintes in 1648. Bastide asked that Surin be sent to him, and he treated him with kindness and respect. Father Surin recovered step by step. His asthmalike breathing difficulties disappeared. But it was 1657 before he was able to write as much as three pages. Three years later he began to walk again. He discovered that there was a beautiful outside world, with green lawns and flowers, and no thought of devils. Now came visions, ecstasies, psychic experiences of the euphoric kind. Eventually, though, Surin grew calm and ordinary enough to preach, hear confessions, and advise others in letters or conversations. He wrote of his experiences in Loudun and the years that followed in a memoir, *Science Experimentale*. He died, peacefully, in 1665.

Surin had freed Sister Jeanne of her devils; there, he had been victorious. But he fell victim to the very evil over which he had triumphed. On a far less tragic level, the Reverend Blumhardt succeeded in ousting the 425 demons that infested Gottliebin Dittus, but at the price of giving her a home. Theophilus Riesinger in Earling, Iowa, and Carl Wickland in Chicago and Los Angeles put demons and ignorant spirits in their places through highly personal mixtures of dogmatism and self-assurance. Everyone of them may have been the victim of self-delusion; but all saw themselves as victors in a struggle with darkness.

4. "Just Don't Call Me an Exorcist!"

The clergyman who today is possibly one of the most knowledgeable and successful exorcists totally dislikes the word *exorcism*. He is Canon John D. Pearce-Higgins, former canon residentiary and vice-provost of Southwark Cathedral in London. He is a founder-member of the Churches' Fellowship for Psychical and Spiritual studies, and chairman of its Psychic Phenomena Committee. When discussing his numerous encounters with haunted minds and haunted houses the Anglican cleric insists, "Just don't call me an exorcist! The concept of exorcism in Christianity took on the meaning of 'binding' and implies 'cursing' or condemning an entity to the Lake of Everlasting Fire. The idea of binding a demon, restraining it or driving it out has so far hardly entered into my work at all."

Canon Pearce-Higgins, a slender, soft-spoken man in his late sixties, has developed a procedure for freeing men, women, or houses from "possession" that is designed to persuade rather than to threaten. His approach is based on the conviction that the possessing entity is neither a devil, a demon, or an "evil spirit," but an earthbound, possibly confused spirit who is attached to a person or a place.

Canon Pearce-Higgins, who has long been a member of the Society for Psychical Research and a student of parapsychology, came into this work through pastoral calls for help, and at first dealt only with haunted houses. "Not having the slightest idea," he says, "or any help from the church as to how to deal with these requests, I had to start by using mediums, not least Mrs. Ena Twigg, the well-known British sensitive." Later he worked for a time with a trance medium whose guide advised him that it would be a great help if he were to take a service of Holy Communion before the medium went under control. Subsequently he found it was possible for him to deal with cases alone, without a medium present. This arose because on a number of occasions the medium was not able to be present, and the guide instructed him to go alone, having given some diagnosis of what the particular haunting involved.

After a time, owing to the publicity his work received, clergy and others began to write to him for help. He was instructed by the trance personalities to send the form of service which he had evolved (basically a perfectly orthodox, but somewhat shortened form of the Anglican liturgy—a Requiem Mass with certain special prayers) to the priest or minister concerned, which he did. In the majority of cases the priest would write and tell him some time later that the service had been successful; the phenomena had ceased immediately. There were, however, as Pearce-Higgins puts it, "some failures because of lack of motivation and sincerity of purpose—all important in such matters."

Since early in 1971 the canon has worked with a husband-and-wife team, Roy and Joan Broster, who about that time appear to have received a charismatic gift for physical healing. With the help and encouragement of the canon they soon developed a capacity for dealing with psychic and mental cases. The statistics of this team of three during an eighteen-month period in 1971/72 when they dealt with some 3,000 cases, of which the majority were physical but 540 were claimed psychic—hauntings or possessions—are interesting. One hundred and eighty were claimed hauntings, but of these only 40 proved to be genuine. Of the remainder, 113 were genuine cases of possession. The rest were what the healers call "all-in-the-mind" cases—schizophrenia, hysterical hallucinations, anxiety states, and other forms of mental or emotional disturbance. While these initial figures indicate 5 percent genuine cases, a recent six-month set of figures give what is probably nearer the normal incidence percentage.

Of 430 claimed psychic cases (note however the percent increase out of the total number, for this six-month period) only 20 were considered genuinely psychic—about fifty-fifty hauntings and possessions. Since the team only became known for their work in 1971, it looks as if there had been a backlog of psychic cases which sought help once the sufferers had at last found someone who could help their condition. By 1974, the curve evened out to 5 percent. Canon Pearce-Higgins found it alarming that "an increasing incidence of mental disturbances employ the language and symbolism of an obviously spurious brand of Spiritualism."

Neither of the Brosters would call themselves mediums; their special sensitivities take the form of physical and mental healing—the husband having perhaps the greater healing power, the wife, who is Irish, the greater intuitive and diagnostic ability. Pearce-Higgins regards this as important, because "quite apart from the many who come, having incorrectly diagnosed their own condition, there also are a number of phonies who come for less worthy motives, not least to try to trip up the healers." The canon, a modest man, would not claim any special prowess in all this, but rather that "success is due to teamwork (where two or three are gathered together in Christ's name) which thus forms a greater channel than an individual working alone.

"In contact healing we work with a minimum of ritual or dressing up, particularly in cases of personal possession," the canon says, "as the power which flows through my healer friends' hands seems sufficient to extrude the possessing entity. Sometimes this produces various stretchings or contortions of the patient's body, but no words are spoken until the end, when I modify the prayer of 'exorcism' into a thanksgiving that God has removed the entity. This fact becomes apparent from the changes in the possessed person's appearance and manner—a cure in fact."

Citing one case, Pearce-Higgins notes a possessed man wriggled and stretched during the healing process, then "fell into a mildly catatonic state, suddenly slid right off his chair and finished up with kneeling on the floor." Most of the possessed pass through a light trance during the healing process. Their bodies respond to the various healing stages and to the exit of the controlling entity from the possessed body. Canon Pearce-Higgins and his helpers visited a young woman who it seems was inhabited by the spirit of "a young man who had been stabbed to death during an altercation outside the woman's house, and who had somehow managed to possess her for a short time." The process of extrusion seemed to move upwards from the lower part of the young woman's body. In the process of this upward exodus, the woman's neck swelled as if she had a "huge goitre," and returned to normal at the entity's departure presumably through the back of the neck. The woman was more or less in trance during the whole proceeding. She came back to consciousness when it was completed, but felt quite exhausted. Pearce-Higgins reports, "After a good night's sleep, she telephoned me in the morning and said she felt fine."

The canon says that in haunting cases he goes either alone or with his two healer-friends to the place involved and conducts "a short service of Holy Communion, a Requiem Mass for the release of the earthbound spirit." Afterwards, he goes through the house with a bowl of Holy or Blessed Water, makes the sign of a Celtic Cross in the name of the Holy Trinity on each wall, door, window and mirror in the rooms that seem to have been affected by the spirit entity. With haunted houses and possessed individuals, Canon Pearce-Higgins insists on avoiding the pattern of "demonic belief, because of the fear it injects into a situation which might be neither dangerous nor frightening, were it not for the fear of demons and devils which certain outdated 'exorcism' methods inject or project into it."

This nondemonic approach clashes with other interpretations within the Anglican and Episcopal churches, the Roman Catholic church, and certain Protestant denominations. Canon Pearce-Higgins points out that "we have no words by Jesus himself about what he did, only Mark's interpretation of most of the healing miracles." In the canon's view, "there is no evidence of what Jesus really thought about the cases he cured, whether he knew through his clairvoyant powers that some cases were caused by discarnate entities and other by 'elementals,' or something quite different."

Christian theologians find it difficult to restate the early concepts of devils, demons, evil spirits—and angels—in modern terms. Most of them ignore the problem and avoid up-to-date definitions. Pearce-Higgins wonders whether "there might not be a multiplicity of spirits who are undergoing an evolutionary process." He feels that evolution need not be seen exclusively in terms of man on earth, physical forms, and skeletal shapes, "but from the very smallest known or unknown unit to the very highest, on all levels of consciousness." He says:

"We should keep in mind that a belief in so-called demons really involves us in a most complicated theological problem of Dualism. If these demons and 'The Devil' really exist in their own right, then we have an unabashed Dualism which is difficult to accommodate to monotheism. The alternative, and I believe this to be the correct biblical answer, is a doctrine of Fallen Angels. Demons would then be Fallen Angels and fallen humans who have said, like Macbeth, 'Evil be thou my good.' If so, they still remain Children of God and, as Origen—a remarkably enlightened second-century thinker—saw it, may be ultimately redeemable."

Pearce-Higgins finds that his own approach closely resembles that used earlier by Dr. Carl Wickland in the United States. On the whole, the canon's approach to a possessing spirit is not "judgmental" but a mixture of kindness and firmness very similar to Wickland's. "After all," he says, "who am I to stand there and condemn any entity to eternal damnation—not that our condemnation can probably really affect what the powers-that-be do with them! And even when I feel moved to use the more powerful medieval form of exorcism, I alter the words to say, 'In the authority of Christ, I command you to be taken hence and bound fast as with chains and cast into darkness, from which there is no return save through repentance,' or 'until the day of repentance, so that you trouble no more the servants of God.' In other words, in those cases when real damage or evil is being caused, it is equivalent to a prison sentence for the sake of society, to remain in effect until they have mended their ways; they must, so to speak, be under lock and key to protect the rest of us."

Obviously, the Pearce-Higgins approach owes a good deal to the practice and ideas of Spiritualism. His library of recording tapes contains a great number of conversations through trance mediums which suggest that haunted minds and haunted houses are caused by misguided spirits. Over and over again, the canon seeks to impress on the entities that they have "really died." He regards as "one extraordinary 'new' truth that has emerged through Spiritualism: it is possible to have died without knowing you are dead."

For all his gentle manner in dealing with spirits and people, Canon Pearce-Higgins is something of a stormy petrel within the Church of England. He finds himself at odds with much of the Church Establishment. The problem he faces was illustrated by a conversation with Bishop John Robinson, author of *Honest to God*. He asked the bishop why he did not put more stock in psychical research and the evidence for human survival after death. Robinson replied that the church was not really interested in survival, but in Eternal Life. Pearce-Higgins agreed that this, of course, was the ultimate goal, but that surely Eternal Life, being a quality of life which was worthy of survival, implied survival as a precondition. The bishop suggested that this was irrelevant, as it all depended upon our present relationship with God. Pearce-Higgins answered that this would immensely curtail the number of people "making the grade," as only a small percentage of ordinary men and women appear to have much consciousness of God, whereas evidence which he himself believed to be valid indicated that even if people did not "make the grade" in this life, there were plenty of opportunities in the "many mansions, or stages, of the hereafter" for them to come to such an awareness and conscious relationship. The bishop did not appear greatly interested in this line of argument.

This attitude appears to Pearce-Higgins as typical of much in modern theology which professes great concern for individuals while they live, but loses all concern after they pass beyond the point of death which to so many seems impenetrable. An understanding of death and afterlife is, in Pearce-Higgins's view, essential to knowledge of everyday existence and to a fuller understanding of the meaning of life on earth.

The canon found "little trace of a gentler approach" in the church pamphlet *Exorcism* (1972), which presented the findings of a commission appointed by the Bishop of Exeter and edited by Dom Robert Petitpierre, an Anglican Benedictine monk. The commission addressed its findings not only to the clergy, but also to doctors, psychiatrists, social workers, and others. It issued the report because of an "increasing, and too often unhealthy, interest in witchcraft, magic and the occult," which makes it important for the church to "have a clear mind about the spiritual casualties so often involved and how to deal with them." The report contains the following definition:

"Christian exorcism is the binding of evil powers by the triumph of Christ Jesus, through the application of the power demonstrated by that triumph, in and by his Church. The New Testament not only assumes the existence of non-human powers of evil, it asserts repeatedly the fact of the triumph of Christ Jesus over them. The prominence given in the gospels to the exorcisms done by our Lord is evidence of this, as is also the close association with them in the word *exousia*.

"It will be as well at the outset to note that in Christian usage the verb *to exorcise* applies strictly only to demons. It is possible to speak loosely about exorcizing persons or places, but what is meant in the exorcizing of the demonic forces of evil *in* those persons or places. Exorcism is an exercise of *exousia:* it commands and binds."

The report notes a need to "reduce the present unfortunate emphasis on exorcism as an action concerned exclusively with so-called demonic 'possession'" and adds that "until the more Christian concept of general exorcism returns to the conscious-ness of the Church, she is likely to be faced—indeed is being faced—with demands for such 'possession' exorcism." The report says "it cannot be overstressed that, as it is usually understood, this concept of demonic 'possession' is extremely dubious."

The Anglican commission emphasizes that "the exorcism of a person must not be performed until possible mental or physical illness has been excluded" through consultation with medical practitioners. Only a priest acting "under the authority of the bishop" should engage in actual exorcism, as "it is not a field which forms a part of the ordinary duties of the pastoral ministry for which a parish priest may properly be assumed to be com-petent." The commission adds the caution that failure of medical treatment is not necessarily evidence that "the illness is spiri-tual," as "psychological medicine is still limited in scope, empiri-cal in form, and rapidly changing." It emphasizes the need for after-care of the patient, because "Our Lord tells us that when the evil spirit is gone out of a man, the house, if left empty, will be occupied by evil and the last state will be worse than the first." Finally, "those who have been exorcised must be warned about this, and encouraged by all means possible to lead a prayerful life in union with the Church, to study Holy Scripture, and to receive the sacraments regularly."

This official approach of the Anglican church, or at least of this particular commission, speaks of exorcising "demons" but also refers to an "evil spirit."

Canon Pearce-Higgins would take issue with much of this part of the report. "It would be foolish of me or anyone," he says, "categorically to state that 'demons' or 'evil forces' do not exist. We have seen far too much terrible evil and cruelty in our time not to recognize the existence of a demonic element in human nature and sometimes in its environment. These forces appear to be purposively malevolent and destructive; in other words, they appear to be using reason for bad ends. The thought behind them is evil. That this thought can clothe itself in the traditional visual, auditory or sensory imagery of 'the devil'—with horns, hooves, tails and smells—and terrifying sensory hallucinations is regrettably probable. But in the normal cases which we find in haunted houses and in cases of mental and behavioral disturbance due to possession by low grade, discarnate spirits, the exorcising of 'demons' as a formula, in my experience simply does not work." He also entirely approves of the need for "after-care."

Pearce-Higgins was called to an old farmhouse in Sussex after two visits by a professional clerical demon-exorciser had failed to remove typical poltergeist phenomena. The clerical exorcist had diagnosed that in the top attic there was a very evil demon. On his second visit he went up alone to wrestle with it and returned looking hot and disheveled some fifteen minutes later saying he had defeated it. Unfortunately, the phenomena returned within a few days, unabated. The troubled occupants then called Pearce-Higgins. Accompanied by a medium, he found that this attic was indeed the main focus of disturbance, but the medium diagnosed the presence of a dead Roundhead (a soldier from the seventeenth-century civil-war period) who had been nearly maddened by a head wound and desperately trying to escape. The medium went into trance and was apparently controlled by this entity who started fighting the canon, until Pearce-Higgins realized that the soldier was desperately trying to leave the room. He opened the door and allowed him to go: "I have never in my life seen anyone, whether conscious or in trance, rush down three flights of stairs at the speed that the medium did! I chased after him for fear he should fall down and hurt himself, until he got to the front door, which I threw open for him. Once outside the medium halted, and presently returned to normal consciousness." From that moment the phenomena ceased.

The canon also wonders whether, as the report suggests, only those under the authority of the bishop who are considered "properly competent" should undertake this work. Here the real problem is diagnosis. If the diagnosis is not right, exorcism will not work. Clearly, in the above case the clerical exorcist had wrongly diagnosed a "demonic" presence when the real answer was far simpler—it was an unhappy almost crazed human being "on the other side of life" frenziedly seeking escape. He needed releasing, not cursing.

Since it is this sort of entity that he mostly encounters, the canon thinks that all this exorcising of demons passes right over the head of someone like the Roundhead, who would not recognize himself as a demon addressed by the priest. But when approached with comforting, admonitory, and explanatory words —as a fellow human being—in the course of a Requiem Mass, he finds someone who is talking to "his condition" and reacts accordingly.

The form of service which the canon uses has been sent, in reply to legitimate requests, all over the world. Recently a request was received from an Anglican chaplain in Ethiopia, who said he had a haunted house on his hands, and that he had reason to believe that in the house, now occupied by a German woman, there was still hanging around the restless spirit of an Ethiopian who some twelve years earlier had lived there and had been murdered by a burglar. The canon sent the form of service, which included an address to the earthbound spirit, explaining what had happened to him. The text was translated into Amharic, the local language, and after the service had been performed the house was "completely clear." Apparently, addressed in his own language, the Ethiopian "got the message."

Even more striking was a case in Wales, where extremely vicious, possibly black magic, activities had been perpetrated against the occupants. Most of this was cleared by prayer, but there remained the typical symptom of deathly cold in four of the rooms. The lady of the house was visited by her sister, a woman of considerable spiritual strength, who said, "Betty, we can't have this going on any longer. You have got Canon Pearce-

Higgins's prayers; get a bowl of water and we will clear these rooms." As was reported to the canon, as they said the prayers and made the sign of the cross in the rooms, "great gusts of warm air entered the place, rather as though the heater in a car had been turned on."

The canon concludes that, while episcopal ordination or commission may well be valuable, it is not the only essential; and, in view of the accepted Anglican idea of the universal priesthood of all true believers, a sincere layperson can also better get rid of an earthbound spirit than an insincere priest: "What is most required is complete trust and faith that God will fulfill his promises in Jesus Christ and that where two or three are gathered together in His name, His promise of help will be fulfilled. While in the majority of cases the priest using the prayers succeeds in his aim, there have been cases of failure, apparently due to the fact that the priest does not really believe in what he is doing. It is well nigh impossible to take a service effectively if you have your tongue in your cheek."

The canon warns that "anyone taking such a service must be prepared to find himself exhausted for some hours or even a day afterwards." This "draining" will almost certainly be evidence that the "exorcism" has been successful. After a report of a successful healing has been reported in the press or the media, Pearce-Higgins usually receives a batch of possession cases in the next mail. He does not seek publicity for its own sake, but only because it "provides an opportunity for genuine sufferers to know where they can seek help." The canon has provoked a reexamination of concepts by rejecting the "demon" category and insisting that spirits of the "type we normally encounter in England" are, "if genuine, always discarnate, earthbound human spirits, lost souls in need of help and prayers." Certainly, the term demon has about it something so otherwordly and irresistible that it conveys an aura of unreasoning fear.

Pearce-Higgins is careful to separate cases of emotional illness from possession. And yet, does not his own well-established view provoke the response which the possessed assume he expects of them? Possession tends to rub off on people. To put it more scientifically, it has qualities encountered in contagion and epidemics. It reminds me of a British cabinet minister's response to pressure to build more highways to reduce traffic congestion. "Building roads," he said, "is like feeding pigeons; more of them come flocking around." People hear of possession cases and, presto, they discover possession within themselves! Or, to put it another way, they interpret their discomforts and anxieties in terms of possession. This thinking in terms of possession, says the canon, is "a new phenomenon; it would not have happened even twenty-five years ago." It certainly happened in the U.S. in 1974, when the motion picture "The Exorcist" was released.

The history of exorcism is full of evidence that tells us, "If you're looking for devils, devils you'll get; if you look for demons, demons you'll get; and if you look for evil, malignant, ignorant or earthbound spirits, for hungry ghosts or spirits of foxes, those are precisely what you'll get!" The Freudian psychotherapist encounters an Oedipus complex, the surgeon a much-needed appendectomy, and the nutritionist a vitamin deficiency. Pearce-Higgins expects to encounter earthbound spirits, and he does.

It depends on what comes first, concept or evidence. Canon Pearce-Higgins insists that cumulative evidence, not a preconceived idea of the nature of possession, prompted his viewpoint. He is not dogmatic: "God forbid that we should return to the mentality of the times of the 'Devils of Loudun,' which—a priori—saw diabolism or witchcraft in every shadow, in every unusual physical or mental state. But surely the massive achievements of the scientific method are a sufficient protection against this. Here we are dealing with the frontier area between the normal and the paranormal, the psychological and the parapsychological, whose existence science is loath to admit, while yet being unable to account for or deal with it."

The Church of England's Commission on Exorcism speaks of

changing concepts in psychological medicine, but does not define where emotional illness ends and where possession, in the church's sense, begins. Like a physician who, after decades of practicing medicine and seeing thousands of patients, achieves a conditioned know-how regarding human illness, so Pearce-Higgins and his team have developed a "feel" for spirit possession, and can distinguish persons suffering from something truly outside themselves (objective) from those whose experiences are psychological and internal (subjective).

When someone comes to Pearce-Higgins claiming to be possessed by an entity, he or Mr. and Mrs. Broster will place their hands on the person's head and in front of his face. If there are rapid, flickering movements of lids and eyelashes, the team regard the problem as a psychological one stemming from the subconscious; but if there is no such flickering, they consider the likelihood of possession by an external entity. It is easy enough to write this sort of thing off as amateurish pretension, but Pearce-Higgins is alert to the kind of criticism that scoffs, "Oh, but it is all the old spiritualist guff, entities, auras, guides, the lot!" He is well aware of the many faces of Spiritualism, from genuine aid to the bereaved to the dangers of dabbling in such occult devices as "Ouija" boards.

The canon claims that he has a complete answer to this type of criticism: "The Freudian, Jungian or even behaviorist therapist uses a hypothetical model of the human psyche to which he himself has a key he can use when the patient has accepted the psychiatrist's model, to unlock the mind's barred doors, but this type of psychiatry is not usually able to deal with cases of possession. We contact genuine discarnate spirits for whose former earthly existence in many cases it is possible to produce documentary and other factual evidence. The former reality of such entities is often totally unknown to the patients and healers, and only subsequently established by searching in burial and other records. Furthermore, the cures are more or less instantaneous, the moment the entity is removed, as were Dr. Wickland's."

The canon is not a "starry-eyed spiritualist"; indeed, he considers that "a great many spiritualist mediums do untold harm diagnosing 'spirit-possession' when in fact there is no possession at all." Further, he would "not dream of using" his technique and service for dealing with cases which appear to be entirely due to emotional repression in adolescents, which appears to be true for many well-known instances of poltergeist phenomena. Such cases, he says, "clearly show that they are an emotional protest against authority, whether parental or sociological or economic or religious—some form of authority which has produced an intolerable internal tension for which the adolescent concerned can find no overt outlet but somehow unloads unconsciously by externalizing his or her repressed energies in causing external physical (poltergeist) disturbances. To conduct a service of exorcism or even a Requiem when no spirit entity is involved is worse than useless."

Pearce-Higgins adds: "The Church is probably still the highest form of authority. The poltergeist activity is a protest against authority, what Freud calls the 'Superego.' If the Church arrives with all its pomp and importance and a service is conducted, the result may be temporary abatement, but very soon the phenomena begin again because the adolescent has only been temporarily cowed into compliance. But the Church represents that very authority-in-society against which the poltergeist phenomena are a protest, therefore, far from releasing the tension, it increases it. While private prayer for a disturbed adolescent can do no harm, a public service does more harm than good. What is needed is love and wise counselling by some competent child psychiatrist. Such cases do not respond to a Requiem. But genuine psychic-spirit cases do. You cannot exorcize, or release a nonexistent ghost! Per contra, you cannot analyse away a real 'spirit.'"

The evidence and conclusions presented by Canon Pearce-Higgins must be judged against the background of his career and credentials. He was educated at Rugby School and Gonville

and Caius College, Cambridge, and was Winter Warr postgraduate research student in ancient philosophy at the University of
Vienna. Pearce-Higgins later attended Ripon Hall Theological
College, Oxford, and was ordained to the ministry in 1937.
During World War II, the young clergyman served as chaplain to
the British armed forces in North Africa and Italy, where he
suffered a leg injury. From 1945 to 1953, John Pearce-Higgins
was vicar at Hanley Castle, Worcester, and also became senior
divinity lecturer at the City of Worcester College of Education.
From 1953 to 1963, he served as vicar of Putney Parish, London,
and then began his ministry at Southwark Cathedral which he
continued until his retirement in 1971.

Canon Pearce-Higgins is married and the father of two sons
and three daughters. He is the joint author of *Life, Death and
Psychical Reseach* (1973). His many lectures have included two
tours of the United States, in 1968 and 1972, during which he
was asked to deal with several possession cases, including a severe
one in Ohio and another in New York State. His visits to the U.S.
were sponsored by the Spiritual Frontiers Fellowship. He has
made many radio broadcasts, both in Great Britain and the
U.S.A.

If, in this day and age, one has the good luck to come face to
face with an experienced exorcist—although he refuses to accept
the title—there are obviously a few questions one must ask.
When, in addition, this nonexorcist is a worldly, knowledgeable
man, with a life spent in parish work, theology, and the British
army and equipped with a puckish sense of humor, the questions
come thick and fast. Above all, how does someone who can speak
of "all the old Spiritualist guff" and loathes ouija boards, have a
firm belief in spirits?

Canon Pearce-Higgins simply feels that he has encountered
enough of them, and talked to them so often and at such length,
that he knows their existence as well or better than someone who
has made frequent visits to a foreign country whose language
happens to be his own. He says: "Over and over again, we are

called to go to a house whose occupants are being bothered by hauntings or possession. I have worked with several mediums, and it is striking how often I can take them to a place that they have never seen before, meet people who are strangers, and come up with a clairvoyant description or trance contact with a person who turns up to be a former resident of the place." Pearce-Higgins tells this particular story, an example of both types of mediumship:

"One of the first cases I was asked to help was in a vicarage in southeast London. The former vicar had died of cardiac asthma, rather suddenly at the end. The new young vicar and his wife had come to the house several days before their children in order to put things straight. They had immediately sensed an atmosphere of great depression. The children arrived and the oldest, a boy of about eleven, asked to have the vicar's bedroom, but after one night refused to sleep there. At times steps were heard going up and downstairs, nearly always ending at the study door, which had just been blocked up during alterations. The wife also felt herself being continually watched when in the kitchen, and the door would open mysteriously. But above all it was the atmosphere of depression and heaviness which irked them.

"Mrs. Twigg came with her husband one evening, and together with the vicar and his wife, we had a sitting, Very soon Mrs. Twigg began to describe a sad middle-aged man, a bachelor, a priest, whom the vicar easily recognized as his late predecessor. (I should say at this point that I had never known him, and that neither Mrs. Twigg nor I had ever been inside either the vicarage or the church.)

"She next reported him as saying, 'I lived here alone, I died alone, I am tied to this place by the sense of what I left undone.' We tried in vain to comfort him, saying we believed he had done faithful service here. Then he began to talk about changes in the vicarage, the blocked study door, his books all dispersed, the brown paint altered, etc. He also began to speak to the vicar about parish matters and especially two boys in the church youth club, mentioned by name, who had been in trouble with the police. Finally, we told him he must go on because he was frightening the children. 'Oh, but I did not mean to; I love children; I come back because of the children; children were the only people I could really communicate with when here.' Again we urged him to leave and to go on up into the light. 'But I do not know where to go,' he said plaintively. We continued to try and explain to him, and then he burst into tears, we were told. After a time the atmosphere seemed to lighten and presently he was reported as saying: 'Thank you for coming, you have set me free; now I can arise and go to my Father.' After some further conversation with the vicar about changes inside the church, and especially a memorial being made to himself, he bade the vicar and his wife farewell.

"Then he turned to the medium and said, 'Thank you for your help; had I known you when alive I would have said you were of the devil.' He has asked us to pray for him as he departed, and this I did. A few days later the vicar rang me and said all was well; all noises had ceased and the atmosphere had cleared.

"But a fortnight later he rang me urgently again. 'The house is clear but we now have disturbances in the choir vestry' (the church was about 250 yards away). On this occasion the bishop of Southwark was with us, and Mrs. Twigg was unable to come so I engaged a trance medium who pronounced the vicarage clear and walked over to the church with the bishop. What happened next was reported to me by the bishop as I was detailed to look after the wife, who was clearly very psychic and somewhat distressed. The medium went into the church, knelt down before the altar and then went into the choir vestry where he was entranced. The former vicar spoke to the bishop and in distress asked for forgiveness for his sins and errors, and the bishop gave him absolution. And that was the end of the trouble.

"Both mediums did well. Mrs. Twigg picked up the poor man's character, as well as details about the vicarage and church unknown to her. The trance contact enabled the poor man to be released. A lonely withdrawn bachelor, he had been too fond of boys, it seemed, and the sacrament of confession and absolution was what he most needed. This was an early case and only confirmed me in feeling that a medium was needed in such cases. It was only later that I learned the value of a service, and that such cases could be cleared without the presence of a medium."

Canon Pearce-Higgins sees his work and ideas as a bridge between biblical tradition and modern discoveries. "We read in the New Testament that Jesus was able to cast out evil spirits, and my own experiences and those of other clergymen are a continuation of this form of healing. Misguided spirits, then, have been and are a reality, so there is absolutely no need—to use a word that is a favorite with some theologians—to 'demythologize' the scriptural accounts we have. Some of the physical healings Jesus did may also have been cases of possession.

"We can choose from three alternatives: either, Jesus knew that possession was a fact and was able to deal with it; or, he knew it was not a fact but played up to his contemporaries' belief in possession (who then described his cures in their own language and thought form) ; or, Jesus believed that possession was a fact, but was wrong in thinking this, and his cures, if correctly recorded, were similar to those reported at Lourdes. Personally, I can only accept the first alternative as correct: Jesus knew what he was doing, what needed doing, and he did it."

Pearce-Higgins says that the strongest evidence for his methods and views is in the evidence of the immediate change in either the atmosphere of a house or the behavior of a person. A most recent and striking case may be cited as a final piece of evidence. Just before Christmas, 1973, a woman in tears telephoned. Her family life was being wrecked by appalling behavior on the part of her second daughter, Kay, aged eight. She had a sweet elder daughter, Betty, aged ten, and a son, James, aged four. All names have been changed.

Kay's almost diabolical behavior had started as soon as James was born. Pearce-Higgins thought this was a typical case of jealousy, but when he heard the account of the quite pathological viciousness inside the home directed not only at the small brother but also at the family in general (although Kay's behavior in school was exemplary) he sent them for diagnosis to his colleagues. Mrs. Broster diagnosed possession; she and her husband then dealt with the case, as they are well able to do, without his being present. They reported a successful "exorcism." Two days later the mother telephoned the canon in joy to say that Kay was completely back to normal. She rang a week later, and said, "Now I am in tears—tears of joy, not of despair as I had the first time."

The child had for three and a half years been under treatment by a psychiatrist and a psychoanalyst at the London children's clinic, and there had been absolutely no improvement; indeed, the analyst had turned her attention to the mother: when the child was next taken to the hospital, they were amazed at the change, and tried to claim the credit for their own treatment which had at last borne fruit. Pearce-Higgins say: "The mother knew better. I wrote, at the mother's request, a fairly full letter [to the therapist], outlining what we thought we had done—to which I received a curt three-line acknowledgement! This, I feel, was hardly science!"

On the basis of his experiences and study, Canon Pearce-Higgins hopes that medicine and, in particular, psychiatry will take a fresh look at symptoms pointing to possession, and that the various religious denominations also reexamine their attitude toward exorcism. He says: "Really, it is time the churches began to teach people something sensible about what happens after the death of the physical body, the reality of the spirit body of which St. Paul spoke, and of the continuance of consciousness. I believe that there are more haunted minds and haunted houses than we suspect, and it is surely partly to be laid at the Church's door that this is so, due to its own ignorance and its failure to teach the truth to others."

V. Conclusion: Know
Your Demon!

1. Know Your Demon!

Exorcism, to put it simply, is a special form of healing a human soul in distress. Setting, ritual details and human involvement may vary, but all essentials are identical. Labels don't really matter, except as categorical symbols. Are we dealing with a demon or a compulsion neurosis? Is the "possessed" man or woman suffering from diabolical intrusion, from hysteria, schizophrenia, unresolved aggressive impulses, manipulation by a "hungry ghost," an evil, unclean, or ignorant spirit? Words change their meanings with the times and places in which they are used, within the context of cultural environment. Psychology long ago abandoned "hysteria," along with "split personality," and there are so many forms and shadings of "schizophrenia" that this term, too, will doubtless be discarded before long.

Without adopting either total rigidity or total tolerance, we would be wise to approach our conclusions concerning possession and exorcism free of set ideas. That includes avoiding the clichés of various schools of psychology, from those riddled with clinical statistics to those which maintain that, in an allegedly mad society, madness is The New Sanity.

When viewed against the background of competing or contradictory concepts of man's psychophysical functions, the idea that our troubles are due to vicious invisible beings has all the seductive charm of simplicity. That's why it was so popular in earlier and in primitive societies. And we shouldn't be haughty about this approach, either. Nothing pleases us more, to this day, than to blame others—visible, for the most part—for our unhappinesses, failures, and frustration. If for nothing else, Freud became popular because we all have parents, and he gave us the alibi that our father, mother, or both, were the causes of our misfortunes. The stupid boss, the ignorant investment broker, the crooked politician, the lazy employee, the ungrateful child, the haphazard doctor, the spendthrift wife, the negligent lawyer, the blind umpire, the inattentive husband, the sloppy repairman, the officious traffic cop—they are all (not always undeserved) targets of our wrathful self-justification, or, of our "projections."

In the 1970s, the U.S. television comedian "Flip" Wilson popularized his female impersonation, called Geraldine, who forever got herself into trouble that prompted her to say, "The Devil made me do it!" It was clear to TV viewers that scheming Geraldine somehow got what she really wanted, and that her invocation of the devil was a delightful, transparent alibi. But, if nothing else, her gimicky excuse served to put any potential critic in a difficult position. (Purely by association with Wilson's stage name, we might mention that the possessing personality is often what we might call the "flip side," or opposite, contradictory side of the possessed person's personality. Colloquial language recognizes this when we say that somebody "has flipped.")

Possession, as well as the exorcism ritual, is a dramatic extension of common motives and situations. Every bureaucrat who ever learned the fine art of passing the buck, of leaving responsibility to others ("I only followed orders"), to the point where ultimate responsibility or neglect can simply not be fixed, knows the value of avoidance. The poor workman blames his tools, because to acknowledge lack of expertise or skill would degrade his self-respect as a craftsman.

Self-image is all-important. Our personal jungle of desires, hates, aggressions, and yearnings is so vast and dark that we find it difficult to acknowledge its existence. This is hardly a new concept, and, at best, religious confession has served long and well as a mini-exorcism. And yet, for a nun to acknowledge sexual yearnings, for example, to the very confessor for whom she

feels them, could hardly be acceptable as anything but a diaboli-
cally induced thought. Even a small child will feel demeaned if
he is forced, once too often, to say, "I'm sorry," or to beg forgiveness for some trespass. And, certainly, marriages are poisoned at
their roots when man and wife continually blame each other—
become each other's demon—for whatever domestic disaster has
occurred.

While it is easy to blame invisible entities for illness or other
misfortune, it is certainly awkward when daily life becomes a
round of defensive rituals. Again, we are dealing with degrees of
involvement: if you check the door at night, try the handle to see
if it's locked, you are being prudent; if you go around the house
three or four times, checking every door and window and then
sleep uneasily because you may have missed one, then compulsion has got the better of you. Exorcism, in our time, has its
secular equivalent in the various forms of psychotherapy. In
essence, all are designed to bring out the "demon" within the
patient, to have him state his name, burst fully into the fore-
ground, and then be talked into leaving by various stages of
withdrawal. The "talking cure," one label for modern psychotherapy, has its direct antecedent in the violent dialogue between
exorcist and demon. A good deal of the value in modern medicine, at least to the patient, lies precisely in the labeling of illness
and therapeutic methods. A thing without a name, invisible and
unformed, is doubly fearsome. The woman who says, "I don't
know what ails me," is looking for a firm reply, or at least for the
convincing illusion of identification, such as, "This is a slight,
but quite manageable case of hyperglycemia . . ."

Know your demon! It is the first step toward getting rid of it.
In modern society, with its elusive responsibilities, gargantuan
multinational corporations and self-perpetuating bureaucracies,
even "Leviathan" would be an insufficient demonic label. And so
we have vague monsters, such as The Establishment, the Military-
Industrial Complex or Neocolonialism (as well as labels on the
reverse side of the political-economic coin) to take the place of

the likes of Beelzebub. Modern China no longer speaks of the outside world as "foreign devils," but as influenced by "Revisionists" (Soviet Union) and "Imperialists" (U.S.A.). It is demonology in nineteenth-century dress, but not quite out of fashion in the twentieth century.

We are lacking demonic personalities in contemporary history, however, just as the generation of great statesmen died with Winston Churchill and Charles De Gaulle. World War II created no antiwar movements to speak of, because Adolf Hitler was so clearly a man-demon intent on enslaving the world. By contrast, North Vietnam never furnished a demonic image: Ho Chi Minh projected the benign picture of the oriental sage, and his successors were a faceless group of interchangeable political and military leaders. When Joseph Stalin died, ending his career in several years of irrational slashing-out in all directions, the affairs of the world were in psychological disarray: The Red Devil had left the Kremlin, and yesterday's clear-cut lines of demarcation and antagonisms were no longer valid.

The world has become de-demonized in the traditional sense. Its Nouveau Demons are such entities as Drug Traffic, Energy Crisis, Overpopulation, Crime in the Streets, and Pollution. Malefactors of Great Wealth, as Theodore Roosevelt called them, have faded, and their place has been taken by corporations with such initials as IT&T. The most impressive villains, even in gangsterdom, are now to be found in fiction rather than in real life, where their demonic stature has been blurred. Hollywood, which created such stars as "The Man You Love to Hate," is no longer a den of sin, and its villains lack dramatic individuality.

Reluctantly, we discover that the age of giants in good and evil, is no more. And yet, our insight into the demonic within ourselves remains unsure. Our Greco-Roman terms, such as psychosomatic, are more fashionable than precise; much of the verbiage in academic journals might as well be the language of alchemists. As for the theologicans, they are retreating in disarray, tripping over each other's cassocks, or mixing with a secular crowd in all-too-modern dress. The churches have rediscovered the ministry of healing, which is indeed their legitimate concern; but pastoral psychology, an excellent concept, is always in danger of being crowded out by heavy parish schedules, financial crises, and angry disputes over tradition versus reform. Exorcism, in its contemporary sense, is a form of pastoral healing, because it places the bewildered, problem-possessed parishioner within a religious setting that he or she may have known since childhood, finds reassurance in smell, touch, and sound (provided the new church building, the pastor, the liturgy, or various committee chairmen do not alienate him). The dialogue between parishioner and clergyman follows the age-old pattern of that between possessed and exorcist, complete with established values and a ritual setting. To be successful, it requires maximum faith and understanding on both sides.

Maximum understanding demands that we be aware how minimal our knowledge is. The symptoms described by traditional exorcists often parallel those seen today. But just what symptoms are induced or spontaneous, just how preconditioning or environment plays its part, or what the actual give-and-take in the healing process achieves—that we do not know. There are, of course, various stages in any disease, physical or emotional: ascent to a plateau and, if treatment is successful, return to full health. We do not know how many patients recover entirely by themselves, without any therapy. It is quite clear, however, that an overeager exorcist can provoke symptoms and create a crescendo of suffering which is the very opposite of well-being and tranquillity; just as the overindulged patient may become hospital-prone or overdependent on his therapist. Quickly prescribed tranquilizers and antibiotics may have no more and no less effect than a placebo; they both inspire the patient's belief that something definite is being done to help him.

The lessons to be learned from exorcism lie mainly in the relationship between patient and physician. In our day, when computerized diagnosis and treatment instructions are just around the corner, the doctor-patient relationship—by whatever name—is becoming crucial. Bureaucratized medicine and the imbalanced ratio between doctors and patients tend to make their contacts increasingly impersonal. What psychoanalysis calls transference and countertransference, the intimate roles played by analyst and analysand in the psychotherapeutic setting, are delicate, fluctuating relationships for which we have a terminology, but of which we know next to nothing.

Dr. Henri Ellenberger cites several views that compare the exorcist with the psychotherapist who, in order to be effective, is not merely "analyzing his own countertransference," but is concerned with "working on his own personality" and "developing in himself a genuine wish to help the patient." Quoting Alphonse Maeder, he writes: "In that active procedure, the patient first calls for help (this is the 'appeal process') ; the therapist responds with his will and readiness to help and then calls for the self-healing tendencies within the patient. The latter answers by projecting upon the therapist the 'archetype of the Saviour,' with gradual activation of his self-healing tendencies, although the therapist must sometimes induce this reaction with special techniques." The possession victim demands the attention of the exorcist-therapist, if need be with increasingly violent symptoms and language; the exorcism is successful when the exorcist becomes fully engaged in the ritual and dialogue.

In realistic contemporary terms, the time-consuming and energy-demanding procedure of exorcism is quite impossible today. Who has the time to spend days, weeks, or months with a single patient, put everything else aside, and devote himself exclusively and with exhausting emotional involvement to just one case? In terms of man-hours alone, the prospect is forbidding. Depending on the possessed patient's social position, treatment may range from frequent fifty-minute sessions to wholesale tranquilizer disbursement in a state mental institution. Spirit or no spirit, few clergymen have the time to spend on dealing with haunted minds and haunted houses as does Canon Pearce-Higgins in England.

We can see from possession and exorcism that much symptom-
ology is a cry for attention; call it a ritualized tantrum, if you
like—at any rate, the patient calls attention to himself for a
variety of social, emotional, or even economic reasons. He, or
more frequently she, dramatizes a cry for help, including more or
less sublimated demands for sexual attention. And the exorcist
probably appoints himself to the "savior" role for complex
emotional reasons of his own. Traditional exorcists often said
bluntly that they were following in Jesus' footsteps; today's
doctors are accused of "playing God" to the point where such
new stereotypes appear in television comedies. This gets us into
the intriguing question of just why, exactly, men choose to
become doctors and priests in the first place; no doubt, detailed
inquiry would find a great variety of reasons ranging from the
totally idealistic to the easy safety and superiority provided by a
respected and well-defined position in society. The exorcist-type
of medical man, whether engaged in the treatment of physiological or psychological symptoms, must (a) believe in his own
calling fully, (b) be convinced that his manner of treatment is
correct, indeed the only proper means of treatment, (c) throw
himself wholeheartedly into the healing process, battling the
visible or invisible foe which is the illness, and (d) proceed
regardless of his possibly ambivalent feelings about the patient,
driven only by his passionate desire to effect a cure, to oust the
illness.

In purely economic terms, only a millionaire's full-time attending psychiatrist could undertake such neo-exorcism today. And
yet, it is well to remember that saturation treatment is one thing
we learn from exorcism. Saturation treatment might be one
shortcut to cure we have neglected, ever since enlightenment
pushed the exorcist's craft into the background. No doubt, a
modern ritualistic setting might create a pattern to facilitate
treatment. Group Therapy, Encounter Therapy, Biofeedback,
Meditation—the whole panorama of experimentation that has
attracted Humanistic Psychology—offer new scenes and rites.
These have invited the attention of some religious leaders.

Indeed, the name of Jesus has of late been associated with numerous raucous quasi-religious and quasi-psychological movements that profess to heal the ills of our society, *en gros* and *en detail.*

In the ferment of our time, how can something as esoteric as exorcism provide us with useful insight? Isn't it all a little bit too primitive, too encumbered with religious and other superstitions to be of use in our jet-propelled, computer-ridden civilization?

But anything that can teach us about the relation of people to people, and of people to themselves, has meaning today. We are fascinated with the mysterious past, with gods from outer space, Lost Continents, Magical Powers of the Ancients—what, then, are we looking for? We are searching, within the limits of our present attitudes, for a rational explanation of the irrational. That is, of course, the purest kind of contradiction in terms, and irrational in itself. Still, it is part of our continuing effort to solve the riddle that is ourselves.

One self-experiment in possession was undertaken, early in the century, by a German professor who combined the more or less irrational (philosophy and theology) with the more or less rational (biology and chemistry). This man of dual interests, Dr. Ludwig Staudenmaier, professor of experimental chemistry at the Royal Lyceum at Freising, described his personal experiences in *Magie als experimentelle Naturwissenschaft (Magic as an Experiment in Natural Science,* 1912/1968). The Staudenmaier experiment, which got him much deeper into the irrational than he had planned, provides unique details of possession from the inside; he remained self-aware while his personality was controlled by a succession of entities.

Staudenmaier told his readers that he had "undergone two quite different types of education, partly at war with each other, one oriented toward medieval thinking, the other totally modern." He saw himself as a "crude" natural scientist who preferred natural explanations wherever the border between "the natural and the supernatural, between pathological and real devils, between magical arts and miracle" was somewhat blurred.

At the age of thirty-six, Professor Staudenmaier was asked by a friend to study phosphorescent images he had seen at mediumistic séances. Perhaps, the man said, he could find physical or chemical explanations for them. Staudenmaier answered that, as far as he knew, "all Spiritualism is based on fraud." But his acquaintance had been so impressed by what he saw that he was eager to know what a hard-nosed experimental scientist could make of it all. He told the skeptical professor that some spiritualists were using "automatic writing" to develop mediumistic powers, but Staudenmaier's first attempts were unsuccessful and the whole thing seemed a waste of time. Then everything changed:

"A few days later I experienced a strange pull in my fingertips. They seemed to want to push the pencil from left to right, on an upward slant. This pressure increased. I tried to hold the pencil as lightly as possible and to support the writing tendency with my own thoughts. Within two weeks, the process became quite easy."

Staudenmaier was then reading books on spiritualism, and in one of them he encountered the name "Julie Norne." Promptly, one evening, the pencil spelled, "Julie Norne is here." In his thoughts, the experimenter asked whether a spirit was present, received an affirmative reply, and characteristically gave the entity a test in chemistry "to assess her intelligence level." While his hand was writing one letter, the next one came clearly to mind, but he had difficulty guessing the next word.

Quite soon, the experiment expanded out of control. Numerous spirits announced their presence, "including inferior, and even morally defective and malignant entities." Staudenmaier not only knew in advance what would be written, but now began to hear words ahead of time. His hand simply scribbled rapidly, while he heard the voices with increasing clarity. Soon, he threw the pencil aside, simply listened to the words as they were spoken and began to answer with his thoughts.

Shortly afterwards, the experimenter not only heard but saw entities: "For several days I was being visited by a pretty young lady who made a considerable impression on me. But this feeling faded when she quickly disappeared. A few days later I was lying in bed at night, my body turned to the left, all the while speaking with one of the interior voices. When I turned to the right, I discovered to my surprise that the young lady's head emerged from the bed as if she were lying next to me. It was magically transfigured, of delightful beauty and ethereally transparent in the near-dark room; only a distant street lamp threw a soft light."

Briefly, Staudenmaier was totally dazzled by this miraculous appearance, but quickly realized that it must be some sort of delusion. At the same time, he heard a crude, deep voice whispering to him in a taunting manner. Annoyed, he turned back to his left. When a friendly interior voice said later, "The young lady is gone," he turned to the right, saw that nothing remained, and fell asleep. Professor Staudenmaier's experience is virtually identical to an incident reported by C. G. Jung: in 1920, he was visiting English friends at their country home, and during the night half of a woman's head, with one eye wide open, "materialized" on the pillow next to him—it disappeared quickly, but Jung spent the rest of the night sitting in an armchair. Staudenmaier's experiment turned malignant:

"Antagonistic phenomena took various forms. At times, pandemonium reigned. For long periods of time, I saw devilishly grimacing faces with total clarity and sharpness. Once, lying in bed, I had the distinct feeling that someone was tying a chain around my neck. Immediately afterwards, I smelled the particularly repelling odor of sulfuric acid and a threatening voice said, 'Now you are my prisoner. I won't let you go. I am the devil.'"

Staudenmaier comments: "There could be no doubt: in naïve-medieval terms, I was possessed. I had to face these uncomfortable alternatives: I am either on the trail of basic discoveries which might enable me to illuminate the puzzle of human existence from a totally new viewpoint, or I am a fool, who is about to sacrifice years of his existence, health, and possibly life itself, to irresponsible stubbornness."

Throughout this difficult period, while in almost constant and frightening dialogue with devils and other entities, Staudenmaier managed to retain control over his external life. Occasionally he would act on information given him by possessing entities, but he tried to check on it before taking action. Once, he asked his demon the identity of a tenant who had moved into a house across the street. He was told that the man was one Captain von Müller. This turned out to be wrong. Staudenmaier "gently" reproached his personal demon for having led him astray. He received a "sincere reply" which revealed the vicissitudes of low-level entities: "We just can't act differently. We are forced to tell lies. After all, we are evil spirits, and so you mustn't hold it against us!"

Clues to the dynamics of apparently possessing personalities, their role in expressing Staudenmaier's own character facets, emerged clearly. At one point, possessed by Napoleon, he walked "with a feeling of loftiness, and my attitude became one at once energetic and military." When less forceful character aspects came to the fore, he "became more relaxed." But soon still other "personalities of high rank" took over, and an idea of personal "grandeur and nobility gradually developed."

One of Staudenmaier's possessing spirits, whom he called "My Highness," was impatient with his modest way of living. He bullied and threatened him to attend military parades, lead a more fashionable life, furnish his home elegantly, perfect an upright military bearing and take a greater interest in physical exercise, hunting, and other sports. "My Highness," he wrote, "dislikes children, all common things, joking and gaiety. He particularly detests illustrated magazines, satirical cartoons, teetotalers, and such; moreover, I am somewhat too short for his taste."

Something "in" Staudenmaier, no doubt, resented that he wasn't taller, more elegant or distinguished—but something else was charmingly infantile. This surfaced when "The Child" took control of the professor, displaying "wonderfully tender and innocent ways, such as no real child could show in such an open and touching manner." The child entity called Professor Staudenmaier "putzi," or just "My dear Zi." He had to go along with its demands and stop in front of toy-shop windows, buy himself toys, even join children in dancing in a circle, behaving with a total absence of "loftiness," in contrast to the "My Highness" personality. Staudenmaier felt that these traits, surfacing in the form of strongly dramatized and controlling entities, enriched his life:

"Since The Child personification gained great influence over me, not only has my interest in childish ways, toys and even shops increased, but so has my search for childish satisfactions and innocent joys of the heart. This has influenced my body, rejuvenating and refreshing it, and driving away many of the cares of the grown man, who becomes more and more accustomed to the use of his intelligence."

Just what might have happened, had his colleagues observed him buying himself toys and dancing in playgrounds, Staudenmaier does not say; but he appears to have remained circumspect in acting out his impulses—or obeying his possessing entities—outside his own home. He felt that a number of other personalities had a "beneficial influence" on him. He developed an interest in the arts, notably those of antiquity and the Middle Ages, because some of "my personalities are passionately interested in them and continually impel me to devote attention to them."

Like other possessed, and like some mediums in trance, Staudenmaier discovered that his facial expressions reflected those of his entities, from the stern visage of "My Highness" to the bland sweetness of "The Child." Staudenmaier wrote that his face "often showed a character of its own, so that I no longer displayed my known, habitual features, a fact which did not escape persons who knew me well."

Oesterreich, using Staudenmaier's experience to explain possession cases generally, comments that they reveal "a very remarkable inter-relationship between the possessed and the personality imposing itself upon him." He also finds: "It is not merely impulses and inhibitions which traverse the normal life of the individual and may, as in the cause of Staudenmaier, disturb it so little that those around him have no knowledge of them, because the possessed retains a sane judgment of his state and is not, therefore, deranged in the strict sense; but phenomena of obsession can take forms which at first sight disconcert the modern psychologist and oblige him to reexamine his views to gain new insights into psychological processes."

Oesterreich urges that modern psychology examine the relatively rare, or at least rarely reported, cases of possession for elusive evidence concerning the human psyche. Step by step, like a growth in nature, the possessed, "filled with the idea that a strange spirit has entered into him, behaves towards his abnormal state in a manner consistent with this belief. Like Staudenmaier he addresses the demon in his soul, talks to him, petitions him" and generally "treats him as an ordinary living person" who then "gives replies, makes promises, feels repentance, just like a real person."

"In possession," Oesterreich observes, "everything is accentuated. It is not in imagination that the possessed hears someone answer him, his own organs of speech enter into movement which is not voluntary, but automatic and compulsive. Thus there occurs the singular spectacle of two persons appearing to express themselves through the same body." This process spills over into the exorcism setting, where "the possessing spirit talks with the exorcist, grows angry with him, insults him, attacks him, replies to questions—in short behaves as if a demon had entered into the body of the possessed."

The Staudenmaier case, which ended with the professor regaining control of his body and mind through a form of step-by-step self-exorcism, illuminates the anteroom to more violent types of possession. It is unique in that it provides autobiographical insight into states of mind that led the man to tell himself that, in a certain sense, he was indeed "possessed." Experimenting with automatic writing—a ouija board might have brought the same results—and reading spiritistic literature created a structure of expectation, and Staudenmaier's mind lived up to these expectations.

The Umbanda possession in Brazil also creates such a structure. With personal variants that express individual needs and desires, the possession experience fulfills these expectations. Everywhere, the possessed person and her devils, demons, and spirits conform to what is expected of them. For good or bad, they practice Dr. Ehrenwald's "doctrinal compliance," bringing forth the proper kind of entity to conform to the expectations of their audience, their exorcists or the families they seek to influence.

I have referred to Ehrenwald's ideas several times in this book, because they are relevant to possession and exorcism in a uniquely modern and imaginative way. It is his view that a patient may not only bring out, or create, the kind of material his psychotherapist expects or desires, simply by guessing what is expected of him, but that the patient may actually obtain this insight by "telepathic leakage" from the therapist's own mind. Ehrenwald feels that a therapist, even though his avowed purpose be only to cure a patient, "may at the same time have an altogether different motive at the back of his mind, namely, to prove the validity of his own pet theories of psychotherapy." He adds that to prove one's theories to be right can be as valid and strong a motive as the desire to cure, but under such circumstances the patient may "oblige" and "by some act of psychologic legerdemain, telepathic or otherwise, conjure up the expected evidence."

Writing in the *American Journal of Psychotherapy* (April 1957), Dr. Ehrenwald refers to the exorcisms at the Ursuline convent at Loudun, and especially to the experiences of Father Surin. He also recalls that at the time of the Loudun trial Cardinal Richelieu was the most powerful personage in France. One exorcist, Laubardemont, asked one of the demoniacs, "What

do you say about the great Cardinal, the Protector of France?"
The devil, speaking through the demoniac, promptly answered,
"He is the scourge of all my friends." Asked who his friends were,
the devil replied, "The heretics." This kind of thing, Ehrenwald
says, "was exactly what the exorcist wanted to hear—and the
hysterical nun, subjected to many weeks of harrowing interrogation, obliged. It is impossible to decide whether or not a telepathic element was involved in her performance." Dr. Ehrenwald
says that it isn't permissible "to describe the procedures of the
inquisitioners in terms of anything like modern psychotherapy,"
and adds:

"But there are three ingredients of the therapeutic situation
which can be recognized in the medieval setting: The patient's
profound emotional disturbance, reminiscent of hysteria in our
sense; a 'healer' seeking to effect her 'cure' by psychological
means; and a 'transference relationship' between the two, however warped and distorted this may have been. The result was
unmistakable: the grafting of a new iatrogenic neurosis upon the
existing mental disorder. As it happened, the new syndrome
seemed to be just what the doctor ordered: it amounted to a
perfect corroboration of the exorcist's expectations. It met the
needs of his own selfish and frankly sadistic countertransference."

The physical abuse of possessed people has at all times had this
rationalization: by making the human body, inhabited by devil
or demon, uncomfortable, the entity would be forced to leave it;
Dr. Wickland's electric shocks are an illustration of this point.
But we have a psychological novelty, here and now, that con-
forms to this pattern: aversion therapy. Simply put, this therapy
is designed to condition a patient away from personality problems ranging as widely as cigarette smoking, obesity, alcoholism
and homosexuality. For example, an alcoholic may receive a
painful electric charge whenever he reaches for a whisky bottle,
or a homosexual may be conditioned to feel repugnance at the
sight of a male body. Shocks are only one means of aversion
therapy; nausea-causing drugs and suggestions of fear and anx-

iety are also employed. Within a cultural framework that accepts demon possession, all these forms of treatment might easily be seen as exorcism techniques.

If the reader, at any point, has felt that the author of this book is stopping short of any particular conclusion, some definite or definitive appraisal of the exorcism enigma, he is quite right. Any bridge between traditional exorcism concepts and modern thought would have to be built like a zigzagging roller coaster, carpeted with a crazy quilt. Still, daring architects can be found, and one of them is Dr. Wilson Van Dusen, associate professor of psychology, J. F. Kennedy University, Martinez, California. In his booklet, *The Presence of Spirits in Madness,* published by the Swedenborg Foundation (New York, 1972), Van Dusen states that "by an extraordinary series of circumstances a confirmation appears to have been found for one of Emanuel Swedenborg's more unusual doctrines—that man's life depends on his relationship to a hierarchy of spirits." Swedenborg (1688–1772), a man of many gifts, wrote extensively about his encounters with the spirit world and had a profound influence on leading writers and artists of the nineteenth century. Dr. Van Dusen found that his patients' experiences were strikingly similar to Swedenborg's descriptions of the spirit world.

As chief psychologist at Mendocino State Hospital in Talmage, California, Van Dusen examined a great number of patients who thought they were in contact with spiritlike entities. He overcame their reluctance, and in many cases was able to address these entities directly and to elicit the patients' own candid opinions of them. Dr. Van Dusen found that about one-fifth of these entities were of a "high order" and the rest of a "low order," corresponding to a hierarchy of spirits as Swedenborg had described it. His patients resisted the concept of "hallucinations"—these entities, whether angelic, demonic, or whatever, were real to them. According to Van Dusen, "all of the lower order are irreligious or anti-religious." Most of the patients regarded these entities as ordinary people, until "they appeared as conventional devils and referred to themselves as demons." Attempts at partial possession seemed relatively frequent: a spirit would try to control a part of a person's anatomy. Van Dusen, aware of potential doctor-to-patient suggestion, writes that he encountered a relatively narrow pattern in these manifestations and says, "Some people might suspect that my manner of questioning fed back to the patients what I wanted to hear, but after I addressed on hallucinations an audience including patients, many warmly commended me for capturing their own experience too." He found "many impressive similarities between the patients' experiences of lower-order hallucinations and Swedenborg's obsession and possession by evil spirits."

Was Swedenborg "simply mad," and is that why his own experiences parallel those of some mental patients? Van Dusen answers this question by referring to Swedenborg's active and constructive life, quite different from that of patients who become so enmeshed with hallucinations that they are unable to function in society. Dr. Van Dusen wonders whether such "spirits" are merely "pieces of the unconscious or is the unconscious simply a reflection of this interaction with spirits? That is, which is the more substantive reality—the unconscious or the world of spirits?" Van Dusen thinks "the two are the same," and that Swedenborg may have been right when he saw our own existence as "the little free space" between "giant higher and lower spiritual hierarchies." Van Dusen views patients as traversing this region "by an alienation from the sources of their own thoughts and feelings, so they experience underpinnings of their mind as alien forces."

One epidemic that would surely have been classified as mass possession and in need of exorcism, in earlier times, occurred in the Alabama town of Berry in 1973. The local elementary school was hit by an epidemic of scratching, fainting, vomiting, crying, and screaming for about one week that affected about one-third of its 400 students. On May 11, ambulances took more than 70 children to the county hospital in nearby Fayette. Of these,

20 were unconscious, and, as the *Wall Street Journal* reported (November 16, 1973), "frantic parents arrived to take home their children, some of whom had scratched themselves bloody, convinced along with school and local authorities that some disease or toxic substance or perhaps a swarm of biting insects was to blame." If this had been sixteenth-century South Germany, for example, some inoffensive but possibly repulsive local crone might have been accused of witchcraft, tortured, brought to confession, and even burned at the stake.

The parallels with possession cases, such as those occurring among teen-age nuns, are striking. As analyzed by Dr. Richard J. Levine of the U.S. Public Health Service, the mass illness began when a fifth-grade girl scratched a long-standing skin rash so vigorously that the teacher asked her to sit in the hall. During the 10:30 class break, her classmates joined her, commiserated with her, and began scratching themselves. The epidemic spread from class to class, with pupils imitating each other's behavior. By 1:00 P.M., students complained of burning eyes and throats, numbness, and chest pains. The principal rang the fire alarm and the building was evacuated. After the epidemic subsided, it was found that no toxic substance was involved, and Dr. Levine ascribed the symptoms to "hyperventilation," or overbreathing. Psychologists from the University of Alabama found that the more prominent victims were more sensitive and more demanding than others, as well as "attention-seekers."

The lush variety of possessions is governed by differences in historical period, geography, religiocultural patterns, social structure, and personal interrelations between possessed, society, and exorcist. Self-assertion, self-flagellation, dominance, victimization, fraud, or total surrender to the phenomena are among the often contradictory elements that have been recorded. Indeed, possession cannot really be definitively outlined; it spills over into noisy poltergeist phenomena, contains elements of multiple personality, of mediumistic and hypnotic trances, of individual and mass suggestion, and other psychological, parapsychological, and religious categories.

Two recent studies, indirectly related to possession, illustrate the "border traffic" between several of these areas. The first, *The Search for a Soul*, by Jess Stearn (1973), is based on a series of hypnotic sessions undergone by the novelist Taylor Caldwell. They appear to show that Miss Caldwell, whose historical novels enjoy great popularity, remembered numerous dramatic earlier incarnations. Under hypnosis, the novelist "recalled" that she had been an Irish scullery maid in the household of the Victorian novelist George Eliot; falsely accused of stealing, she was sent to the workhouse, where she hanged herself. In the fifteenth century, she was a nun and a follower of Savonarola, burned at the stake as a heretic; she was imprisoned in a bell tower. Five centuries before Christ, she was a woman surgeon in Athens. She was also the mother of Mary Magdalen, saw her daughter stoned to death, but was herself saved by Jesus.

Naturally, it has occurred to Taylor and Stearn that these previous incarnations might be creations of her fertile novelist's imagination. But some patterns of these personalities are related to Miss Caldwell's own. Do her chronic neck pains go back to the day she hung herself, in a previous incarnation? Is her impaired hearing due to the incessant clanging of bells, while imprisoned in a clock tower? At least two medium-psychiatrist teams have published cases of severe neurotic symptoms which were apparently cured when identified as the results of traumatic events in previous incarnations. The parallel to the psychodynamics of exorcism are, here, very close, just as clinical cases of multiple personality might have been diagnosed as diabolic possession in previous centuries.

The second book in an adjacent field does, in fact, deal with a complex case of multiple personality. It is *Sybil* (1973) by Flora Rheta Schreiber, and it deals with the case of Sybil Dorset, a pseudonym for a patient of the psychoanalyst Cornelia Wilbur. At the age of three, apparently to shut herself off from her sadistic, emotionally ill mother, Sybil began to go into amnesia states during which she was somebody else; in other words, total escape into a different being. In all, seventeen personalities, each complete with attitude, mannerisms, and speech peculiarities, took turns in "possessing" Sybil. Dr. Wilbur's exorcism took the form of eleven years of psychoanalysis, supplemented by treatment with sodium pentothal and hypnosis.

The wish to be somebody else, or at least to shut out another presence, was also cited by Eileen J. Garrett (See Sec. IV, Ch. 1, "Ghost Against Ghost") as the initial stage of her mediumship. Constantly upbraided by the aunt who brought her up, Mrs. Garrett as a child developed the capacity of shutting off the aunt's voice, much as one turns off the sound on a TV set; she could see her lips move but did not hear the words she was saying. From then on, she developed invisible playmates, trance states akin to amnesia, and eventually mediumship. Dr. Nandor Fodor, psychic researcher and New York psychoanalyst, treated several patients who reported disturbing evidence that might have indicated some form of "possession" by discarnate entities and intermittent trance states; he helped these patients to channel what might otherwise be socially unacceptable symptoms or capacities into mediumship and thus establish personally satisfactory outlets and social identities.

The concepts of possession and exorcism, as we have noted, do not merely overlap into other psychic phenomena but can be applied to a wide panorama of sociopolitical factors. Aldous Huxley, who anticipated much of the interest in mind expansion and altered states of consciousness, wrote in *The Devils of Loudun* that "an urge to self-transcendence is almost as widespread and, at times, quite as powerful as the urge to self-assertion. Men desire to intensify their consciousness of being what they have come to regard as 'themselves,' but they also desire—and desire, very often, with irresistible violence—the consciousness of being someone else. In a word, they long to get out of themselves, to pass beyond the limits of that tiny island universe, within which every individual finds himself confined."

Huxley touches on the "disgusting vice of herd-intoxication—of downward self-transcendence into subhumanity by the process of getting together in a mob." In fact, if Satan be real, a good case can be made that he hasn't really bothered possessing individuals for some time, finding a more effective and receptive vessel in mass man, whether in the lynch mob, the military or civilian crowd set upon massacre, the rioters, the self-degraders who—by means of word, drug, or drum—turn into a thousand-footed superanimal. They may be soldiers who mass-murder minorities or enemy civilians, ironically call themselves Hell's Angels, or executors of this or that revolution and counterrevolution. Huxley notes that "being one with a multitude delivers a man from his consciousness of being an insulated self and carries him down into a less than personal realm, where there are no responsibilities, no right or wrong, no need for thought or judgment or discrimination."

That, precisely, is the pleasure of being possessed: not to be responsible for one's own action, only to be "following orders," presumably defined and irresistibly executed by an all-powerful diabolical force. The Satanic Mob has been with us since recorded time, often enough in the name of Christ (in the Crusades, the Thirty Years' War, down to the Catholic-Protestant fratricide of Northern Ireland). Often, the leader of a mob has the diabolical charisma of a Hitler, practicing the oratorical seductiveness of one possessed by an overwhelming idea.

To be possessed by an idea, to be the single-minded True Believer, is perhaps the most prevalent from of "possession" in our day. It is also the form culturally most easily accepted, even desired, and highly valued. Militancy, single-mindedness, exercise of the driving force that comes with a politico-ideological concept of aggressive simplicity, can unleash the halfhearted and confused from the need to make a carefully balanced decision. To be possessed by an idea means to assert that "those who are not with me are against me," and to wage social warfare with the certainty of an *idée fixe*. As Huxley saw it, "the crowd-delirium can be indulged in, not merely without a bad conscience, but actually, in many cases, with a positive glow of conscious virtue."

The outlines of human personality, of individual identity, are much less finite than we would like to believe. Possession and exorcism provide us with a dramatic glimpse into the area where individuals act upon each other, singly and in groups. The urge to be noted, to win approval or at least attention, brings out submerged facets of personality. Chameleonlike, now this and now that personality hue comes to the surface in a desire to conform, to be accepted, to shock, to escape one's own identity, or to become someone else. It is going on all around us, beginning with the relatively innocent "games people play" and including the self-denial or self-destruction that dramatize a nagging restlessness with everyday existence.

To be aware of submerged personality facets, to "Know Your Demon," must be part of everyone's self-understanding. Socrates maintained that an invisible demon used to whisper to him, advising against rash action. He knew his demon and accepted his advice, even when it amounted to the silent acceptance of treason charges and a death sentence of drinking poison hemlock. Perhaps the demon, in this instance, was no more than the ancient Greek philosopher's own desire for dramatic martyrdom. Socrates may have known his demon, known that it was his other self. If so, like most of us, he had the demon he truly desired.

Selected Bibliography

ARCHER, ETHEL. "A Note on Exorcisms." London: *The Occult Review,* May 1928.

BALDUCCI, CORRADO. *Gli indemoniati.* Rome, 1959.

BALDUCCI, CORRADO. "Parapsychology and Diabolic Possession." *International Journal of Parapsychology* 8, no. 2 (1966).

BLATTY, WILLIAM PETER. *The Exorcist.* New York: Harper & Row, 1971.

BLUMHARDT, JOHANN C. *Krankheitsgeschichte der G.D.* [Gottliebin Dittus] *in Möttlingen.* Full text in Mandel, Theodor H., *Der Sieg von Möttlingen im Lichte des Glaubens und der Wissenschaft.* Leipzig, 1886.

BOECHER, OTTO. *Dämonenfurcht und Dämonenabwehr.* Stuttgart: Verlag W. Kohlhammer, 1970.

CHARLES, LUCILLE H. "Drama in Shaman Exorcism." *Journal of American Folklore* 66, no. 260 (1953).

DELATTE, LOUIS. "Un office Byzantin d'exorcisme." Brussels: Académie Royale de Belgique, *Mémoires,* collection in–8⁰, 2ᵉ série, 1957.

DE JESUS-MARIE, BRUNO, ed. *Satan.* New York: Sheed and Ward, 1952.

DES ANGES, JEANNE. *Soeur Jeanne des Anges, supérieure des Ursulines de Loudun.* Paris, 1886.

DIECKHÖFER, KLEMENS. "Zum Problem der Besessenheit." Basle: *Confinia Psychiatrica,* no. 14 (1971).

DODDS, E. R. "Supernormal Phenomena in Classical Antiquity." London: *Proceedings of the Society for Psychical Research* 55, part 203 (1971).

EBON, MARTIN. *They Knew the Unknown.* New York: World Publishing Company, 1971.

ELIADE, MIRCEA. *Shamanism.* New York: Pantheon Books, 1963.

ELLENBERGER, HENRI F. *The Discovery of the Unconscious.* New York: Basic Books, 1970.

243

ERICKSON, MILTON H., and KUBIE, LAWRENCE S. "The Permanent Relief of an Obsessional Phobia by Means of Communications with an Unsuspected Dual Personality." *The Psychoanalytic Quarterly* 8, no. 4 (1939).

EYNATTEN, MAXIMILIANUS. *Manuale Exorcismorum*. Antwerp, 1626.

FREI, GEBHARD. "Probleme der Parapsychologie." Munich: *Imago Mundi* 2 (1971). Paderborn: Verlag Ferdinand Schöningh.

FREUD, SIGMUND. *Totem and Taboo*. New York: Random House (Vintage Books). Undated.

HORTON, WALTER M. "The Origin and Psychological Function of Religion According to Pierre Janet." *The American Journal of Psychology*, 35 no. 1 (1924).

HUXLEY, ALDOUS. *The Devils of Loudun*. New York: Harper & Row, 1952.

JANET, PIERRE. "Un cas de possession et d'exorcisme moderne." Paris: *Névroses et idées fixes* 1 (1898).

KELLY, HENRY ANSGAR. *The Devil, Demonology and Witchcraft*. New York: Doubleday, 1968.

KERNER, JUSTINUS. *Geschichten Besessener neuerer Zeit*. Stuttgart, 1834.

LaBARRE, WESTON. *The Ghost Dance*. Garden City, N.Y.: Doubleday, 1970.

LEWIS, I. M. *Ecstatic Religion: An Anthropological Study of Spirit Possession and Shamanism*. Middlesex, England: Penguin Books, 1971.

MESSING, SIMON D. "Group Therapy and Social Status in the Zar Cult of Ethiopia." *The American Anthropologist*, no. 60 (1958).

MISCHEL, WALTER and FRANCES. "Psychological Aspects of Spirit Possession." *The American Anthropologist*, Vol. 60, (1958).

MISCHO, JOHN. "Psychologische Aspekte der Besessenheit." Freiburg, *Zeitschrift für Parapsychologie und Grenzgebiete der Psychologie* 13, no. 2 (1971).

MOUSSEAU, JACQUES. "Freud in Perspective: A Conversation with Henri F. Ellenberger." *Psychology Today*, March 1973.

OESTERREICH, T. K. *Possession: Demoniacal and Other*. New Hyde Park, N.Y.: University Books, 1966.

OTTO, RUDOLF. *The Idea of the Holy*. Middlesex, England: Penguin Books, 1959.

PEARCE-HIGGINS, JOHN D. "Twentieth Century 'Exorcism.'" *Spiritual Frontiers*, Winter 1969.

PETITPIERRE, DOM ROBERT, ed. *Exorcism: The Findings of a Commission Convened by the Bishop of Exeter*. London: S.P.C.K., 1972.

RODEWYK, ADOLF. *Die dämonische Besessenheit.* Aschaffenburg: Pattloch Verlag, 1963.

SARGANT, WILLIAM. "Possession," in *Man, Myth and Magic.* London, 1972.

SERVADIO, EMILIO. *Psychology Today.* New York: Garrett Publications, 1965.

STAUDENMAIER, LUDWIG. *Die Magie als experimentelle Naturwissenschaft.* Leipzig, 1912.

TRACHTENBERG, JOSHUA. *Jewish Magic and Superstition.* New York, 1939.

TYLOR, EDWARD B. *Primitive Culture: Researches into the Development of Mythology, Philosophy, Religion, Art and Custom.* London, 1871.

VANDENDRIESSCHE, G. *The Parapraxis of the Haizmann Case of Sigmund Freud.* Louvain, Belgium: Publications Universitaires, 1965.

VOGL, CARL. *Begone Satan!* Rockford, Ill.: Tan Books, 1973.

WALTER, W. GREY. "Viewpoints of Mental Illness: Neurophysiologic Aspects." *Seminars in Psychiatry* 4, no. 3 (1972).

WICKLAND, CARL A. *Thirty Years Among the Dead.* Los Angeles, 1924.

ZILBOORG, GREGORY. *A History of Medical Psychology.* New York: W. W. Norton, 1941.

About the Author

MARTIN EBON served as administrative secretary of the Parapsychology Foundation for twelve years, while editing the magazines *Tomorrow* and *International Journal of Parapsychology*. Recently, he was editor of *Spiritual Frontiers,* the journal of Spiritual Frontiers Fellowship, a nationwide organization concerned with the interrelation of religion and psychical research. Mr. Ebon has lectured at the New School for Social Research in New York City, as well as at New York University, and has given guest lectures at numerous other educational institutions.

Mr. Ebon's writings encompass the areas of biography, political affairs, the psychology of economics and, most notably, the field of extrasensory perception; in the latter area, his books include *Prophecy in Our Time* and *They Knew The Unknown,* as well as the anthology, *Exorcism: Fact, Not Fiction.* The author divides his writing and research activities between New York City and Athens, Greece.

74 75 76 77 10 9 8 7 6 5 4 3 2